COMPETING FOR INTEGRATION

Waves of globalization threaten to reduce each corner of the globe to look-alike fragments in a nearly uniform world economy—that at least is the impression created by some superficial and sensational reports that have economic, political, and cultural linkages spectacularly increased throughout the 1990s. As the authors of this book demonstrate, this is a highly misleading picture.

In the introductory section, the economists Faber, Van Dijck, and Kagami demonstrate what the effect of reducing trade barriers through the WTO processes are, and their implications for our understanding of market forces, the diminishing capacity of governments, consumer power, and the role of international agreements dealing with the negative effects of transboundary deals. While paying due respect to the role of the United States, they provide fascinating details of how the European Union and Japan develop their own strategies toward emerging Asian and Latin American states, their use of WTO rules, and their tactics with regard to the use of foreign direct investment and official development aids as part of their attempt to increase their leverage in the complex processes of international competition. A young Chinese official, Yang Zerui, provides his personal views on the implications of China's accession to the WTO. In the second section, the focus shifts mainly toward integration processes in Latin America, analyzed by a Brazilian and a European academic specializing in the study of the effects of Neoliberalism on this vast continent.

The book concludes with an attempt by British political economist Paul Cammack to provide a coherent interpretation of the political principles underlying the complex economic policies of the main actors in today's global economy, focusing on development strategies offered by the World Bank.

COMPETING FOR INTEGRATION

JAPAN, EUROPE, LATIN AMERICA, AND THEIR STRATEGIC PARTNERS

KURT W. RADTKE AND
MARIANNE WIESEBRON
EDITORS

AN EAST GATE BOOK

M.E. Sharpe
Armonk, New York
London, England

An East Gate Book

Serialized in *The Japanese Economy: Translations and Studies,* Volume 26, nos. 2, 3, and 4.

Library of Congress Cataloging-in-Publication Data

Competing for integration : Japan, Europe, Latin America and their strategic partners /
edited by Kurt W. Radtke and Marianne Wiesebron.
 p. cm.
"An East gate Book"
Includes bibliographical references and index.
ISBN 0-7656-0962-2 (alk. paper)
 1. Latin America—Economic integration. 2. East Asia—Economic integration. 3.
Europe—Economic integration. 4. Regionalism (International organization) 5. Trade
blocs. I. Radtke, Kurt W. (Kurt Werner), 1945– II. Wiesebron, Marianne.

HC125.C65157 2002
337.1—dc21   2002019091

Contents

EUROPEAN PERSPECTIVES

ASIAN PERSPECTIVES

LATIN AMERICAN PERSPECTIVES

PREFACE

This book is one of the results of a medium term project focusing on relations and co-operation involving countries in Latin America, the European Union and East Asia. This project comprised various workshops and conferences, as well as an intensive course on Asia, Europe and Latin America, for graduate students from Latin America (see below, project "Cabral"). Two symposia were held, "South-South Relations" and "Towards the Millennium Round: Asia, The European Union and Latin America." Scholars and graduates from three Latin American countries (Brazil, Argentina, Chile) and Asia (Japan, China, India, and Korea) participated in these projects. In addition, a "Masterclass" was conducted in 2000 as part of the Advanced Master's Program of the Centre of Non-Western Studies of Leiden University.

"Project Cabral" was a professionalisation course for twelve Latin American post-graduate students and assistants on the theme of continental and intercontinental integration, held at the coordinating institution, Leiden University, in 1999. One student from Mainz and five from Leiden participated also in that project. It was a project in the framework of "Network ASALFA" sponsored by the European Commission and the following institutions and representatives:
Universidade Federal do Rio Grande do Sul, Prof. Dr. Paulo G.F. Vizentini (Brazil); Universidad de Chile, Prof. Dr. Hernan Gutierrez; Universidad Nacional de Cordoba, Prof. Dr. Jaime Silbert (Argentina); the Center for Asian Pacific Studies, Universitet Stockholm, Prof. Dr. B. Edstrom (Sweden); Universität Mainz, Prof. Dr. M. Mols and Universität Trier, Prof. Dr. K.H. Pohl (both Germany); Leiden University, Prof. Dr. K.W. Radtke and Dr. M.L. Wiesebron (the Netherlands).
Associate institutions and their representatives were: Centro de Estudios y Documentacion de America Latina, Amsterdam, Dr. P. Van Dijck (the

Netherlands), and the International Institute of Social History, Amsterdam, Prof. Dr. J. Lucassen and Prof. Dr. W. Van Schendel.

The symposium "South-South relations" was held in February 1998 at the University of Leiden, and focused on recent developments in relations between Latin America and Asia (organizers: K.W. Radtke and M.L. Wiesebron). The workshop "Towards the Millennium Round: The WTO and Deepening Integration in Asia, The European Union and Latin America" was held in March 2000 (organizers: M.L. Wiesebron and K.W. Radtke).

The contributors to this book participated at least in one of the activities listed above. The editors of this book conferred with the contributors on numerous occasions, gathered during the various activities listed above, and commissioned the papers collected in this book.

We should like to take this occasion to express our gratitude to all those who participated, and to the sponsors listed above. The co-ordination of activities concerning universities, scholars and graduate students in Latin America was shouldered by Dr. Paulo Vizentini (Universidade Federal do Rio Grande do Sul), who was also the holder of the Chair of Brazilian Studies in Leiden during the intensive ASALFA program, and Dr. Pitou van Dijck (University of Amsterdam) in collaboration with Dr. Marianne L. Wiesebron (Leiden University). Dr. Kurt W. Radtke (Waseda University, Tokyo) liaisoned with scholars and institutes in Japan and China. In particular we should like to mention Professor Raymond Buve (Professor emeritus, Leiden University) who played an indispensable role during the workshops and other activities, as well as in the preparation of this book. We are also grateful to Nel Buve-Kelderhuis for her involvement in the production, and Mrs. Rosemary Robson (KITLV, Leiden) and Rab Paterson (Ph.D. Candidate, Waseda University) for language editing.

Last, but not least, the editors should like to thank all scholars and students involved in this project, and who directly and indirectly contributed to its success.

LIST OF ABBREVIATIONS

ACP	Africa, Caribbean, Pacific, the ACP countries (77 in 2000)
AFTA	ASEAN Free Trade Area
AIA	ASEAN Investment Area
ALADI	Latin American Integration Association and the Caribbean
ANZCER	Australia-New Zealand Closer Economic Relationship (Treaty Agreement)
APEC	Asian Pacific Economic Cooperation
ARF	Asian Regional Forum
ASEAN Plus Three	ASEAN Ten and Japan, China and South Korea
ASEAN	ASEAN Ten
ASEAN	Association of Southeast Asian Nations (Ten members)
ASEM	Asia-Europe Meeting
BLT	Build, Lease, and Transfer
BOO	Build, Own, and Operate
BOT	Build, Operate, and Transfer
BRT	Business Roundtable
CACM	Central American Common Market
CAP	Common Agricultural Policy
CARICOM	Caribbean Common Market
CARIFTA	Caribbean Free Trade Area Association
CDs	Compact Disks
CEEC	Central and Eastern European Countries
CEO	Chief Executive Officer
CET	Common External Tariff
CFC	Chloro Fluor Carbons
CGE	Computable General Equilibrium
CM	Common Market
CSN	*Companhia Siderúrgica National*, National Siderurgy Company
CTBT	Comprehensive Nuclear Test-Ban Treaty

CU	Customs Union
CUSFTA	Canada-US Free Trade Agreement
CVRD	*Companhia do Vale do Rio Doce*, Rio Doce Valley Company
DAC	Development Assistance Committee (OECD)
DSU	Dispute Settlement Understanding
EAEC	East Asian Economic Caucus cooperation
EALAF	East Asia-Latin America Forum
EAs	Europe Agreements
EASG	East Asian Study Group
ECLA	United Nations Economic Commission for Latin America
EEA	European Economic Area
EEC	European Economic Community
EU	European Union
FDI	Foreign Direct Investment
FTA	Free Trade Agreement, Free Trade Area
FTAA	Free Trade Area of the Americas
G 15	(in 1989, 15 countries, in 2000 19) Algeria, Argentina, Brazil, Chile, Colombia, Egypt, India, Indonesia, Iran, Jamaica, Kenya, Malaysia, Mexico, Nigeria, Peru, Senegal, Sri Lanka, Venezuela, Zimbabwe
GATT	General Agreement on Tariffs and Trade
GCC	Gulf Cooperation Council
GDP	Gross Domestic Product
GMOs	Genetically Modified Organisms
GNP	Gross National Product
IAEA	International Atomic Energy Agency
IBRD	International Bank for Reconstruction and Development
IDB	Inter-American Development Bank
IMF	International Monetary Fund
IPPs	Independent Power Producers
ITO	International Trade Organization
JETRO	Japan External Trade Organization
KEDO	Korean peninsula Energy Development Organization

LDCs	Less Developed Countries
LNG	Liquified Natural Gaz
MAI	Multilateral Agreement on Investments
MEBF	Mercosur-European Union Business Forum
MENA	Middle Eastern and North African countries
MFN	Most-Favored Nation Treatment
MNCs	Multinational Corporations
MOFTEC	Ministry of Foreign Trade and Commerce (China)
MTCR	Missile Technology Control Regime
NAFTA	North American Free Trade Agreement
NAS	New Asia Strategy
NGO	Non-Governmental Organization
NIEs	Newly Industrialized Economies
NPT	Non-Proliferation Treaty
ODA	Official Development Assistance
OECD	Organization for Economic Cooperation and Development
OPEC	Organization of Petroleum Exporting Countries
PEMEX	Petróleos de Mexico, Mexican Oil Company
PFI	Private Finance Initiative
PPP	Purchasing Power Parity
PT	*Partido dos Trabalhadores*, Workers' Party
PTAs	Preferential Trade Areas
QR(s)	Quantitative Restrictions
SAARC	South Asia Association for Regional Cooperation
SAFTA	South American Free Trade Area
SEANWFZ	South East Asia Nuclear Weapon Free Zone
SOEs	State-Owned Enterprises
SPSM	Agreement on the Application of Sanitary and Phytosanitary Measures
TAFTA	Transatlantic Free Trade Area
TBD	Transatlantic Business Dialogue
TBT	Agreement on Technical Barriers to Trade
TOE	Tons of Energy
TRIPs	Agreement on Trade-related Aspects of Intellectual Property within WTO

TPA	Trade Promotion Authority
UDN	*União Democrática Nacional*, Democratic National Union
UN	United Nations
UNCLOS	United Nations Conference on the Law of the Sea
USA	United States of America
VERs	Voluntary Export Restraints
WB	World Bank
WC	Wealthy Countries
WTO	World Trade Organization
ZPCSA	Zone of Peace and Cooperation in the South Atlantic

COMPETING FOR INTEGRATION

INTRODUCTION AND OVERVIEW

Kurt W. Radtke

This book focuses on the role of regional integration as a means for societies, economies, and states to survive in the struggle called globalization. Members of the Triad, the USA, Japan and the European Union, have developed different types of networks to enhance their competitive strengths.[1] While acting globally, each of the three players has been engaged in shaping geographically contingent regions to fit into integrated networks, subordinating weaker economies.[2] It is not by chance that the countries that maintain closer relations are often those who in the past were bound to each other in a colonial type of relationship. Since their respective 'backyards' are structured differently, politically, economically, but also culturally, it comes as no surprise that the web of relations developed by members of the Triad differs in many respects. Weaker countries take part in integration schemes led by Triad members, and at the same time attempt to develop their own network of institutions in the form of regionalism to better withstand pressures from members of

---

1. Among the vast literature on the topic I should like to mention here only a few recent publications: M. Kagami and T. Masatsugu, eds. *Privatization, Deregulation and Economic Efficiency. A Comparative Analysis of Asia, Europe and the Americas*; W. Pape, *Models of Integration in Asia and Europe: Generating Public Space for our common Futures.* B. Belen, *Europe Inc.: Regional and Global Restructuring and the Rise of Corporate Power*; M. Reiterer, "ASEM–The Third Summit in Seoul 2000: A Roadmap to Consolidate the Partnership between Asia and Europe," in *European Foreign Affairs Review*, June 2001, pp. 1–30; W.A. Lovett, et al. *U.S. Trade Policy: History, Theory, and the WTO*; M. Schulz, F. Svderbaum and J. Vjendal, eds. *Rationalization in a Globalizing World. A Comparative Perspective on Forms, Actors and Processes.*

2. For two Japanese views criticizing the current financial world order, see H. Yoonosuke (Professor, Tokyo University, Research Institute of East Asian Cultures), *Ajiagata keizai shisutemu*; Y. Takahashi, *Shin sekai chitujo.*

the Triad, and other possible competitors. Processes of integration thus occur at many levels and layers; competition promotes integration, but various forms of integration processes in turn sharpen competition among all participants.

Some expected the World Trade Organization [WTO] to become an overarching network of rules which would subsume separate regions. When we planned for the publication of this book—originally scheduled to appear in the second half of 2000—most contributors were fairly optimistic that they would have some idea about the contents of the new round of trade negotiations within the WTO framework by the time they submitted their manuscripts. The breakdown of talks in Seattle in 1999, and uncertainties surrounding even the planned meeting for the 141 member countries in the Gulf emirate of Qatar in November 2001 following the attack on New York in September, added to doubts about the future course of the WTO itself.[3] In recent years the increasing number of bilateral Free Trade Agreements (Preferential Trade Areas) have given cause for concern that this may affect the principle of multilateralism embodied in the WTO process. Institutions such as the WTO, International Monetary Fund [IMF], the World Bank [WB] and others have come to be seen by some as tools for 'globalization' pushed by the USA as the sole global hegemonic power. The contributors of this book from Asia, Europe and Latin America, despite their different scholarly disciplines and political persuasion, agree that increasing global interaction has sharpened competition, and that this is a major force driving global and regional integration. Far from stopping at creating customs and free trade areas' traditional style, developed countries are pushing the process of 'deep integration' including new sectors such as investment, competition and the environment onto the negotiating agenda. They are opposed by developing countries that fear that their relative competitive power will be eroded in the process.

'Globalization' has produced a torrent of publications by institutions, governments and individual scholars, yet few have attempted to analyze the integration process from a comparative perspective, focusing on Asia, Europe, and Latin America and their strategic partners.[4] The joint effort by contributors to this book supports the view that differences within, and among the regions of the globe are a major reason why 'globalization'

---

3. G.P. Sampson, *Trade, Environment, and the WTO: The Post-Seattle Agenda.*
4. See W. Pape, *Models of Integration ...*, and M. Schulz et al., *Rationalization ...*

is not a simple one-way road towards a future homogenous global economic and (perhaps even political) order. 'Globalization' is not just a material event and an unavoidable historic development, it clearly is also a political project.[5] It plays a role as an ideology, or as Solinger has put it, as an 'ideational component' that has exercised considerable influence on policy making in China.[6] Similarly, the rise of market economics may be seen in the context of the rise of Darwinism in the social sciences, and we may define economics as institutionalized economic Darwinism, an institutional framework for selecting the economically 'fittest' producer (and, at the same time, creating the ideal consumer).

A caricature of this process of globalization sees the United States, universally recognized as the unchallengeable hegemonic power of this age, as its main architect. It sets patterns for international co-operation, and organizations such as the WB, the IMF, and the WTO appear to many as mere tools to strengthen U.S. domination of an integrated global system, characterized by a highly sophisticated and efficient division of labor promising the greatest of riches to the greatest number of people. 'Global capitalism' seems to reorganize financial markets along the slogans of 'neo-liberalism' as a major means to influence and 'moderate' government policies around the globe, ensuring that they are not interfered with by the whims of populist governments of whatever color. Indeed, a major economist has argued that to some macro-economists, differences in the micro-economic structure of countries, their history, or even the distribution of income simply do not matter.[7]

The global superiority of the United States in the field of military strength is undisputed, but this does not simply translate in the ability to dictate a global order. True enough, the other members of the Triad are Japan and a European Union in which a united Germany plays a major role. Their special status as former aggressor nations, and their resulting strong links with the United States are important factors in circumscribing their potential for becoming politically more independent from the United States. More than anything else it is the symbiotic relationship with the United States that has led Japan to equate U.S. leadership with internationalization, and U.S. standards with global standards.

---

5. L. Thurow, *Yomiuri Shinbun*.

6. D.J. Solinger, "Globalization and the Paradox of Participation: The Chinese Case," in *Global Governance*, Vol.2, 2, Apr.–June 2001, p. 180.

7. J. Stiglitz, "What I Learned at the World Economic Crisis," *The New Republic*.

Embedded in the association called the European Union, in size and population comparable to the USA, Germany, Great Britain, France and others have built a web of economic and political relationships whose structure differs remarkably from the type of linkages that exist between the USA and Latin America, China and Japan. Japan and China, on the other hand, rely mainly on bilateral agreements to give shape to the global reach of their economies. Whatever the relationship between companies and governments, it is premature to underestimate the (admittedly, changing) role of governments and states. Together with other international institutions they constitute a framework for necessary political mediation that cannot be provided for by 'independent' markets—whether it concerns the setting of interest rates by the major central banks, mediating between the often conflicting demands of business, and last but not least by providing the security machines without which global order would collapse fairly rapidly. Political mediation at home is not necessarily identical with democratic decision-making. It is not exceptional, nor accidental, when 'market forces' are mentioned before democratic institutions. Commenting on the Japanese Prime Minister's plan for the reform and restructuring of the economy, the U.S. Assistant Secretary of State for East Asian and Pacific Affairs, James Kelly remarked:

> They are, of course, up to the Japanese government to develop, but they will have to be convincing to the markets and the Japanese people.[8]

Somewhat similarly, (macro) economists are often averse to 'politics' that in their view tends to unduly interfere with rational economic policies.

Where markets are institutions acting as 'playing fields' in (mainly economic) exchanges, global institutions such as the WTO and institutions for regional cooperation and integration should first of all be interpreted as 'playing fields' for negotiating the terms of exchanges in areas that reach from trade and investment to agreements on building an architecture of (cooperative) security. 'Regionalism' is therefore not an aim in itself, or a means to create new 'super states'. Even 'open regionalism' should

8. Special Report–James Kelly on Asia Pacific, 12 June 2001, Office of International Information Programs, U.S. Dept. of State (www.usinfo.state.gov). Transcript of U.S. Assistant Secretary of State for East Asian and Pacific Affairs James A. Kelly's testimony before the Subcommittee on East Asia and the Pacific and the House Committee on International Relations on 12 June 2001.

not be equated with global free trade—regionalism, just like preferential trade agreements—exists by the grace of establishing boundaries that influence the dynamics of the global order.[9] Typically, networks of such boundaries are created by wealthy countries [WC] to ensure and stabilize access to markets for goods, as well as financial or other products. This is by no means a new phenomenon, nor is it necessarily a peaceful process: the opening of Japan by Commodore Perry was pushed through in the presence of more than a hundred cannons aboard his ships, as he proudly noticed in his diary. The attempt by the USA to implement an 'Open Door Policy' for China a century ago had little to do with liberalism. Without asking for Chinese approval it was an early attempt to prevent exclusive spheres of influence in China by the 'powers' that might shut out the USA from the lure of the 'China market'.

Although assessments differ, it remains questionable to what extent attempts at regionalism by medium and smaller powers can be called a success. In discussing the effectiveness of trade blocs, Foroutan concluded that among other prominent regional groups involving only developing countries ASEAN was among those which have thus far not proved effective.[10]

Having initially suspected that Asian Pacific Economic Cooperation [APEC] may undermine U.S. access to Asia the USA turned to using the APEC process as one of its levers to push its own global agenda—aiming amongst other things to intimidate its main economic rival, the European Union. Needless to say, other countries like China regard participation in the APEC process from the vantage point of their own national interest. Rather than going into specifics described in the contributions to this book, I should like to return once more to the role of the WTO as an instrument for political mediation. Common misperceptions regard the WTO as an appropriate instrument for setting up a system of a common global market following the same, legally enforceable rules. As pointed out by several contributors to this volume, one of the central innovations of the WTO is the introduction of compulsory dispute resolution, but this is different from establishing a utopian global judicial authority whose judgments are directly enforceable. In the absence of such a court, all that

---

9. "*Free trade can only be implemented properly through common external borders*". P. Gerhard, "Trade, Treaties and Treason ...," in *European Foreign Affairs Review*, 6, p. 122.

10. F. Foroutan, "Does Membership in a Regional Preferential Trade Arrangement Make a Country More or Less Protectionist?"

can be achieved is institutionalization and formalization of economic competition and conflict resolution through mechanisms requiring political mediation. States and governments remain the main actors through which such political mediation is effected. This process is made even more complex by the fact that 'national' interests and the interests of companies do not necessarily coincide, as Joseph Nye pointed out. U.S. enterprise is far from abiding by what the U.S. government may see as its national interest.[11] What may be regarded as a 'failure' of the WTO—the non-adoption of a legally enforceable system of dispute resolution—is not simply due to differences in existing legal cultures. The deep reason for this inability lies in the fact that circumstances under which states and governments operate are too diverse to admit for a global unification of rules. Also, trade policy and the formulation of rules do not always easily go together—as G. Soros has emphasized, decision making institutions such as the European Union seek to implement policies by formulating rules, but this approach lacks the necessary flexibility to succeed.[12]

The forum of the WTO is an important, but not the only institution stabilizing the modalities of trade relations. Like multilateralism, the WTO does not present a value by itself, but is only accepted as a useful venue and approach towards dealing with the extremely complex and asymmetrical architecture of world trade relations.[13] This had led to the lengthening of some negotiating processes to such an extent that negotiating partners may decide to bypass the WTO process when judged convenient, raising the question to what extent the 'lock-in' effect is sufficient to force actors to abide by the rules of existing institutions. This will depend very much on judgments of the relative benefits and damages in the short, middle and long term. In the final account, it is not the 'principles' of multilateralism, open markets or regionalism that governs the course of structural development of the global economy, but the (in)ability of the players to see cooperation as being in their advantage. Imposing 'principles' contrary to common sense may in fact erode the authority of existing processes for cooperation.

---

11. Needless to add, 'multinational' companies are not 'footloose' but continue to be closely associated with national economies. See W. Ruigrok and R. van Tulder, *The Logic of International Restructuring*.

12. Soros is sometimes referred to in Chinese sources as a 'financial terrorist', due to his part in bringing about the 1997 Asian financial crisis.

13. R. Wilkinson, *Multilateralism and the World Trade Organization*.

In the early '90s, East Asian countries had liberalized their financial, and capital markets—not because they needed to attract more funds (savings rates were already 30 percent or more) but because of international pressure, including some from the U.S.-Treasury Department.[14]

Such sudden, uncontrolled liberalization leading to unlimited influx of capital is likely to have a devastating corruptive effect on the behavior of actors in markets—the functioning of market mechanisms is by itself not a sufficient condition for 'rational' economic behavior. Globalization has often been portrayed as an inevitable consequence of market forces portrayed as having inherently the potential for impartial justice independent from the human will. The slogans of the day—from 'market economics' to 'democracy'—and its rather unnatural offspring, 'market democracy', and further on to 'protectionism', 'distortion' (of market mechanisms) and 'decoupling' (of subsidies) suggest a world view that contrasts openness with closeness, transparency with darkness, fairness with corruption, and the rule of light against the threat of unknown darkness.[15] Leaving aside the unintended poetics of that kind of language use, it needs little effort to point out that market economics under the aegis of national treasuries, politically motivated manipulation of interest rates, speculation by institutional and other investors against short and long term market flows is characterized by anything but openness. Neither the U.S. Treasury nor comparable European or Japanese institutions are known for transparency or democratic decision making.[16] Systemically, it is impossible to separate markets for short, medium and long term dealings, and this is one important factor impeding a truly rational flow of investments. The division of labor according to the rational, i.e., cost efficient application of capital in the production of goods, rests on the assumption that production costs are a fair reflection of the ability of a producer to organize production more efficiently than other competitors. The large scale, direct and indirect subsidies wealthy countries can afford to give their agricultural producers is the most conspicuous example of intentional distortion of production costs, usually concealed from the

---

14. J. Stiglitz, "What I Learned ..."

15. Democracy, by definition, allows citizens irrespective of their income and wealth to participate in decision making; in the market bargaining strength is strictly related to economic power.

16. J. Berthelot, paper presented to the Symposium on issues confronting the world trading system, World Trade Organization-Geneva, 6–7 July 2001.

consumer, and accompanied by misleading or outright false information provided to organizations such as the WTO.[17] The cost of capital needed for production is highly dependent not only on unpredictable financial markets, but also dependent on the presence or absence of general infrastructure, which permanently benefits producers in wealthy countries, irrespective of their comparative individual efficiency. Public debates on policy issues have become crowded with rational sounding slogans of 'fair' market mechanisms which conceal more than they reveal. Symbiosis between producers and political institutions is not the prerogative of Asian 'cronyism'. The symbiosis between agricultural producers and institutions of wealthy countries has led Jacques Berthelot to conclude that 'WCs are almost transforming their farmers into civil servants.'[18] In fact, the 'special relationship' existing also in some other areas of the economy such as the defense industry raises doubts to what extent we can hand down clear distinctions between 'private' and 'public' enterprise.

The proper functioning of markets requires informed customers, especially since increasing sophistication and complexity of production processes make it more difficult for governments to provide protective mechanisms. As suggested by Faber (see below) this may partially be met by improving product information enabling the customer to choose himself, without being guided by a protective government. Yet even the USA, 'paragon of transparency', is actively engaged in concealing product information, ranging from jealously guarding the secrets of the ingredients of Coca Cola to the presence of genetically modified agricultural products in goods sold to the consumer.[19]

The ideal of 'private' (i.e., 'free') enterprise active in non-distorted markets underestimates the instinctive behavior of individuals, (economic)

---

17. Berthelot, paper.

18. Berthelot, paper.

19. According to one report, Wichai Chokwiwat, secretary-general of the Thai Food and Drug Administration, revealed on 13 February 2001 that the threats to invoke Section 301 of the U.S. trade laws were made during an official visit on 13 February this year. "*I explained to them that the Thai government had resolved in 1999 to have food products carry a GM label to protect consumers,*" said Wichai, adding that the regulations would merely involve a special label reading "*manufactured with genetically modified soybean/corn*" for products having a GM concentration higher than 3 percent. (Posted from ag-impact@iatp.org Wednesday, 25 July 2001, posted by smurphy@iatp.org (see also www.just-food.com/news_detail.asp?art=37810&c=1, 19 July 2001, archive: www.gene.ch/genet.html).

institutions and states to maintain, perpetuate and expand existing positions of advantage, privileges and its extreme form, monopolies, and bypass rules (and loopholes) in their pursuit of these. After all, the ideology of market economics shares with theoretical socialism utopian assumptions about human behavior that are disproved in our everyday experience— deviations tend to be conceptualized as lesser or greater examples of 'corruption'. It has been argued that the discipline imposed by accession to the WTO is one of the means to combat illegal and corrupt practices in the Chinese economy. Similarly, Indonesian economic officials were willing to cooperate with the WB and the IMF in order to break the hold of the corrupt Suharto elites on the Indonesian economy. It is no secret that the debacle of the Indonesian economy was closely followed by Chinese officials, concerned about similar consequences as a result of accession to the WTO. Several well known China specialists have expressed their apprehension about China's ability to cope with the repercussions.[20]

Together with North Korea and Vietnam, China is one of the last examples of a state that professes a 'socialist' system. Integration in the institutions of the global economy is also regarded as a means to achieve the irreversible introduction of a market economy in China (albeit called 'socialist market economy'). This alone, however, does not guarantee the breakdown of international barriers inherited from the age of the global confrontation between a 'communist' and an 'anti-Communist' camp. While China has cooperated with the USA and other countries in some areas of security, deep differences and suspicions remain, affecting cooperation in other areas. The heritage of the Cold War is not the only barrier dividing Asia. Regional cooperation of the kind that enabled the creation of the present day European Union is unthinkable in other parts of the world (including the USA) since it requires the ceding of parts of state sovereignty to supra-state institutions. Moreover, no country in Asia is ready, willing or able to grant a leadership role to any of its rivals. The essential inability of Asia to embark on true regionalism is one of the

---

20. P. Drysdale, and S. Ligang, eds. *China's Entry to the WTO: Strategic Issues and Quantitative Assessments*; M.A. Groombridge, *Tiger by the Tail: China and the World Trade Organization*, for examples of Chinese publications, Hou Shusen, *WTO gei Zhongguo baixing dailai sheme?* [How will the WTO affect ordinary Chinese people?], and Deng Zhihai et al. eds., *Shimao zuzhi wenti jieda* [Questions and answers concerning the WTO], Zhongguo duiwai jingji maoyi.

foundations of the ability of the USA to entertain active relations with all Asian players without having to fear being excluded from this largest continent in the short and medium term.

The potential for an area to transform itself into a region also depends in good measure on the consensus of its elites and the population at large about the direction of development. Participation as citizen, and social citizenship are important ingredients, but some of the effects of globalization rob many people of their social citizenship.[21] It is acknowledged that the changing forms of citizenship influence not only domestic politics, but also affect international relations, but little research has been done on *"how identities have changed over time."*[22]

Just as in Asia common concerns about powerful neighbors—be they China or Japan—have not led smaller powers to form a close web of co-operative relations, so have developing nations around the globe failed to join ranks against the aspiration of regional and global hegemonic powers.

> Big developing countries, especially India and Brazil, are well entrenched in Geneva and will use their diplomatic wiles to ensure that China's entry does not undercut their influence too much...[they] resent the way China has become an export platform for foreign multinationals even while its domestic economy has remained only partly market driven.[23]

Despite profiting from China as a production base for industry, countries such as the USA and Japan are concerned lest China develop into a serious competitor, and are wondering whether it is wise to maintain the current size and speed of investments in a country that may one day challenge the military authority of the USA.[24]

Before presenting a brief overview and summaries of the contributions to this book, I should like to conclude with a few thoughts about much vaunted 'neo-liberalism'. Similar to other 'isms' of the twentieth century this 'ism', too, presents itself as a universally applicable ideology. One

---

21. For the social disenfranchisement of Chinese citizens, see D.J. Solinger, "Globalization ..." p. 173.

22. P. Dombrowski, and T. Rice, "Changing Identities and International Relations Theory: A Cautionary Note," in *Nationalism and Ethnic Politics*, p. 85.

23. P. Bowring, "Foreign-Invested Enterprises Account for Half of China's Exports," *International Herald Tribune*, 29 June 2001.

24. Robert Kapp, president of the US-China Business Council, referring to Senator Sarbanes testimony at www.uschina.org (June 14 hearing of the U.S.-China Security Review Commission www.uschina.org/public/june14press.html).

may wonder whether after all it is not an expression of a widely-propagated image of Anglo-Saxon (economic) culture, which may or may not reflect reality.

> *The marketplace promotes American values: trade encourages more freedom and individual liberties. U.S. investment establishes higher standards of enterprise behavior in regard to corporate governance, labor relations, or even environmental attention.*[25]

Raymond Feddema introduces the historical background to the issues of global interaction and the role of the WTO. He emphasizes that in order to grasp the dynamics of the WTO, we need to take into account the historical setting and the shift in economic power among countries, the rise of regional groupings and the role of non-state actors. Rather than taking the 'building block perspective' of institutionalism he approaches the issues by selecting suitable themes which illustrate both the dynamics of institutions, but also the changing character of the players. Trade itself is only one among many other factors, but a very tangible one especially in a period where one economic hegemony—the United States—attempts to impose its own economic structure on numerous other actors and institutions. The rationale proposed by the USA—Neo-liberalism advocating free trade and open markets—is considered the 'victorious and sole doctrine' of the 'new world order'. Ideology and practice tend to differ, and Feddema chooses the Dispute Settlement Understanding [DSU], claimed to be a major achievement of the WTO, as a major issue to prove his case. Another topic presented here is how the agendas of negotiation rounds are determined. It appears that contrary to what might be expected, it is only one regional grouping that shows a consistent approach towards agenda and issue setting—the European Union. Other regional groupings in Asia and Latin America (ASEAN, South Asia Association for Regional Cooperation [SAARC], Mercosur/l and North American Free Trade Agreement [NAFTA]) were incapable of agreeing on issues they would raise as one group. This feature should be taken as one indication that trade relations, and global order in the wider sense, cannot simply be modeled along the line of a hierarchical order in which micro-regions, regions, states, cross-border regions and their institutions would form a Hegelian order of ascending integration. Reflecting on the policy behavior

---

25. Special Report–James Kelly on Asia Pacific, 12 June 2001. (See note 8.)

of business groups (mainly Chief Executive Officers [CEOs]) from the USA and the EU who want to dictate their governments' new regulatory frameworks for specific trade issues, Feddema raises the question of the democratic content of the developing global trade order.

Faber approaches multilateralism through an examination of 'deep integration'. Following the reduction of tariff barriers and other quantitative restrictions the importance of other regulatory barriers has increased. Their removal leads towards deep integration between the economies of partners to such agreements. They do, however, also affect global rule setting. Having discussed the reasons for the creation of regulatory trade barriers, Faber outlines the progress of deep integration in the global economy, in particular its effect on reducing regulatory trade barriers, and ventures a prognosis of future developments. The course of negotiations is influenced by models advocating trade liberalization as a means to increase overall welfare in the long term, and politicians who maneuver between different pressure groups and the formulation of a collective interest. The existence of regional integration makes it easier for politicians to push for liberalization. Different from tariff and quantitative restrictions that are often the result of domestic protectionist demands, regulatory intervention frequently originates as a means to correct market failures. This includes mediating the tensions that exist between the pattern of short/medium term costs and benefits at the individual level, compared to those relevant at the level of the community and in the long term. Such market failures are not just the result of technical issues such as insufficient information or speculative behavior; they may also differ according to levels of income, resource endowments and group culture, the latter comprising a vast array of factors such as the direction of education as well as religious values. As a result, governments also adopt widely differing means to correct such market failures affecting trade flows. Faber points out that the present trading order and further trade liberalization can only be maintained if the diversity in regulation is reduced. This raises the question of whose regulatory standards should prevail in the drive towards regulatory harmonization. This is one area where economists—opposing differences in regulations—and politicians may differ. Rather than giving preference to either, Faber suggests a pragmatic approach, starting by accepting the existence of regulatory trade barriers as a matter of fact. New and more restrictive standards are introduced, and trade preferences, bans and quotas used as levers to gain favorable positions vis-à-vis trading partners. The existing tensions between various interest groups require political mediation which an institution such as the EU can provide. The WTO, however, lacks powers to set the regulatory standards of its members. As a result, the WTO may come under pressure from two fronts, free traders on the one hand, and consumer and environmental groups on the other. I (K.W.R.) would add that governments are far from forming a cohesive group on either side, and are likely to maximize national interests by 'playing' issues accordingly. Faber warns that the 'broadening agenda of trade liberalization may turn out to be too much for the WTO', and that this may produce serious problems for the world trading order as such. After outlining the main features of the history of the development of regulatory standards he concludes that 'the global integration process brought forward by the negotiations in the GATT (General Agreement on Tariffs and Trade) and the WTO has increasingly limited the freedom of public regulators to introduce regulations that aim at the correction of market failures, by formulating specific norms in international organizations, and at the same time introducing constraints for the introduction of stricter norms than internationally agreed. The harmonization of food standards has led to major conflicts. Also, conflicts have erupted over process (e.g., labor) standards, and the use of genetically modified organisms [GMOs]. Last, but not least, there has been no unanimity on the harmonization of national policies with respect to direct investment. Product standards are often not sufficient, or indeed actually inefficient, in controlling deleterious effects beyond national borders, as in the case of pollution. Yet slow progress in achieving international agreements is likely to increase pressure for product norms, resulting in increasing regulatory trade barriers. Technological progress, and increasing complexities of production, have meant that the ability of governments to establish specific regulatory mechanisms (resulting in compulsory product information, for example) has been lowered. Import and export of products traded or ordered via internet (books, designs, financial products) is difficult to control. Faber concludes that on the one hand, market forces and diminished governmental regulatory capacity result in lowered regulatory trade barriers. Yet there is also pressure on governments by various groups—producer lobbies as well as consumer groups—to increase new regulations, even where they are not supported by rational evidence. Rather than risking loss of faith in the international trading order by harmonizing regulatory schemes against political pressure, he suggests that demanding increased transparency in product information may be a workable compromise. Rather than shutting out products from poorer countries, the adoption of safer production technologies in those countries, and facilitating imports from those countries into the markets of developed countries, may be a suitable way of alleviating political pressures.

From a different perspective, Pitou van Dijck also reaches the conclusion that the developing global trade order is multilayered, and also shows regional preferences for particular trade relationships that co-exist next to the regional and global trade regimes. He pays particular attention to the role of preferential trade areas [PTAs] and other different types of special relationships with countries and groups of countries in the EU's strategy. Van Dijck stresses that the EU's strategy towards emerging Asia differs fundamentally from the way the EU traditionally tends to frame its external economic relations. He points out that the combined value of EU exports to Latin America and developing Asia now equals the combined EU exports to the other powers of the Triad, the USA and Japan. Altogether, the USA, developing Europe and developing Asia have become three major trade partners of the EU of more or less equal size when measured according to EU exports. Moreover, China (including Hong Kong) has been the single most important destination of EU exports to the region in 1997, and in 1998 even more significant than Japan. Against this background van Dijck proceeds to focus first on the role of PTAs in shaping a cobweb of relationships. Different from

> the era of import-substitution policies emerging economies now aim at supporting the fairly radical programs of trade and investment liberalization initiated unilaterally in the context of comprehensive stabilization and reform programs.

The spread of regionalism is one of the factors that forces large institutions such as the EU to rethink its strategies towards its main competitors (the USA and Japan). The enlargement of the EU that will include Central and Eastern European Countries [CEECs] as its new members will also impact on the overall strategies of the EU towards the WTO. Although the USA is "by far its major trade and investment partner" there are numerous differences—including deeper ones concerning the architecture of the world trade and economic order. After a brief review of the ASEAN Free Trade Area (established in 1992) and APEC (1989) van Dijck emphasizes that East Asian *open regionalism is characterized by concerted unilateral trade liberalization on an MFN basis, which has distinguished APEC from the PTAs in Europe and the Americas.*

At issue here is that the USA, which wishes to extend concessions to outsiders on a reciprocal basis to maintain leverage against other countries, differs from Japan and other Asian emerging economies which favor *"unconditional and non-discriminatory treatment of outsiders."* The creation of an *"implicit Asian or Pacific trade bloc favors trade in a discriminatory fashion,"* and may disadvantage the EU in expanding trade with its partners in that region. Like several other authors, Van Dijck also refers to market distortions of *"regional or group-wise harmonization of standards,"* as well as investment diversion and higher transaction costs. This is likely to become an important issue since we have now reached a stage where countries in Asia-Pacific, including the USA and Japan, are changing their previous strategies and are now actively engaged in creating a web of bilateral PTAs or special trade relations. It is highly unlikely that East Asia—the Koreas, Japan, China, Mongolia and Russia—will move in the direction of 'regionalism', which is most pronounced in Europe, but also widespread in Latin America. We are now in a transitional phase where it is not yet clear how far attempts to create a new 'super-region', the Free Trade Area for the Americas [FTAA] will result in a trading bloc marked by 'deep integration'. At the time the contributions for this book had already been finalized, the financial crisis originating in Argentine had already severely affected the Brazilian economy as well. Since this customs union unites two major Latin American economies with a combined production of over 40 percent of the region-wide GNP measured at Purchasing Power Parity [PPP], the course and outcome of the crisis is likely to affect not only Mercosur/l itself, but also further developments towards creating the Free Trade Area of the Americas [FTAA]. Since the FTAA is able to accommodate to a large extent (conditionally, though) existing bilateral and sub-regional PTAs there is a certain risk that non-members may become outsiders in these markets. Japan, like numerous other countries in (South) East Asia, has relations with the USA that combine strong economic with political and often military ties. They are unlikely to form a third 'independent' leg in a triadic game between the USA, Europe and Asia. In 1994, at the initiative of ASEAN countries, a regular forum for dialogue between Asian nations and the EU was established whose themes go beyond economics, and include politics and other areas. One of the interests of the Asian side lies in a shared strategic interest with the EU to maintain access to all global markets. Van Dijck goes into details concerning the EU proposals and strategy towards the agenda of the next round of talks. It was in fact the EU that has contributed strongly to the worldwide spread of preferential trade relations. Together with the emergence of 'mega' PTAs in East Asia, the America's and between the EU and South America which involve the USA, Japan and the EU there is always a danger that these developments may undermine strict WTO rules aimed towards maintaining a truly multilateral trade regime.

Another contributor from Japan, Kikuchi Tsutomu focuses on the interaction of regional and global governance and the way in which this may improve regional cooperation in East Asia. Nesting of regional forms of cooperation in global institutions is one way to achieve this, and this chapter analyzes the role a relatively new form of cooperation, ASEAN Plus Three (i.e., the ASEAN Ten Plus Three) has to play here. This is particularly important when seen against the difficulties of setting up a new global round of negotiations within the WTO framework. Regional cooperation may promote multilayered governance, which will eventually strengthen global cooperation as a whole. Japan's contribution was essential to get the ASEAN Plus Three process working. In addition to the "Joint Statement on East Asian Cooperation" of 1999, ASEAN Plus Three concluded bilateral currency swap agreements in May 2001 following the Chiang Mai Initiative of Finance Ministers in May 2000. Further topics on their agenda are discussions on an "East Asian Free Trade Agreement" and the holding of an "East Asian Summit." As in Latin America, the (South) East Asian region displays a complex set of factors favoring regional cooperation, but also has its fair share of factors encumbering such cooperation. According to Kikuchi, the driving force towards regionalism is the consensus among elites on the need to develop a common business agenda, and the will to cooperate to shape the future direction of capitalism. States and their governments are equally interested, since this may be one of the instruments for asserting strategic trade interests. If regional institutions of economic cooperation such as NAFTA, the EU and FTAA prove successful, this may force East Asia to accelerate cooperation in order to be able to face these challenges; cooperation for integration assists the build up of competitive strength. Successful integration in one part of the world, in turn, accelerates the need for building integrated structures in other regions. In East Asia as in Latin America, integration is seen as one of the means to defend national autonomy and development. In a globalizing Asia, the crisis of 1997 was deeply humiliating for Asian countries that had to bow to the demands of global institutions under USA guidance. Interestingly, integration does not simply adopt a conservative posture, but is used by commercial and political elites for conducting an autonomous restructuring of their domestic political and commercial institutions, and eroding domestic forces opposed to change. At the same time, ASEAN governments need to act together to avoid marginalization in the face of China and Japan, economic giants on the global scene.

Mitsuhiro Kagami's contribution on "Japan and Latin America" first presents an historical survey of Japan's relations with Latin America, pointing out that business relations with Latin America during the past one or two decades were fairly limited. This also applies to foreign direct investment and official development assistance. After a survey of Japan's trade with Latin America, the main thrust of his paper focuses on an analysis of Japan's FDI (Foreign Direct Investment) and ODA (Official Development Assistance) to Latin America, followed by a discussion on possible roles for Japan in the context of the new wave of bilateral free trade arrangements related to Latin America. The nineties saw three new developments in Latin America: the establishment of macroeconomic stability, moves towards regional integration providing new opportunities and markets, and also increased volatility in financial markets and monetary crises as a result of financial globalization. Regional trade blocs such as NAFTA and Mercosur/l contribute to the creation of new markets, including markets for investment. Their establishment may actually create new opportunities both for high-tech production from East Asia, but also promote FDI inflows. Kagami discusses the relationship of short-term capital markets in Latin America and (South) East Asia which may destabilize money markets if not properly handled. Japan's FDI was partially the result of high interest rate policies by the USA and the UK that produced a large difference between Japan's internal interest rates and the global markets. The direction of flows was to some extent determined by the better economic performance of (South) East Asia compared to that of Latin America. However, the nineties saw a limited return of Japanese FDI to Latin America, aided not only by policies of privatization, and the private sector's participation in infrastructure investments, but also the importance of the strategic location of Mexico and Brazil in the context of new developments in patterns of regional cooperation and integration, i.e. NAFTA (Mexico) and Mercosur/l (Brazil).

Japanese ODA has been used to facilitate the participation of the private sector in infrastructure building. Kagami includes detailed references to the positive impact of Japanese ODA policies, including its vital role in easing the effects of external debt crises. At the political level, Japanese ODA has a positive effect on the poor and the weak, who are left behind under liberalization and the free market mechanism. From a strategic point of view, the Japanese and Latin American economies are highly complementary, since Japan imports food, raw materials and fuel while Latin America imports Japanese manufactured goods, and this should further strengthen the linkage between both economic areas. In the areas of food and energy, not only Japan, but also China and Indonesia will increasingly be looking for new sources of supply, and Latin America is high on the list of candidates. Diversification of supplies has been a long-standing Japanese strategy. From that point of view Japan's heavy dependence on U.S. primary products is rather surprising, and may be reduced by paying greater attention to Latin America as a supplier of such goods. In the final paragraph, Kagami sums up the potential for Japan's role with regard to Latin America. As long as Latin America maintains economic stability it can compete for FDI while growth is weak in East Asia. Since the size of the Japanese ODA budget will decrease as a result of budgetary constraints its efficiency needs to be increased further, also strengthening the role in business of those who have a shared Japanese/ Latin American background (migrants, and returnees). In the light of the wave of FTAs which are increasingly regarded as a pragmatic way of achieving global liberalization, Japan has also formed study teams for FTAs with Mexico, Korea and more recently with Singapore and Chile.[26]

However, a number of factors stand in the way of a smooth path towards integration. Different perceptions of security interests, and lack of harmonization in the areas of domestic competition and business rules, continue to thwart a fast track towards integration. Political instability fosters repression and attitudes that encourage state-led development. Complementarity in the region is also threatened by competition for attracting foreign direct investments and the battle for markets especially in the face of a rapidly growing Chinese economy. Measures taken by Japan and South Korea to protect their respective agricultural sectors is

---

26. On proposals for a Free Trade Zone between Japan and South Korea (RoK), see the Research Report Yamazawa Ippei (chief researcher) *21seiki no nikkan keizai kankei wa ika ni arubeki ka* [Proposals for Japanese-Korean Relations in the Twenty-first Century].

another indicator for future friction. Since trade rules continue to be provided both by global institutions such as GATT and regional bilateral free trade agreements, it will not be easy to achieve an "East Asian Free Trade Agreement." The interaction with global institutions is accompanied by other circumstances that would make it difficult to conceive of regional cooperation in terms that would exclude countries from outside the geographical region of (South) East Asia. Following Barry Buzan's definition of security networks, Kikuchi points to the existence of networks such as the participation of "USA–Europe–Australia" in "East Asian" financial interactions. Kikuchi thus avoids limiting 'regional interactions' to narrow geographical definitions of the term region. Regional governance likewise is multilayered and involves regional and global rules of governance, exemplified in institutions such as the WTO and IMF, and also present in security networks where Korean Peninsula Energy Development Organization [KEDO] exists alongside the Non-Proliferation Treaty [NPT] and the International Atomic Energy Agency [IAEA]. The Asian Regional Forum would not be operable without simultaneous cooperation in institutions such as the UN, the Comprehensive Nuclear Test-Ban Treaty [CTBT], and United Nations Conference on the Law of the Sea [UNCLOS].

Perhaps somewhat similar to the principle of subsidiary operating within the European Union, Kikuchi sees the role of regional sets of rules of governance as supplementary to global rules, which enable members of a region to 'soften' the impact of single-minded globalization. The important difference lies in the fact that most approaches towards convergence in rules of governance in (South) East Asia rely on a kind of process of socialization whereby elite's and governments from various countries informally agree on regionally endorsed norms, rules and codes of conduct, without relying on their enforcement through sanctions.

In addition to the points mentioned above, such cooperation acts to reduce the chance of developing nationalist tendencies, as well as constituting an additional force making countries of the region abide by international norms. Specifically, the ASEAN Plus Three process has turned out to be an efficient and productive means to lock China into cooperation.

Yang Zerui takes up the issue of the perception of China as a growing threat by comparing the scale of the impact of China's accession to the WTO with that of Japan's accession to GATT several decades earlier. By analyzing the factors behind the high rates of economic growth, and export growth in particular, Yang suggests some possible scenarios for the future. As long as the political-economic system indicated by the term 'socialism with Chinese characteristics' continues to dominate Chinese thinking, restrictions on the activities of the private sector will continue. At the same time, imports will increase, while export growth may slow down or be cut to zero. Predictions are made difficult by the fact that we have little to go on to estimate chances for improved competitiveness of China's state-owned enterprises and FDI investment. In such a situation the Chinese government may resort to protective measures, including calls for 'voluntary' export restrictions by foreign exporters to the Chinese market. Some statistical computations indicate that there are few reasons to expect that China's accession to the WTO will have a major impact on world trade, certainly less than Japan's membership of GATT had.

Marianne Wiesebron pays much attention to the question of internal economic, social and political stability, presenting an overview of the Latin American continent that takes in most countries. She recognizes the prime importance of relations with the USA, she also discusses Latin American relations with the United States of America, the European Union and recent developments in relations with Asia from a larger perspective. Her focus includes the position of Mexico, a key country in the integration processes of North and South America since it was the first important Latin American country to enter into a close and direct relationship with its giant northern neighbor through membership in NAFTA. Not only is the USA important to South American countries, the USA itself has a major trade interest in the region, which in terms of share, exceeds the relative role of any other region for the USA including both the EU and Japan: in 1996 the area accounted for 40 percent of total U.S. foreign sales, equivalent to the combined markets of Japan, China and East Asia, nearly double that of the EU. Barchefsky expected that by 2010 Latin America will be a bigger market than Japan and the EU together. Yet the FTAA concept has not found it smooth going, despite U.S. pressure. Not only is Latin America beset by economic problems, social and political instability may be worsened by prematurely rushing into the kind of pressure presented by integration processes. Like some of the other contributors, she refers to the diversity of interests of countries in the region, which also prevents possibly interesting alliances with developing countries in Africa and Asia in particular. Brazil had initially established a special relationship with India that went beyond common economic interests and technological cooperation, and included joint efforts to permit both countries to be permanently presented on the Security Council in moves to reform the Council, but relations were seriously damaged in the wake of Indian nuclear tests. While Peru enjoys traditionally close relations with Japan, Brazil and some other Latin American countries feel a greater political affinity with China. In the end, the room for political maneuver both in domestic and international politics is limited, partly due to conditionalities imposed by the IMF. In summing up she concludes that the direction of future regional integration will be a crucial factor in answering the question whether Latin American countries will be able to cope with instability brought about by increasing global interaction.

The problems faced by Latin America are of quite a different order and nature. Paulo G. F. Vizentini discusses integration processes in the context of that region undertaking needed economic reforms, while attempting to preserve the ability for independent policy making vis-à-vis its North American giant neighbor. Various attempts at integration have failed to provide a definite answer. The USA reply to the region's so far only promising attempt at regional institution building—Mercosur/l—has been an attempt to construct an even larger Free Trade Area of the Americas under U.S. leadership. However, neither scheme has had a smooth sailing so far. For Mercosur/l the alternatives are a deepening of the process, the creation of supranational institutions and the widening of membership, or a slow down of objectives and timetables in search of a more realistic approach. In order to provide answers to this question Vizentini proceeds to analyze the main factors behind the current crisis that began with the global aftershocks in the wake of the 1997 Asian financial crisis and resulted in a massive flight of capital from the region. This reduced imports from Argentina, whose economy has since then slid into a very serious crisis for the Argentinian economy as a whole, and led some to predict the end of attempts to keep the regional integration process going. The crisis is worsened by the deterioration of the social situation, and the difficulties of building stable governments able to conduct the necessary reforms without destabilizing the social structure beyond acceptable limits. The crisis is not limited to Brazil and Argentina, since both economies play a key role in South America as a whole, decisions on the future of the continent hinge very much on these two countries. Business has come to appreciate that Mercosur/l may provide the kind of environment that will enable them to survive global competition. The limitations of the institutional architecture of Mercosur/l has been held responsible by some for the slow speed with which integration proceeds, but according to

Vizentini the realities of Latin America, both in domestic and international (regional) politics, prevent the region from following the integration model of the EU. The crisis has also affected governability in general, and there has been an increasing realization that cooperation is the only key to survival for all countries of that continent. This leads Vizentini to suggest that the construction of an even wider form of cooperation, namely the South American Free Trade Area [SAFTA], associated in some form with Mercosur/l, may be the best alternative. Success can, however, only be achieved by establishing sound relations with other poles of world power, such as the United States/NAFTA, the EU and Eastern Asia. Through regional integration the countries of South America may achieve the kind of negotiating position versus the USA that will ensure better conditions for economic development. It is important to regain the initiative, and avoid merely reacting to U.S. policies. As a specific proposal Vizentini refers to an emergency program proposed by Samuel Pinheiro Guimarães, Director of the Institute of International Relations Research of the Ministry of Foreign Relations as one of the few options that may lead Brazil, and the continent as a whole, out of the crisis.

In his contribution, "Mercosur/l and Latin American Integration" Paul Cammack adopts a 'new materialist' approach, a more recent attempt to further develop principles first set out by Marx. The object of his inquiry is the changing relationship between state and society in the context of the rise of global capitalism. Although states never controlled global capitalism, he recognizes (with Panitch) that states author globalization in circumstances in which the determining power of capital is more powerful than ever before, and states seek to "*construct international regimes which define and guarantee the global and domestic rights of capital.*" Regional association may even in turn influence the project of station formation, and the construction and transformation of state identity. As other contributors of this volume have also noted, local, regional, supra-regional, international, state and non-state institutions do not form a neatly compartmentalized construct. They constitute fora for the negotiation of conflicting, and the formulation of common interests; the shaping of agendas is one area where relative strength and hierarchy becomes visible. On the basis of this methodological approach, Cammack pursues the analysis of the regional and local contexts of Mercosur/l. The inclusion of Paraguay and Uruguay barely affected an essentially bilateral arrangement between Brazil and Argentina, which in addition to its cross-border strategic character, also aimed at reorienting social relations in those countries and imposing the discipline of capital over labor, commenced in Brazil in 1990 under President Fernando Collor de Mello and by President Carlos Saul Menem in Argentina since 1991. Like the creation of other regional schemes of cooperation, Mercosur/l too, was partly prompted in reaction to U.S. moves towards schemes of cooperation with Canada and Mexico. The weak domestic basis of Collor de Mello was one of the reasons why he attempted to use the agenda of regionalism to strengthen his domestic political position. This was not easy since as in Argentina, liberal civilian traditions had been weak, and both countries looked back on currents of developmentalist, corporatist and interventionist ideas held since the 1930s. Mercosur/l itself is hampered by the very fact that it is mainly carried by Brazil and Argentina and any friction in their bilateral relationship immediately translates into the weakening of Mercosur/l as an institution—and Brazil as the stronger party by far, is prone to act unilaterally if judged necessary. Also, the consolidation of the WTO, and the greatly strengthened power of the IMF and the WB have eclipsed the usefulness of Mercosur/l in enforcing the neo-liberal agenda. From this macro-perspective, Cammack concludes that Mercosur/l *"appears to be an institution whose best days are behind it."*

Echoing Mao Zedong's saying that *"making revolution is not like going to a party"* one may add that globalization and efforts to cope with it are not undivided pleasures either. The pressures of competition are not merely the consequence of any particular ideology. Individuals and institutions may genuinely dislike competition and integration, but man's existence as a social being forces him to meet these challenges—preferably in a way that allows him to lead a humane existence.

EUROPEAN
PERSPECTIVES

THE WTO, GOVERNMENTS AND GLOBAL BUSINESS
WHO DECIDES THE SHAPE OF INTERNATIONAL TRADE RELATIONS?

Raymond Feddema

For the past two decades three major international economic institutions have gone through difficult times. Two of them, the IMF and the WB, succeeded in triggering controversies for considerable periods of time. The third institution, the GATT, in 1995 renamed the WTO, was already in crisis long before its crisis-stricken meeting in Seattle in December 1999. This attracted the attention of a larger public only after numerous interest groups took to the streets of Seattle to express their discontent with the WTO's policies, protests that were widely covered by the mass media. There is a pressing need to explore what went wrong with these international institutions. This article will analyze problematic issues confronted by GATT, and currently by the WTO.

The WTO, like its predecessor the GATT, has been under attack for some time because of strong doubts about the effects of its policies on human development, which WTO advocates so often claimed to be positive. A fair judgment points to the fact that its benefits are unevenly distributed, and that its disadvantages have a negative impact on the daily life of vast numbers of people all over the world.

In discussing the relationship between trade and the changing power relations in the world, we may wonder why trade should be taken as the

I would like to express my gratitude for the useful comments made by Kurt Radtke on an earlier draft of this article.

core issue for an analysis of changing global power relations. The answer is both simple and complicated. Trade and trade relations are among the most prominent expressions of relations between nations or groups of countries. In sharp contrast with official statements, most of the time phrased in diplomatic jargon and suitably expressed futuristic slogans, from heads of states, ministers, or high officials issued at the conclusion of international meetings, trade is a tangible reality and a straight indicator of the state of relations, acquiring formal shape in the establishment's (mal)functioning trade arrangements.[1]

It was not until the first half of the twentieth century that countries felt the need for a more structured framework for international trade relations, it's outline finally taking shape during the Second World War. It was the United States, at the time already the major economic power in the Western world, which took a leading role in this process. Not surprisingly, it was also the USA that left it's mark on the international trading order after the war.

A number of factors contributed to a change in power relations: European and Asian economies achieved a growing independence after a period of reconstruction, followed by the successful formation of a strong regional grouping in Europe, and the decolonization and subsequent emancipation of less developed countries. Several decades later the collapse of the socialist block and the end of the Cold War left the USA as the only hegemonic power in the military field. International institutions that took shape in the 1940s failed to adapt to the changing world order and came to face a number of crises. The limitations built in GATT from the very start—especially the lack of compulsory rulings—were not completely removed when the WTO was established, and it may be argued that the WTO—like the GATT before—has been unable to meet with the challenges of rapidly changing international (trade) relations. In the nineties the United States, by far the most powerful nation at the time the multilateral institutions were founded, continued to act as if it still dominated the global economy, and this has been one of the factors impeding necessary change.

In order to analyze the complexity of the present crisis in the WTO we studied the development of international trade arrangements and the

---

1. In modern history for example, one can think about the so-called 'unequal treaties' forced upon some Asian countries and trade relations between Western colonial powers, their colonial possessions, and third countries.

organizational structures against the background of changes in the international political and economic order. We will discuss these developments at the level of the GATT/WTO, the government level of their member-countries, and also take in the growing influence of private enterprise. The growing importance of multinational corporations in the global economy has also left its mark on trade relations and arrangements. Last but not least we must pay attention to the changes in flows of global trade: not only did the composition of world trade change, so did the share that different countries have in the total trade of manufactured goods. These changes had a great impact on the international trade agenda, and made it all the more difficult to agree on an agenda for a new round of trade talks for the WTO. In order to understand the dynamics of the current situation we will present a brief historical survey of the predecessors of the WTO.

The Stillborn ITO and GATT

After World War II, the United States took the lead in building a new trading system. Great Britain, the former hegemonic power, had already lost its leading position in the world economy decades earlier, and was now confronted with a wave of decolonization. Between 1947 and 1970 over fifty countries (re)gained their independence and a voice in world affairs.

As early as 1941 the United States and some West European countries made the first steps to set up a world trading system which was to be based on principles of non-discrimination and free exchange of goods and services.[2] During the following years discussions were held between the United States, Great Britain, and Canada on the establishment of a post-war economic system. The first concrete results were achieved at the Bretton Woods conference in 1944.

Named after the conference venue where an institutional framework for the world economy was constructed, the Bretton Woods Institutions established at the end of the Second World War and in subsequent years were intended to provide the institutional framework of the postwar world economy and an order for international trade. The Bretton Woods conference itself established the IMF and the International Bank for

---

2. These were among the aims laid down in the Atlantic Charter in August 1941, and the Lend-Lease Agreements in February 1942.

Reconstruction and Development (IBRD), later mostly referred to as the World Bank.[3]

Both the United States and the United Kingdom were in favor of free trade at the Bretton Woods conference, yet the British negotiators were apprehensive that the United States would force them to open up their markets due to the American economic supremacy. The United Kingdom was not prepared to give up essential domestic economic autonomy concerning issues such as full employment and the economic policies vis-a-vis their colonies. In the end the UK and the USA agreed that many unresolved trade issues would be dealt with in the course of time, and that the International Trade Organization (ITO) would function as a framework for working out the modalities. The ITO was meant to work closely together with the IMF. According to the original plan, supervision over international trade would be a prime task of these institutions. Supervision on the reduction of import quotas and commercial policies in general was to be the main task of the ITO, while the IMF would take care of the abolition of monetary controls over international payments.

From the onset, United States negotiators aimed for the implementation of the ideological notion of 'free trade' as the foremost aim in their talks on trade regulations with other countries. However, the initial attempt to establish a global trading system leading to a gradual liberalization of trade through the ITO, a specialized agency of the United Nations, failed. The origin of the failure must be sought in the Havana Charter, the founding document of the future ITO. The Havana Charter had been composed by the Preparatory Committee in its First Session.[4] The United States drew up the draft that formed the basis for the discussions in the Preparatory Committee. Following the Havana Charter, the Preparatory Committee started drafting the ITO charter in 1946–1947. At the same time and independently, Committee members conducted negotiations to reduce tariffs in anticipation of the establishment of the ITO charter. These negotiations resulted in an interim agreement, the General Agreement on

---

3. For the negotiations on the establishment of the IMF and the IBRD and their outcome, see: W.M. Scammel, *International Monetary Policy*. For the period after: B. Eichengreen, *Globalizing Capital: A History of the International Monetary System*, H. James, *International Monetary Cooperation since Bretton Woods*.

4. Besides the United States, the United Kingdom, the Soviet Union, China, India, France, Brazil, Canada, South Africa, the Netherlands, Chili, Australia, Czechoslovakia, Austria, Cuba, Belgium, New Zealand, Norway, Lebanon, and Luxembourg were members of this committee.

Tariffs and Trade that was signed by 23 nations on October 30, 1947.[5] On January 1, 1948, the GATT came into force as a provisional body to formalize interim trade rules and agreements on tariff reductions. After the completion of the ITO and ratification of its charter by the legislature of its members, parts of the GATT arrangements would be incorporated in or covered by the ITO and the Havana Charter. The Havana Charter covered many more issues than the GATT, and was therefore considered a more comprehensive framework.[6] With the exception of tariff reductions and Most Favored Nation obligations, all other legal commitments of GATT would be suspended. Events took another turn when the U.S. Senate, dominated by an isolationist mood, made it clear that it would not approve the Havana Charter in case the U.S. government submitted it to Congress. As a result, the American president did not submit the Havana Charter, causing other countries not to ratify the Charter and submit it to the United Nations as the depository for the Havana Charter accessions. This clearly demonstrated the economic and political power the United States could exercise at that time in the world.

The contradictions in the trade policies of the U.S. government in the 1940s are similar to the position taken by the USA at present. The American president was certain of defeat in Congress because by ratifying the ITO and Havana Charter, Congress would accept the ITO principles and hand over the power to make changes in duties and trade practices to a multilateral body. That was considered as an unacceptable loss of sovereignty. The economist Jacob Viner analyzed the 1947 situation in this respect as follows:

> *The free trader objects to trade barriers both as obstacles to international special-ization of production in accordance with comparative national advantages for pro-duction, and as sources of international friction.*[7]

But although the message of lifting trade barriers has been trumpeted by the United States government time and again, Viner concludes that this was a purely ritualistic behavior, and that U.S. policy practice is quite different:

---

5. Among the first signatories were 12 developed nations and 11 developing nations. They agreed upon a provisional codification of trade relations.

6. Issues like dispute settlement under ITO auspices, economic development, employment, and restrictive business practices were among the provisions of the Havana Charter.

7. J. Viner, "Conflicts of Principle in Drafting a Trade Charter," *Foreign Affairs*, July 1947, vol. 25, no. 4, p. 613.

But there are few free traders in the present-day world, no one pays any attention to their views, and no person in authority anywhere advocates free trade. "*[...]'The practical issue turns on whether existing trade barriers should be reduced, and if so, how much; and on this point there is perhaps as much division of opinion within countries as between countries. Despite the fact that the international nego-tiations were launched by the United States Government and undoubtedly would collapse if this country were to lose interest in them, intransigent American protec-tionism is at least as serious an obstacle to the successful realization of the Ameri-can trade proposals as the protectionism of other countries.*[9]

Three years after Viner made this analysis predicting the future behavior of the United States, it was indeed that country that blocked the final establishment of the ITO.

It turned out that the ITO was still-born because almost all nations waited for the ratification by the United States government, while the United States organized simultaneously bilateral talks on trade which resulted in reciprocal tariff concessions embodied in the GATT.[10] The specific task of GATT, to find a general consensus among all signatories on the substantial reduction of tariffs and other trade barriers, and to eliminate discrimination, was all that was left. In conclusion we can say that although some of the functions of the ITO were incorporated in the GATT, and some provisions of the Havana Charter taken over by GATT, the functioning of the latter has been seriously limited by the fact that it was not granted the power to force member countries to dismantle controls or to amend duties which were legislatively sanctioned in their own country. GATT's reach and power were so much more limited than that of the ITO that the two were incomparable.[11]

The Main Problem of GATT: How to Lose its Provisional Status?

As a result of the rejection of the ITO by the United States what remained was a provisional agreement without much authority. Compared with the ITO the scope of GATT's responsibilities had been reduced to an extent

8. J. Viner, "Conflicts ..."
9. J. Viner, "Conflicts ..."
10. The ITO Charter had been drafted and discussed during the Spring and Summer of 1947. Delegates of fifty-six countries discussed the draft at the Havana Conference, which lasted from 21 November 1947 until 24 March 1948, and resulted in the Havana Charter. Two years later, only two countries, Australia and Liberia, had ratified the Havana Charter.
11. In contrast with the ITO, the U.S. Congress considered the GATT as much more loosely knit and therefore it could better serve the interests of U.S. trade.

that it could never function as an adequate framework to handle important trade issues in the 1950s. New issues such as trade in services, intellectual property rights, and foreign direct investment which came up the following decades made it all the more clear that GATT was not suited to dealing with the growing complexity of international trade. At best it served as a negotiating forum with marginal rule-making authority. Pressing problems concerning preferential trade agreements or custom unions could not be solved within GATT because it lacked the necessary authority. In addition, breaches of rules and agreements were the order of the day, and there was no working dispute settlement mechanism to solve the growing number of trade disputes. In addition to its internal weakness, from the very beginning GATT became a political instrument in the Cold War which made it all the more difficult to transform it into a rule-based organization. And finally, the decolonization process, the establishment and growth of the European Economic Community, and the rise of multinational corporations (MNCs) onto the world stage, followed by their fast growing global influence, brought basic changes to the international environment which GATT was not equipped to handle.

Also, GATT was hampered from the start by the fact that agriculture had been omitted from its tasks despite the fact that it was one of the most important issues in international trade. It was the United States that insisted that agriculture be left out of the agreement during the negotiations on GATT, because at the time this was judged to be in the U.S. national interest.[12] In the same vein, the predominant position of the USA in fact undermined GATT in the 1950s and 1960s. As the hegemonic power in the capitalist world, the USA dominated the GATT agenda, and ignored GATT rules whenever they did not serve American interests. Right from its inception GATT supported such unfair trade practices, allowing U.S. markets to be closed to foreign competitors at will.[13]

---

12. Later on the USA regretted this decision. At present it looks as if the U.S. government is not fully aware of the implications of bringing agriculture back onto the WTO agenda. A favorite item of American negotiators is EU agricultural subsidies. The latest figures of the U.S. Department of Agriculture demonstrate that the American Federal government subsidies on agriculture are mounting: $7.5 billion in 1997, $12.2 billion in 1998, $20.6 billion in 1999, and $22.9 billion in 2000. *The Financial Times*, 23 July 2001. In addition to the existing agricultural subsidies, the House approved on 5 October 2001 a far-reaching, 10-year farm bill that expands government payments to traditional farm groups with an the overall $170 billion. *Washington Post*, 6 October 2001.

13. One of the best examples of the way the USA kept its markets closed for foreign competitors is the arms trade. This continues until today. For the early period: Merton,

The issue of unfair trade did not play a role in the GATT or in the United States until the end of the Kennedy Round in 1967. Neither Democrats nor Republicans raised the issue before congressional committees. Witnesses from industry did so only occasionally at congressional hearings. However, the late 1960s saw a drastic change in this respect. The economic resurgence of Western Europe and Japan played a major role in the change of attitude concerning antidumping and countervailing-duty rules in the GATT. During the first two decades after the Second World War, American industry had little to fear from Western European or Japanese competition. However starting in the mid-1960s, U.S. companies had to reckon with growing competition from industries that had recovered from the aftermath of the war, and only one decade later the industries of the newly industrialized countries became additional competitors as well.

Self-interest plays a pivotal role in American trade policies. So-called basic or fundamental ideas like free trade are abandoned whenever they do not serve U.S. interests. A good example is the introduction of *Voluntary Export Restraints* (VERs) on a large scale in the 1950s and 1960s. VERs are clearly contrary to the principle of a self-regulating market and the concept of free trade. VERs can be concluded between two countries, a country and private party in another country, or between two private industries in different countries. In the last case VERs will attract the special attention of anti-trust officials. VERs have been in existence for a long time: the first one dates from 1937, and involved Japan and the USA, when Japan agreed 'voluntarily' to restrict its textile exports to the USA Since the first decade after the Second World War the number of VER has been increasing. In the mid-1950s Japan and the USA agreed on a VER concerning textiles, soon to be followed by more VERs, most of which concluded on the initiative of the United States. In the 1960s VERs were very common—and all of them fell outside the GATT system.[14]

J. Peck and F.M. Scherer, *The Weapons Acquisition Process: An Economic Analysis.* For the more recent period: Gansler, J.S., *Affording Defense*; McNaugher,T.L., *New Weapons, Old Politics: America's Military Procurement Muddle*; Markusen, A.R. and S.S. Costigan, eds., *Arming the Future: A Defense Industry for the 21st Century.*

14. For a more detailed description on the spread and the impact of VERs, see: Nigel Grimwade, *International Trade Policy*, pp. 65–93.

There were other developments in the international economy, which demonstrated the shortcomings of the GATT framework and its inability to react effectively in the face of new developments. The emergence of multinational corporations (MNCs) on the international stage at the end of the 1950s, and their growing influence on international trade had not been foreseen at the time GATT started functioning. Initially it was American companies that felt the need to expand their production activities beyond the domestic market, partly in response to the founding of the European Economic Community (EEC). It did not take long before European industries, followed by Japanese, South Korean and other rapidly industrializing economies took a similar path. MNCs increasingly made use of GATT's dispute settlement mechanism through the representative of their home country in GATT, but the GATT framework turned out to be ill suited to deal with this development.

During this period various parts of the world saw the rise of new forms of cooperation and integration. As mentioned above, Western European countries succeeded in building the European Economic Community, while developing countries, mostly former colonies, assembled in new organizations such as the non-aligned movement. Some East Asian economies that were recovering and developing after the war—the most successful example being Japan—developed into fully industrialized nations. In the face of this, the United States resorted to a mixture of unilateral, bilateral, and multilateral policies, willing to operate outside the GATT framework, and at times ignoring it completely. As a consequence, resentment against such hegemonic behavior started growing especially during the period of détente.

Trade has always been considered by the U.S. government as a strategic issue, and as such inextricably linked to the issue of U.S. national security. During the Cold War trade relations had been under strong surveillance, especially when socialist countries were involved. Protectionist sentiment, which has always been strong in the USA, had been temporarily suppressed during the heyday of the Cold War.[15] Liberal trade policies had been justified by successive administrations because they were considered as

---

15. Industrial circles have been ambivalent on the question of protectionism. Firms operating (almost) exclusively on the home market were in favor of protectionism. However, American multinationals expressed their concern over this policy. "*In October 1967, a number of U.S. business leaders joined together because of a shared concern that a new worldwide trade war was in the making. Proposals to severely restrict imports into the*

one of the best weapons against the threat of communism.[16] For a long time the conventional wisdom was that trade restrictions vis-à-vis the American Cold War allies could undermine their economies, making these countries more susceptible to communism.[17] Trade advantages were therefore granted within the grand design of the Cold War, and as a weapon in the fight against communism.

Trade Rounds and the Deepening Crisis of GATT

Until the 1960s, issues concerning international trade could be negotiated in rather short meetings. The specific task of GATT was to find a general consensus among all signatories on the substantial reduction of tariffs and other trade barriers and to eliminate discrimination. During the following decades numerous amendments were made and agreed upon by the signatories of the GATT. However, the yearly negotiating rounds on the issue of tariff reductions showed diminishing results, while contributing to the complexity of the GATT system in a period when the international economy also witnessed some drastic changes outlined above. In order to cope with these developments the GATT signatories decided to embark on comprehensive rounds of trade negotiations. The first of that kind, the Kennedy Round, was held from 1964 until 1967, lasting longer than originally planned. The next one was the Tokyo Round, focusing on trade liberalization. It lasted six years (1973–1979) due to the complexities of the issues involved. It was generally accepted that this framework was ill suited to initiate another round of talks, since this

---

United States were moving through the Congress. Threats of retaliation by foreign nations were being openly voiced." M.J. Slaughter, *Global Investment, American Returns. Mainstray III: ...*, Introduction.

16. Some of the so-called 'frontline states against communism' enjoyed for some time the fruits of liberal American trade policies. This was the case with Japan for a short time after the war. South Korea and Taiwan benefited in the 1960s and 1970s from the relatively open American markets to sell their products. South Korea and Taiwan were allowed to raise high tariff barriers to protect their own infant industries. However, as soon as they grew stronger and became competitors, the U.S. trade policy toward these countries changed. Since the 1980s bitter legal battles have been fought for the dispute settlement panel of the GATT between the U.S. government and their best allies in the Cold War.

17. D. Verdier, *Democracy and International Trade: Britain, France, and the United States*. R. Baldwin, "The Political Economy of Postwar U.S. Trade Policy," *The Bulletin*, 4.

would require an even longer negotiating period. Added to that were ever-widening policy differences between governments which made it even more difficult to come to an agreement. During the 1980s the United States determined the trade agenda to a large extent, because that country was by far the leading exporter: trade in services grew much faster than that in merchandise and the United States took a firm lead in high-tech industries and investment. The United States adopted various approaches, depending on their national interests: they engaged in multilateral negotiations of the Uruguay Round, opted for bilateralism in negotiating a Free Trade Agreement between the United States and Canada, but did not shy away from unilateralism, as exemplified by the use of Section 301 of the Trade Act of 1974.[18]

Another phenomenon in the 1980s was the trend towards legalization, the introduction of legally binding frameworks and rules. That was often even less compatible with the GATT structure. GATT agreements had allowed too many escape clauses, which emasculated the significance of their commitments. Two examples of the need for legalization are the expanded transparency requirements based on Western legal systems, and the legal base for the protection of investments developed on the basis of North American practice.[19]

During the Uruguay Round that lasted eight years (1986–1994) signatories continued to discuss further liberalization of trade. It turned out to be extremely difficult to negotiate successfully on a number of new issues such as investment, intellectual property, problems concerning subsidies, the application of safeguards, market sharing agreements, and services.[20] In the first years of the Uruguay Round, states were frequently

---

18. Section 301 authorizes unilateral trade action against targeted foreign countries. Justification for, as well as use of this Act generates a great deal of controversy. Similar United States Acts, some of them just as controversial, are the International Emergency Economic Power Act (1977), the International Security and Development Cooperation Act (1985), the Narcotics Control Trade Act (1986), and the Cuban Liberty and Democracy Solidarity (LIBERTAD) Act (1996), better known as the Helms-Burton Act.

19. The legal base for protection of investment has been taken from the North American Free Trade Agreement (NAFTA).

20. The pressures exerted by the United States and the United Kingdom to include services in the trade talks are understandable: over 60 percent of the American GDP is derived from services and accounts for 56 percent of the total employment. The U.K. figures are similar to those of the USA. The measured proportion of services in world trade is nevertheless not growing and is much lower than one might expect. Although

confronted with the severe deficiencies of the GATT system. That confirmed growing consciousness among Western governments in the late 1980s that the GATT did not provide an appropriate framework for the comprehensive trading system needed for the above mentioned 'new' issues. The limited ability of the GATT to respond to the rapid changes in the global economy was a major concern of those Western governments who were strongly in favor of a neo-liberal order. They sought a solution by establishing stronger links between the GATT and the Bretton Woods institutions, the IMF and the WB.

It was finally Canada that proposed the establishment of the WTO as a new institution to cope with the problems, which could not be solved within the framework of GATT. The WTO became a membership organization where the GATT was relegated to the status of a trade agreement between the signatories. The WTO was devised as a strong institutional and legal base for international trade in the most comprehensive sense. All members were to comply with its rules, and a strong dispute settlement system put in place to safeguard adherence to WTO rules. At the same time, the new organization was to cooperate with the IMF and WB in matters of mutual concern, each with their own focus, but always in accordance with the dominant neo-liberal ideology.

The WTO: A Solution for GATT's Shortcoming?

The establishment of the WTO resulted from the Uruguay Round, which concluded in 1994. The WTO is a single overarching institutional framework encompassing the GATT, i.e. all agreements and regulations concluded under its auspices, including the results of the Uruguay Round itself. A main aim of the institutional changes was to strengthen the apparatus for monitoring trade policies.

In order to achieve that aim great emphasis was laid on creating a suitable legal institutional framework. Like other international institutions, the GATT was faced with the question, whether international law can function as a legal framework on a *global* scale because it is not subject to

more and more services have become tradable and have contributed to the rise in foreign trade shares, the measured proportion of services in world trade has remained remarkably stable. The share in services of the total foreign trade amounted to: 1981–1990: 21.5 percent, 1995: 20.4 percent, 1999: 21.2 percent, 2000: 19.9 percent. Bank of International Settlements, *71st Annual Report, 1 April 2000–31 March 2001*, pp. 30–31.

authoritative enforcement by a sovereign. The changes made when the GATT was replaced by the WTO were intended to provide a stronger legal base to the new institution and to provide a certain authoritative enforcement capacity for the new organization.

One of the most contested issues in the GATT as well as the WTO has been the settlement of trade disputes. GATT's dispute settlement mechanism proved to be inadequate to solve the growing number of trade disputes. Already during the Kennedy Round and the Tokyo Round, signatories had been confronted with these limitations. Finally during the Uruguay Round that lasted eight instead of the planned six years, major trading nations decided to turn the GATT into an organization that would have the authority to handle the above mentioned problems. Legal authority and the power and means to enforce its rulings were to be vested in the WTO.

Reservations by the U.S. government against the full acceptance of the WTO rules are understandable if we look at the way the USA has traditionally dealt with the issue of dispute settlement. Under the GATT dispute settlement when a country filed an official complaint against another country, a panel of three independent legal experts was formed to hear arguments of the contending parties and to issue a ruling at the end. That ruling had to be ratified by the GATT signatories. At that stage the losing party was able to refuse signing the ruling, effectively vetoing decisions that went against its interest. Yet even before a ruling was reached, political as well as economic pressures might be exerted to influence the panels' ruling. Compared with other GATT signatories, the compliance of the United States with the judgements of GATT's Dispute Settlement panel was the worst.[21]

After the WTO came into force in 1996, the procedures on the definite decision of the panel changed. The Dispute Settlement Understanding (DSU) required a so-called *negative consensus* in order to reject a decision of the panel.[22] The DSU has been lauded by Ostry as the greatest achievement of the WTO:

---

21. R.E. Hudec, *Enforcing International Trade Law: The Evolution of the Modern GATT Legal System*.

22. In case there exists a consensus among the WTO members to reject a ruling by the DSU we speak about a *negative consensus*.

The most important element of the WTO, the 'jewel in the crown', is the greatly strengthened Dispute Settlement Mechanism.[23]

But is that really the case? Looking at the main purpose of the GATT and its successor, the WTO, it is hard to share Ostry's opinion. The GATT and the WTO were meant to facilitate world trade. So far the results of the Dispute Settlement Mechanism cannot give more than mixed feelings. The number of unsettled disputes has increased over the past years to such a level that the commissioner for Trade of the European Union, Pascal Lamy, gave a warning that the DSU-panel could overwork itself.[24] However not only the number of trade disputes that are finally put to the DSU in a formal manner has increased, so has the number of cases in which a judgment finally leads to trade retaliation measures. The best known cases are the disputes over bananas between the USA and the EU won by the American government, which proceeded to retaliate against the EU to an amount of over $400 million against European products. In the case brought by the EU against the USA over the American corporate tax regime, the EU won, the judgement of the DSU giving the EU the right to retaliate for an amount up to $4 billion. How can one call the DSU the 'jewel in the crown' when it blocks trade instead of facilitating it?[25]

Another, more political than technical problem is the way the USA reacts to the way the DSU functions, as well as to its judgments, beginning with the provision on the DSU made by the U.S. legislation when the Uruguay Round was implemented. One of the conditions to accept rulings was that the USA could revoke its membership in the WTO if the DSU

---

23. S. Ostry, *Reinforcing the WTO*, p. 20. See also: D.P. Steger, "WTO Dispute Settlement" in: P. Ruttley, I. Mac Vey and C. George, eds., *The WTO and International Trade Regulation*.

24. Pascal Lamy at a ministerial meeting of the Organization for Economic Cooperation and Development, 27 June 2000. Lamy proposed to create an alternative forum to settle disputes. Until April 2000, 192 cases have reached the DSU. Only fifty percent of them have been really taken up.

25. The only trade that flourishes is the legal trade. Geneva has witnessed an invasion of legal firms specialized in international trade disputes. Most of the fees that range from $200–$1000 an hour are not paid by the tax payers of the country that files the complaint officially, but by the corporation or interest group that pressured its government to do so. Only the United States Trade Representative and the EU have their own legal staff. *Het Financiële Dagblad*, 25 April 2000.

rules against the USA three times in five years.[26] Like many other member countries, the USA complained about the slow procedures of the DSU. Unlike other complainants though, the USA threatened unilateral sanctions in several cases when procedures were not speeded up.[27]

Looking back over the whole post war period we note that some similarities do exist between the domestic power balance in the USA in 1996 and the one in 1947.[28] However one cannot simply explain the recent U.S. stance by referring to these similarities, as will be demonstrated by an analysis of the preparation phase to the Ministerial Conference in Seattle and the way negotiations were conducted at that conference.

The Seattle Test Case

The first serious test case for the WTO was the organization of a new round of trade talks. According to their planning, the Ministerial Conference was to be held in Seattle in November 1999 and would decide the agenda for the new round.[29] The preparations for the conference started under the worst conditions imaginable. A bitter fight over the election of

---

26. T.C. Fischer, *The United States, the European Union, and the "Globalization" of World Trade*, p. 209.

27. The USA did so in the case of the banana dispute with the EU.

28. Looking at the internal politics in the United States the situation in 1947 resembles to some extent that of 1996. In both cases the United States had a Democrat as president and therefore a Democratic administration but both Congress and Senate were dominated by the Republicans. Vines describes the 1947 situation as follows: '*At this stage of the negotiations* [on the drafting of an ITO Charter, RF], *a special difficulty arises out of the facts that the proposals were initiated by a Democratic Administration, that they involve reduction of the American tariff by executive action without reference to Congress, that the Republicans in both Houses of Congress voted against the Trade Agreements Act under which the Executive has the authority to negotiate reductions in duty, and that the Republicans are now in a majority in both Houses of Congress.*' J. Viner, 'Conflicts of Principle in Drafting a Trade Charter', in: *Foreign Affairs*, July 1947, vol. 25, no. 4, p. 613.

29. The Ministerial Conference is the highest authority of the WTO and is composed of one member of each member state. It convenes at least once every two years to decide on issues concerning multilateral trade agreements. The most important administrative body of the WTO is the General Council, which reports to the Ministerial Council, and which has two main branches: The Trade Policy Review Body and the Dispute Settlement Body. In principle the WTO tries like the GATT to decide with consensus. In case a consensus of all member countries cannot be reached, each with one vote will decide with varying majorities of the votes cast. Depending on the issue at stake required majorities differ. For example admission of a new member requires a two-third majority.

the new chairman of the WTO lasted for almost a year. The fight reflected the deep rift between on the one hand those Western countries supporting wholeheartedly the tenants of neo-liberalism, and on the other hand a large group of Less Developed Countries (LDCs), for the most part newly industrialized nations and some Western countries who supported a candidate whom they thought would support a less dogmatic course. In the end a compromise was reached to let the neo-liberal serve the first two years of the four-year term and the other candidate the following two years. However this struggle certainly set the tone for future debates within the WTO.

The next step to the Seattle conference was the preparatory meetings. The USA, being the host of the conference, expected they could put enough pressure on member countries to agree with the American proposals for the agenda. They certainly underestimated the discontent among the majority of the participants over the arrogance of the American negotiators. Resentments against past USA selfish behavior contributed to the deadlock over the American proposals. The manner in which the USA tried to force their main issues, environmental trade standards and labor laws, upon other countries turned out to be counterproductive.

One of the most remarkable phenomena in the preparatory phase was the absence of common proposals for the agenda by regional groupings. Within NAFTA the USA disagreed on most points with the other two members, Canada and Mexico. The two most powerful members of Mercosur/l, Brazil and Argentina, were engaged in bitter trade disputes over beef and textiles. At one stage both countries feared their trade disputes could lead to the end of Mercosur/l. During the six months prior to the Seattle conference, Mercosur/l did not put one common proposal on the table as a regional grouping. The same goes for the Association of Southeast Asian Nations (ASEAN). In this period, Indonesia, the most powerful country within ASEAN, experienced the deepest crisis since its independence. On the trade front, the only registered trade disputes were between Malaysia and Thailand, but even so ASEAN as an organization for economic cooperation in Southeast Asia did not come up with any common proposal either. The same held true for the regional groupings in South Asia and Africa.

The Asia-Pacific Economic Cooperation (APEC), by some analysts considered as an Asian-American counterpart for the EU, was another regional organization that failed to present itself as a well-structured grouping in Seattle.[30] Within APEC two positions have been developed regarding the structure and future operations of the organization. The United States, with strong support of the Anglo-Saxon member countries of Australia and New Zealand, was heading for an organization that would function as a kind of Pacific Trade Organization with its own legal binding procedures and rules put in place according to fixed time tables and a dispute settlement mechanism which resembles that of the WTO. In sharp contrast with the American view, almost all Asian APEC members want to some extent liberalize their economy, but based on consensus and each with a different speed. Legally binding rules as well as fixed time schedules to implement measures for trade liberalization do not fit their policies.

The only regional grouping that presented itself as a group with a well-defined program on all issues was the EU. Under the leadership of its Commissioner for Trade, Pascal Lamy, the EU maintained an extremely strong position on all major points. The EU succeeded to form coalitions with other countries like Japan, South Korea, Norway and Switzerland on many issues. The explanation for the cohesion within the EU must be attributed to the high level of integration of the member states. The EU has its own dispute settlement mechanism, and trade disputes had been settled and solved within the Union in the past. By way of conclusion it appears that there is no ground for the assumption that regionalism functions as a defense against globalization, in this case embodied in the WTO.

We notice that coalitions were formed on the basis of issues, and not regional groupings during the preparatory phase of the Seattle conference. This pattern reflects what some label the anarchy of the post-Cold War world. For decades one of the pillars on which the American hegemonic power rested and through which they could retain their leading role was the alleged omnipresent menace of communism. With the demise of the

---

30. There are many reasons why the APEC cannot be compared with the EU. The most striking difference between the two is the high level of political, economic, legal, and cultural integration within the EU, whereas integration of whatever kind is almost absent in APEC. In connection with this, the size and with it the coherence that make geographical entities into a region is problematic in the case of APEC. Finally, there is the divergence in views among APEC members concerning the aim of cooperation. Notwithstanding all these differences, some authors still claim that the EU opted at the end of the Uruguay Round for a stronger GATT out of fear of APEC as a successful Asian-American alternative to the GATT. See Lloyd Gruber, *Ruling the World: Power Politics and the Rise of Supranational Institutions.*

Socialist block, the need for American patronage diminished, and new coalitions took shape. It turned out that the USA had fewer 'natural' allies than had been assumed. As a consequence they partly lost control over domains in which they had effectively exercised sovereign rule over a long period of time. The Ministerial Conference in Seattle demonstrated this very clearly, but the U.S. government was unable to understand this. A good example was the behavior of the American negotiator Barchefsky. She conducted the negotiations in the build-up to the conference and held a double position: being chairperson, and at the same time acting as the representative of the U.S. government. However it was not only the head of the American delegation that miscalculated. Leading figures in the WTO did not understand that the drive toward deeper integration is so much more complex and different in scope than during the time of the establishment of the Bretton Woods system and the birth of GATT soon after. Trade is so much more contentious now that we might label the divergences in trade policies the main focus of a new Cold War.

In the preparation for the Seattle meeting and during the meeting itself, the developing countries asked for the establishment of a comprehensive framework for sustainable development. In regard to this, the WTO was conspicuous by its absence. The preamble of the WTO is the only place in the legal framework of that organization where the principle of sustainable development has been formally introduced. Some of the delegates thought they could approach problems of development as their predecessors did in 1947. Now though they were confronted with the growing anger of developing countries, their population partly represented by the NGOs which manifested themselves clearly in Seattle, as well as concerned NGOs acting on a global level. They aired their discontent over the WTO's policies in general, and more specifically its lack of vision on sustainable development and environmental issues.

Another question that angered many delegates in Seattle was the lack of openness. Many important issues were discussed by industrialized nations in closed sessions. Most delegates of the LDCs were kept out, while in the plenary meeting they were admonished to strive for increasing transparency. Instead of holding open discussions leading to the formulation of the trade agenda for the coming decade, the WTO continued to marginalize most groups in society. The group they did not forget was the MNCs. They play a vital role in formulating regulatory frameworks for international trade. Business leaders from different continents have established a network and organize yearly meetings to conclude what they 'urge' their respective governments to do in order to facilitate their business. Such networks have been established between the USA and Europe (The Transatlantic Business Dialogue, TBD), Latin America and the United States, and the EU and Latin America (Mercosur/l–European Union Business Forum, MEBF). In terms of development the last two lag behind the first one. These organizations, especially the TBD, make 'recommendations' to their governments to follow their advice and implement 'fully and timely' their demands. The language is clear:

> We urge the Governments to make such progress that a clear indication can be given at the CEO Conference in Cincinnati that the TBD recommendation will be met.[31]

The new regulations are partly made in these circles, not subject to ordinary procedures. The WTO is directly involved in all this, together with a very select group of (rich) member states. They work towards liberalization of markets on all fronts. A good example is the recommendation adopted in the field of telecommunication:

> The TBD encourage both the U.S. administration and the EU Commission to continue to push for the fast and far-reaching implementation of existing liberalization commitments, for further commitments from the WTO Member States, and for full liberalization of the telecom sector as a condition for the accession of new WTO Members.[32]

It seems clear who gives the directives, and who has to carry them out. LDCs are not involved in the majority of these activities, but they will be directly confronted with the effects of full-scale liberalization. In our assessment the WTO is merely an organization for the MNCs that should serve their particular interests. For them, an analysis of the impact of their policies on the lives of millions of people is apparently irrelevant.

Will There Be a Next Trade Round?

The question whether there will be a new trade round in the near future is hard to predict at this stage. It all depends on some major players such as

---

31. The Transatlantic Business Dialogue, *Cincinnati CEO Conference Briefing Book*, p. 5.

32. The Transatlantic Business Dialogue, *Cincinnati CEO Conference Briefing Book*, p. 37.

the EU and the USA Both trading blocs express their concerns about the future of the WTO in case they will not succeed to set a new trade agenda in November 2001 to start a new round of talks.

The position of the USA has changed since Seattle. After the debacle for which the U.S. government partly is to blame, the USA assumed that they could do without the WTO. But just one year after Seattle, a report of the Business Roundtable (BRT) appeared containing conclusions rather shocking for many Americans.[33] Since the Seattle conference many trade agreements have been signed, and the USA was absent in almost all of them. For the first time since the Second World War, Americans had to reach the conclusion that *"they are not indispensable anymore."*

The question remains to what extent this conclusion of American chief executive officers is shared by other Americans. Most American politicians find their view on the U.S. position in the world better represented by the *New York Times* commentator David Sanger. In his article "A Grand Bargain" he depicted the prevailing American view on the country's position in the world:

> *The new administration comes to power with far greater challenge of preserving America's place atop the world economy while defusing resentments about U.S. economic, cultural, and military might. Washington must convince other nations— both rich and poor—that it is shaping a world economic system for their benefit as well as its own.*[34]

Starting from that point, Sanger views the Seattle debacle as

> *...a remarkable rebellion against American primacy, an assertion that growing American power would meet growing international resistance.*[35]

American politicians are well aware of changes in the world over the past decade. However they refuse to acknowledge the consequences such as the decline of American economic hegemony. On the contrary, the U.S.

---

33. Business Roundtable, *The Case for U.S. Trade Leadership: The United States is Falling Behind,* February 9, 2001. The Business Roundtable is an association of chief executive officers of leading U.S. corporations.

34. D. Sanger, "A Great Bargain," *Foreign Affairs,* Vol. 80, No. 1. January/February 2001, p. 66.

35. Sanger, "A Great Bargain," p. 66.

government and its citizens act on many occasions as if these changes do not affect their position. A reformulation of American policies is therefore not taking place in a proper way and in response to global change.

Reacting to the Seattle failure, Sanger gives two reasons for it. The first reason is a more technical one referring to the voting power of developing nations as a direct result from the change from the GATT to the WTO:

> *For years the world's developing nations were never taken seriously in global trade negotiations. Their economies were too small, and there were too many of them. Instead, the big trade accords in the 1990s were negotiated among the United States, Japan, Canada, and Europe. These countries set the agendas and precooked the results before global negotiations started up. They could afford to do so because the rest of the world desperately needed access to markets. But the WTO's creation changed the balance of power[...] Disenfranchised nations suddenly have the ability to upset the agenda of the large powers. At Seattle they used that power for the first time.*[36]

Sanger's second reason for the Seattle debacle sounds like a conspiracy against the USA instead of a natural reaction to American behavior in the past decades:

> *For the first time, the developing nations—with the help from some wealthy countries that saw an opportunity to protect themselves—resisted what they viewed as a relentless American onslaught to reshape the world economy on Washington's terms.*[37]

Like most Americans, Sanger cannot present a critical analysis of U.S. policies in the past and its selfish behavior that undermined the GATT and later the WTO. That behavior is taken for granted when he discusses for example the U.S. position vis-a-vis the DSU uncritically, concluding:

> *In short, Washington seems willing to heed the rulings of a panel of non-American judges as long as the political stakes are sufficient low.*[38]

The developing countries are a main target in Sanger's analysis. While the U.S. government can carry out protectionist policies by not obeying

---

36. Sanger, "A Great Bargain," p. 69.
37. Sanger, "A Great Bargain," p. 66.
38. Sanger, "A Great Bargain," p. 70.

international rules and regulations when American jobs are at stake, and therefore potentially damaging vital political and economic interests, Asian leaders are labeled as 'weak' when they

> *have little interest in triggering further upheaval by opening markets while they are desperately trying to forestall mass layoffs.[39]*

What the developing world can expect from the USA is 'a Grand Bargain':

> *If ever there was a moment for a grand bargain between rich and poor, now is the time. [...] The world's poorest nations need hard evidence that they will benefit from a global economy rather than become its first victims.[40]*

Does Sanger not understand what kind of havoc the Bretton Woods institutions have caused among poor countries throughout the 1980s and 1990s? Is he really ignorant of the independent evaluations of structural adjustment programs that clearly demonstrated the detrimental effects on societies that they were forced upon?[41]

In case the U.S. government persists in pushing developing countries in the direction proposed by Sanger, the WTO will continue to alienate that group of members. The unequal trade relations from the nineteenth century we referred to in the beginning of this article still exist.

Meanwhile the present director-general of the WTO, Mike Moore, ignores the protests from developing countries against the present trade regulations and practices by saying:

> *The multilateral trading system has probably done more to boost living standards and lift people out of poverty over the past 50 years than any government intervention[42]*

---

39. Sanger, "A Great Bargain," p. 71.

40. Sanger, "A Great Bargain," p. 73.

41. The impact of the IMF and World Bank programs on developing countries have been discussed over the past two decades. The literature on this issue demonstrates the disagreement among scholars on the consequences for the developing world. One of the most balanced analysis on this subject: A. Przeworski and J.R. Vreeland, "The Effect of IMF Programs on Economic Growth," *Journal of Development Economics,* Vol. 62, Issue 2, August 2000, pp. 385–421.

42. Speech by Mike Moore at a meeting of EU ministers and IMF/World Bank officials in London. *The Financial Times,* 20 March 2001.

Moore's words will not convince developing countries to change their objections against the agenda on new trade talks as proposed by the USA and other industrialized countries in Seattle.

The WTO as an organization cannot afford a second debacle, but at present the signs are not so good since progress in the preparatory talks so far has been very limited. This might lead us to the conclusion that the WTO seems to be outdated, like its predecessor the GATT and all the other Bretton Woods institutions. What remains to be seen is whether rules and institutions matter at all where naked power seems to be able to disregard them whenever convenient in the pursuit of national interest.

DEEPENING OF MULTILATERAL INTEGRATION IN THE WORLD TRADE ORGANIZATION

Gerrit Faber

Introduction

The liberalization of world trade is an ongoing process. There is a tradition of many decades dedicated to bringing trade barriers down through multilateral negotiations in the framework of the GATT, which has been continued in the WTO since 1995. Tariffs and quantitative restrictions (QRs) were singled out as the most important factors hampering trade. However, to the extent this trade liberalization has been successful, other barriers have become more important as bottlenecks for trade flows. These other barriers are largely the consequence of public regulation of markets. In order to continue multilateral economic liberalization, these regulatory barriers have been the object of trade negotiations, as have the further lowering of tariffs and quantitative restrictions. This shift in multilateral trade talks has changed the nature of the negotiations. In the past, trade liberalization mainly affected the relative protection of sectors, the area of industrial policy. In the new situation, environmental, social, consumer, public health and cultural policies are drawn into the negotiations as these policies lead to regulatory barriers. This complicates trade negotiations. The number of potential conflicts has increased many times and trade-offs have become more difficult as different policy areas cannot easily be compared. Groups of countries have succeeded in finding ways to diminish

---

The author thanks Sebastiaan Princen for his comments on an earlier draft of this article. The remaining errors are to be attributed to the author.

regulatory barriers. Regional integration of this kind is called 'deep' integration: the existing objective of economic liberalization is realized by common regulation and policies and by constraining the powers of the participating countries.[1] In the European Community (EC), deepening has occurred in the Dassonville and Cassis de Dijon rulings of the European Court of Justice in 1974 and 1979 respectively, and in the Single European Act (1985) and the Treaty of Maastricht (1991). The NAFTA agreement also contains elements of deep integration.[2] This paper discusses deepening of integration at the multilateral level: the harmonization and approximation of regulatory diversity through global mechanisms.

The article is composed as follows. The Section 'Regulation and Integration' discusses the reasons for the existence of regulatory trade barriers. Section 'Harmonization of Regulatory Barriers in the GATT\WTO' briefly describes the progress of deep integration in the world economy, particularly as far as the bringing down of regulatory trade barriers is concerned. Section 'Future Harmonization of Standards' looks into the future of deep integration in the world economy. Section 'Conclusions' summarizes the main conclusions.

Regulation and Integration

The deepening of international integration has a very fundamental reason. In the traditional concept of integration or trade liberalization, the lowering of tariffs and abolition of QRs were the central issues. Through diminishing these trade barriers, trade would increase and would bring welfare gains to the participating countries through consequent static and dynamic effects. This would apply world wide and, if certain conditions were met, would also apply to regional trade liberalization in free trade areas (FTAs) and Customs Unions (CUs). For higher forms of regional integration, (common markets and economic and monetary unions in particular), the simple negative integration would have to be complemented with positive integration. The latter concept is an early formulation of the realization of the necessity to deepen the regional integration process after tariffs and QRs have been abolished. For the purpose of this paper, it is useful to discuss the background of the deepening of integration in general.

---

1. J. Pelkmans, *European Integration. Methods and Economic Analysis.*
2. P. van Dijck, "NAFTA: A model for the WTO," pp. 127–153.

The case for free trade (or trade liberalization) is one of the most non-controversial conclusions among economists. Tariffs and quotas lower the level of welfare of the country that imposes these trade barriers with respect to its international trade. There are a few well-defined exceptions to this conclusion. A large importing country may improve its terms of trade (the optimal tariff case) and a country may reap rents if its exporters capture a dominating market share in the presence of oligopolistic market conditions (the case of strategic trade policy). The truth is that the practical application of these exceptions is difficult or impossible.

Despite the unanimous preference for free trade among economists, the use of tariffs and quotas is widespread. The main explanation for this is twofold. First, for some countries, tariffs are an important source of government income. This applies in particular to less-developed countries. Second, the political economy approach to trade policy has explained the existence of tariffs and quotas by introducing politicians who try to maximize the votes they get in the next election. It can be argued that politicians make a trade-off between the lowering of the general level of welfare that results from tariffs and quotas and the support they get from sectoral groups that profit from protection and from groups that are in favor of trade liberalization.[3] A somewhat different explanation is based on the conservative welfare function politicians are supposed to maximize.[4] In this approach, politicians are supposed to accord an income decline in certain—particularly in lower income—groups a much greater weight than they do general increases in welfare. Sectors that face severe import competition will be protected from a sharp income decline. Empirical studies give broad support to these political economy explanations.

If it is accepted that tariffs and quotas are the outcome of political decision making in which policy makers try to realize their objectives by balancing collective, social and sectoral interests, it follows that trade liberalization can only be achieved if it enables the relevant politicians to strike a balance between the different pressure groups and the collective interest that maximizes their utility function. The GATT principles of non-discrimination and reciprocity are necessary to enable politicians to conclude such package deals. These principles bring about the transparency and predictability that reduce transaction cost sufficiently to make these

---

3. e.g. G.M. Grossman, and E. Helpman, *Protection for Sale*; D. Mitra, "Endogenous Lobby Formation and Endogenous Protection: ...," pp. 1116–1135.
4. W. M. Corden, *Trade Policy and Economic Welfare*.

trade agreements possible and viable.[5] In the framework of regional integration, politicians' transaction cost of liberalization will probably be lower. Among countries that are at a comparable level of development, the risk of inter-industry competition, which may wipe out complete sectors, is much lower than at the global level. Transparency is higher because the number of participants is much lower and cheating is either easily detected or sanctioned. Finally, in regional integration bodies, compensatory mechanisms are easier to introduce than at the global level if the distribution of gains and losses over the participating countries turns out to be more unequal than expected.

How does this relate to deep integration? The first difference with tariffs and QRs is that most of the regulatory barriers that are relevant in this case have not been introduced to support import-competing sectors against low-priced imports. In most cases, and it is assumed here to be general, regulations have been introduced to correct market outcomes.[6] The traditional economic analysis of public intervention starts from the hypothesis that markets serve the interest of economic subjects best through the invisible hand. However, there may be market failures that give rise to too high or too low levels of production and/or consumption of particular goods and services as social costs and benefits differ from private costs and benefits. Reasons for this are negative and positive external effects, the collective nature of certain goods and services and transaction costs. It is generally acknowledged that tariffs and quotas are instruments that may realize the objective of increasing or lowering the production and consumption of certain products, but at a relatively high welfare cost. Generally, it is more efficient to realize the gains from taking away the market failure through the expedient of intervening directly at the source of the deviation of social from private welfare: for instance, by limiting the emissions of polluting matter, taxing the use of certain natural resources, prescribing process and product norms or subsidizing activities that have positive external effects.

A market failure that is the consequence of transaction costs may have several causes. Lack of transparency, opportunistic behavior, asymmetric information are such causes. Asymmetric information arises in the event that a buyer or seller do not have the same knowledge as a result of which one of them pays too much or does not receive enough, or a transaction

---

5. G. Faber, "International Trade ...," pp. 79–105.
6. A. Ogus, *Regulation. Legal Form and Economic Theory.*

does not come about. Asymmetric information has a broad interpretation: consumers are no experts with respect to food safety (such as the effects of additives), the effectiveness—including the side-effects—of medical therapies, the safety of cars and machinery. On the other hand, producers are experts; they have done research and devised production technologies. Sometimes, the buyer has more knowledge than the supplier; this is the case in the insurance industry. Asymmetric information may be countered by a variety of measures: the generally applied principle in the law that protects buyers against hidden defects and the liability of producers for their products may force sellers and producers not to misuse their position of being better informed. Labeling of products may redress the inequality in information. In many cases, governments do not try to correct the information asymmetry, but decide for the less informed party by prescribing the qualities of certain products and forbidding products that do not meet these prescriptions. In many industrialized countries, this applies to products such as medicines, pesticides, cars, electrical machinery, toys and food. For many services, the provider has to meet certain qualifications (diplomas, membership of an institution that guarantees quality and so forth), before he or she is allowed to begin in business.

The correction of market failures differs substantially over countries in two respects. First, the extent to which market failures are recognized and redressed varies. This depends on factors such as income, resource endowments and national culture. Protection of the environment has often been considered to be dependent to a large extent on the level of welfare.[7] Rich countries forbid cars that produce very polluting exhaust gases, while poor countries do not. The same applies for emissions by steel and chemical plants. Other factors, such as surface area, climate and population density, also determine to some extent whether a country will take more or less stringent measures to protect its environment. Cultural differences may play a role as well. If a country attaches more importance to technological innovation than other countries, it will stimulate high tech production more. Religious differences are relevant as well. These differences in national preferences are often difficult to overcome. As some countries do not consider a market failure a problem—or do not even recognize a market failure—the basis for harmonization is absent.

---

7. The World Bank, "Development and the Environment"; *The Economist*, "Dirt Poor. A Survey of Development and the Environment."

Second, given the same perception of market failures, countries try to correct these failures in different ways. As indicated above, there are many instruments that can be applied. Given a certain market failure, a government may use instruments that vary according to the degree of intervention.[8] Information measures require producers to supply buyers with certain facts about the product or service. Prior approval makes it necessary to convince an official agency that the product concerned meets the standards that have been set with respect to health, safety or the environment. In between these two extremes are regulations in the form of standards which allow the product or service to be sold without *ex ante* controls, but use sanctions to enforce compliance. In this in-between category, Ogus distinguishes target, performance and specification standards. A target sanction imposes criminal liability for certain harmful consequences arising from using the product. A performance standard requires certain qualities to be met without exactly prescribing how to realize this while a specification standard compels the supplier to use certain materials and/or production processes or forbids certain materials. Which kind of instrument is preferred depends on several factors. Level of welfare is one of them, as more coercive measures necessitate more precise standards and a greater institutional capacity to formulate and enforce standards. Should the market failure be perceived in the same way by trading partners, harmonization is much easier to bring about than if there is a disagreement on the question whether there is a problem at all. The European Community offers a good illustration of this. In intra-trade, 'measures having equivalent effect' to a QR are forbidden (Art. 28 EC Treaty). Exceptions are allowed "*on grounds of public morality, public policy or public security; the protection of health and life of humans, animals or plants...*" (Art. 30). However, if the regulatory objectives of the member states are equivalent, they have to accept imports from other member states although these states use different regulations. This is the principle of mutual recognition. In the absence of equivalent objectives an EU member state can use the derogation of Art. 30 as long as the measure taken is proportional with respect to the objective and least trade distorting. In that case, a regulatory barrier is accepted.

Differences in regulations will affect international trade in different ways. First, countries fear that international trade may undermine the national standards through importation of products that do not meet the—

---

8. A. Ogus, *Regulation. Legal Form and Economic Theory,* p. 151.

presumably higher or more effective—standards of the importing country. By applying the national standards on imported goods, this effect is prevented. The result is that new trade barriers are created, and trade flows will change. Domestic producers in the standard setting country may profit from market segmentation that is the result of the regulations. However, the high and more interventionist standards will increase their cost of production which may put them in a less competitive position in foreign markets. There is also the possibility that high-standard producers turn the quality of their product into a marketing asset.

Second, if the goods concerned are produced under economies of scale, differences in standards will make large-scale production impossible or less attractive; international specialization is below its potential level and prices are higher than would be the case with uniform standards. Third, producers may shift their plants to production sites where standards are lower.

As a result of these reasons, there is a strong feeling among politicians and NGOs that the present trading order and further trade liberalization can only be maintained if the diversity in regulation is taken away. At the same time, there is a widespread awareness that standards should be harmonized to the highest level. This 'level playing field argument' is reinforced by the conviction in many developed countries that their regulation is based on universal moral notions that should be applied in all countries of the world.[9] The world trading order is used as the mechanism to bring this about. These arguments are different from those used by economists: regulatory trade barriers should be abolished because they diminish international trade and lower welfare compared to the situation where the market failure is corrected without creating trade barriers. However, it can be argued that the differences in regulations do not need to be wiped out in many cases, and that importing countries should not force standards upon other countries as long as exporters do not inflict damage on the social welfare of the importing country. The first reason is that high standards may reflect relative scarcity of certain resources (such as clean air) in the importing country. The lowering of production that uses these resources intensively and a corresponding increase in imports increases the social welfare of the importing country concerned. A second reason for not trying to create a level playing field is

---

9. J. Bhagwati, "The Demands to Reduce ...," pp. 9–41.

that in some cases the realization of the ultimate objective, e.g. the non-occurrence of child labor, is not brought any nearer by harmonized standards.[10] This line of reasoning, although valid, will not be pursued here. Instead, it is concluded here that harmonization of regulation is an issue in international trade negotiations for two reasons.

First, it is a fact that there are regulatory trade barriers. Further integration of the world economy requires the abolition of these barriers. It is interesting to find out how this can be realized under the recognition that countries can have legitimate reasons for different valuations of market failures and their correction. Second, governments and pressure groups are increasingly active to introduce new and more restrictive standards, and to extend their standards to other countries; trade preferences and bans and quotas are used as levers to make other countries accept the standards concerned. The two reasons together may produce tensions. More and stricter standards may not only give rise to further distortions in international trade, it also makes the world trading order the object of intensified political discussions. As the number of 'constituencies' of commercial policy increases, potential conflicts between interest groups and policy makers increases and policy makers may face mounting difficulties in striking a balance between the different interests.[11] At the same time, policy makers may act as brokers between the interest groups and forge coalitions. Vogel has shown that trade liberalization in regional groupings and at the global level has often coincided with the upward harmonization of standards through coalitions between economic interest groups and consumer and environmental organizations.[12] This works in particular as long as there are strong institutions that promote free trade. The EU is a case in point. Given the fact that the WTO is much weaker than the EU as it does not have the powers to set the regulatory standards of its members, the deepening of global integration could cause a growing dissatisfaction with the WTO on the side of both the consumer and environmental groups and the free traders. Consumer and environmental groups blame the WTO for letting low standard countries overexploit their resources (labor, natural resources) and for undermining the high

---

10. J. Bhagwati, "The Agenda of the WTO," pp. 27–61; T.N. Srinivasan, "International Trade and Labour...," pp. 219–245; W. Tims, "New Standards in World Trade Agreements: ...," pp. 307–317.

11. M. Smith, and S. Woolcock, "European Commercial Policy: ...," pp. 439–462.

12. D. Vogel, *Trading Up* ...

standards in their own countries. Groups that have an economic interest in trade liberalization will blame the WTO for not lowering regulatory trade barriers to a sufficient degree. The broadening agenda of trade liberalization may turn out to be too much for the WTO. If that should happen, the world trading order as such would have serious problems.

Harmonization of Regulatory Barriers in the GATT\WTO

From its inception, the General Agreement on Tariffs and Trade (GATT) contained Art. XX that allows contracting parties to enforce measures *'necessary to protect human, animal or plant life or health'* or *'relating to the conservation of exhaustible natural resources'*. These measures are allowed subject to the requirement that they are not applied in a manner *'which would constitute a means of arbitrary or unjustifiable discrimination between countries where the same conditions prevail, or a disguised restriction on international trade...'* This early reference in GATT to the possibility that national policies beyond the trade area may have consequences for international trade, is phrased as an exception to the GATT principles of non-discrimination and national treatment. However, this article does not stimulate deepening of world wide integration through harmonization in the relevant policy areas. On the contrary, it permits the continuation of different policies as long as international trade is not unduly distorted or hampered, the measures are 'necessary' and are related to the particular objective. Only a restrictive interpretation may have prompted international co-operation. This occurred in the tuna-dolphin case, in which the USA was forbidden to enforce its environmental policies outside its jurisdiction; instead, the USA was urged to conclude international agreements with the relevant countries.

In the first three decades of GATT's existence, Art. XX played a marginal role. The breaking down of traditional trade barriers (tariffs and quotas) were the core activities of GATT. The General Agreement started in 1947 with a first round of trade negotiations which led to an agreement to lower tariffs on manufactures. A number of rounds followed—in 1949, 1951, 1956 and 1962—all mainly concerned with tariffs on manufactures. The Kennedy Round (1964-1967) was to expand the negotiations from tariffs on manufactured products to the liberalization of trade in agricultural products. This could only succeed if the contracting parties would have been willing to put their agricultural policies on the negotiating table. An agreement in this area could not be attained as the conflict, primarily between the USA and the EU over the degree and method of agricultural support, could not be resolved.[13] The EU continued to set up its protectionist Common Agricultural Policy (CAP). The main result of the Kennedy Round was, again, a substantial lowering of import tariffs on manufactured products. Thus, the first attempt at the multilateral level to deepen the integration of goods market failed.

A second attempt at deepening was made during the Tokyo Round of Trade Negotiations (1973-1979). This effort was not directed at agriculture but was prompted by the increasing importance of regulatory barriers to international trade. The Round produced eleven agreements or codes, which were separate from the Tokyo Round agreement. Nine of them dealt with non-tariff issues. Of these, the following relate to regulatory barriers to trade: the codes on standards, subsidies, government procurement and on civil aircraft. The codes have been concluded among a subset of the contracting parties, and only applied to these countries (among which were the EC and the USA).

The experience with the codes has been mixed. Generally, the institutional set-up of the codes (committees, dispute settlement) has given rise to exchange of information, consultation, and early settlement of disputes in some codes. Other codes could not solve the conflicts between the signatories on the use of trade distorting measures. This applied in particular for the codes on civil aircraft and on subsidies.[14]

The most generally applicable code was the standards code. It addressed the trade barriers that may arise from standards, technical regulations and certification systems. These standards are motivated by the wish to protect public health, consumers, the environment or exhaustible resources. Although differences in standards are allowed as long as the conditions of Art. XX are fulfilled, a number of contracting parties wanted to diminish the trade reducing effects of these standards. The basic principles of the code are national treatment, non-discrimination and transparency. The code itself does not develop standards, but requires the signatories to use standards in the least trade distorting way. To this end the code urged the signatories to use international standards; it granted foreign manufacturers access to domestic certification systems; and it provided for facilities

---

13. J.W. Evans, *The Kennedy Round in American Trade Policy,* G.P. Casadio, *Transatlantic Trade ...*

14. R. Stern, and B. Hoekman, "The Codes Approach," pp. 59–69.

for foreign manufacturers to gather information on standards and for prior notification of intended standards with a period for comments by trade partners. The code has been effective. It has contributed to the internationalization of product, health and safety standards, to the reduction of various trade-distorting applications of standards and has made the imposition of technical barriers to trade more difficult. Many potential problems have been solved in the permanent Committee on Technical Barriers to Trade meetings and in bilateral consultations between the signatories.[15]

During the Uruguay Round much energy was invested in the further harmonization of regulatory diversity. This produced a number of agreements. First, the Standards Code has been expanded into an Agreement on Technical Barriers to Trade (TBT). Furthermore, an Agreement on the Application of Sanitary and Phytosanitary Measures (SPSM) was concluded. Contrary to the previous codes, these agreements apply to all members of the WTO. A second difference is an even stronger emphasis on the formulation of international standards and on mutual acceptance of national standards.

The TBT agreement prescribes national treatment in the application of technical regulations. The regulations "*shall not be more trade-restrictive than necessary to fulfil a legitimate objective*," according to Art. 2. These legitimate objectives include the protection of human health or safety, animal or plant life or health, or the environment. The necessity of regulations shall be established on the basis of, *inter alia*, 'available scientific and technical information, related processing technology or intended end-uses of products'. A major difference with the previous code is that not only the characteristics of the product itself are taken into account, but also its processing technology. This opening for 'process standards' is relevant to the link between trade and social and environmental protection. The preference for scientific information to motivate standards is striking. If a country introduces a technical regulation that is in accordance with an internationally agreed standard, "*it shall be rebuttably presumed not to create an unnecessary obstacle to international trade* "(art 2.5 TBT Agreement). Stricter regulations are allowed if the international standards do not realize the 'legitimate' objectives of the country concerned. Furthermore, members shall give "*positive consideration*" to the regulations of other members in order to accept them as equivalent even if these differ from their own, "*provided they are*

---

15. L. Eicher, "Technical Regulations and Standards," pp. 137–143.

satisfied that these regulations adequately fulfil the objectives of their own regulations" (Art. 2.7). This goes into the direction of the principle of mutual recognition as used in the EU which is dependent on the existence of equivalence of objectives.

The SPSM agreement heavily relies on international standards as well: they are supposed to fulfil the criteria of Art. XX. These standards are developed in the Codex Alimentarius Commission, the International Office of Epizootics and organizations operating in the framework of the International Plant Protection Convention.

Members are allowed to impose stricter standards if there is a scientific justification and by using risk assessment techniques developed by the relevant international organizations. The burden of proof is with the country that wants stricter regulations than those that have been internationally agreed. If relevant scientific evidence is insufficient, stricter measures may be imposed provisionally 'on the basis of available pertinent information, including that from the relevant international organizations as well as from sanitary or phytosanitary measures applied by other members'. Members are encouraged to recognize the product regulations of other members. If the exporting member has regulations that differ from the importing country's regulations, and the former can show that its measures achieve the importing member's appropriate level of sanitary and phytosanitary protection, the regulations are considered to be equivalent (Art. 4.1). This is again similar to, but less coercive than the EU principle of mutual recognition.

This overview shows that the global integration process brought forward by the negotiations in the GATT and the WTO has increasingly limited the freedom of public regulators to introduce regulations that aim at the correction of market failures. This has been done by stimulating the formulation of standards and specific minimum product norms in international organizations and the formulation of constraints for the introduction of stricter norms than internationally agreed. As a result, regulatory barriers have been abolished or diminished in large sections of world trade. It should be stressed, however, that this harmonization of standards has been far from universal: food safety is largely harmonized by the Codex Alimentarius while technical standards for other products are much less harmonized.[16] It is precisely in the area of food safety regulations where individual countries have introduced stricter rules than

---

16. D.W. Leebron, "Lying Down with Procrustes: ...," pp. 41–118.

those that had been agreed internationally that have led to major conflicts. Thus, regulatory trade barriers remain, or are newly introduced, where no international standards exist and members cannot show equivalence, or where members are allowed to introduce stricter regulations than the international ones. Such trade barriers should again fulfill the criteria of least trade restrictiveness, necessity/proportionality and national treatment. A regulatory area that has largely been left out in the WTO are process standards. The WTO has a preference for product standards that are related to the physical qualities of goods and that can be measured, while process standards relate to technologies that are often difficult to establish at the moment of importation.

Despite the steps that have been taken to lower regulatory barriers at the multilateral level, major conflicts among WTO members have arisen. The WTO Ministerial in Seattle that was to launch the Milennium Round failed as a result of a conflict over process standards, in particular labor standards. The use of hormones in cattle breeding and the use of genetically modified organisms (GMOs) have for many years been a source of tensions between the EU and the USA.[17]

Future Harmonization of Standards

States are defined by their territory. In their territory, states enjoy national sovereignty. Governments decide on the extent to which the economic process is co-ordinated by market forces and intervene with different instruments. Through integration into the world economy, economies are becoming more interdependent. Their economic fate is increasingly determined by what happens outside their territory. This diminishes national sovereignty. The advantages of integration in the world economy and globalization are clear as well: through increasing specialization the global allocation of resources improves, giving rise to increasing levels of welfare. The trade-off between the nationally preferred regulations and economic benefits obtaining from harmonization is hotly debated. In a democratic society, the trade-off should at least be transparent and public in order to lead to decisions that have the required legitimacy.

Technological innovation is stimulating this process of globalization. The results of these developments are contradictory in some respects. As a result of higher incomes, people change their preferences. They want

---

17. P. van Dijck, and G. Faber, "After the Failure of Seattle: ...," pp. 217–355.

better, and more healthy products; they are able to devote more of their energy to care for the environment both in their immediate surroundings and far away; they are better informed about what they consume or could consume. Consumers can make better decisions because their lack of information is being reduced.

New technologies enable consumers to obtain more and better information about their opportunities and about the situation in other countries. On the one hand, this leads to increased demand from national governments for regulation: to take away external effects, to prescribe 'better' products and services and to protect values in other countries, or, in other words, to expand the area of application of domestic regulations to the territory of the other countries. Politicians are prone to give in to such demands, particularly if they are able to link these demands with other pressures. Environmental pressure groups have often made coalitions with economic interest groups in order to induce policy makers to introduce stricter environmental standards, e.g., with respect to exhaust gases of cars. Vogel calls this 'Baptist-bootlegger' coalitions.[18] These coalitions explain the increasing norms and standards that often occur in combination with the lowering of tariffs and quotas.

Given this context, will multilateral harmonization of regulatory diversity continue? In certain well-defined directions, the process is likely to continue. International organizations will continue to produce harmonized standards. The deepening of multilateral integration will also continue through the sectoral agreements that have been concluded in the Uruguay Round that will be implemented gradually; sometimes the agreements provide for further negotiations to give the liberalization and harmonization more substance.

At the same time, there are signs that the deepening process is hitting limits in certain areas. First, the Multilateral Agreement on Investments (MAI) was to provide for harmonization of national policies with respect to direct investment. After a lengthy negotiating period there was no unanimous support by the OECD countries for this agreement. Second, in December 1999, the WTO Ministerial Conference in Seattle that was to launch the Millennium Round failed to live up to the expectations. One of the main reasons for the failure was the insistence by the USA on the application of stricter labor standards in developing countries and threat of sanctions against unwilling countries by the President of the USA. If a

---

18. D. Vogel, *Trading Up* ...

new round is started by the meeting of the Ministerial Meeting of the WTO in Qatar at the end of 2001, there will still be a long way to go before a new set of agreements has been concluded that further deepens the global economy. Third, with respect to GMOs, 130 countries (including the EU) have reached an agreement in the Cartagena Protocol in early 2000 which has been founded on the precautionary principle. Under this Protocol, governments decide, after having made a risk assessment and applying the precautionary principle, whether or not they are willing to accept imports of agricultural products that include GMOs. These decisions will be communicated to an Internet-based Biosafety House. Shipments that may contain GMOs have to be labeled. For products that will be introduced into the environment such as seeds, a stricter Advance Informed Agreement Procedure has been devised. The advantage of the Protocol may be that it creates more transparency in an area where this is noticeably lacking. Moreover, it may act as a precedent in related areas such as hormones. However, a disadvantage of this specific solution may be that the role of scientific evaluations is diminished in favor of a more significant role for consumer preferences and concerns which lend themselves more than science to protectionist manipulation. Perhaps the most important conclusion is that attempts at harmonization of product standards in the area of GMOs have been given up, given the large gap in policy preferences between the participating countries.

A further deepening of multilateral integration requires the ongoing harmonization and approximation of product standards. To answer the question whether this will continue, it is necessary to look more closely at the basic reasons for the introduction of regulations.

External Effects

The first reason is the correction of external effects which cause markets to give wrong price signals. In the case of external effects, the interest of the individual differs from the collective interest. The private market parties inflict losses (or gains) on third parties without paying for that (or being compensated). Using a pecuniary welfare function, it may be argued that an individual will buy a cheaper product if it has the same utility for him compared to a more expensive product that puts a smaller burden on third parties, e.g. through not or less degrading the environment. So the government may either subsidize the 'better' product or tax the 'inferior' product or introduce a product standard that makes it impossible for the 'inferior' product to enter the market in a legal way. There may be good reasons for choosing the latter option—a good that is used in relative large quantities and produced by many suppliers will be difficult to subsidize or tax in an efficient way in the long run. Furthermore, taxes and subsidies create trade barriers as well. If a subsidy causes "...*serious prejudice to the interests of another Member,*" the subsidy is actionable. This serious prejudice exists 'in case of an *ad valorem* subsidization of a product exceeding 5 percent', according to the Uruguay Round Agreement on subsidies and countervailing measures (GATT Secretariat, 1994).

Two cases of external effects should be distinguished. First, the effect may arise when the product is used or consumed or, second, when the product is produced. The first case is straightforward: a product standard solves the problem. The second case is more difficult, as the process may not be measurable from the product, and information about the production process is needed which may be difficult to get in a reliable way. For that reason, the WTO prefers product standards that can be measured from the product in question. One can also argue that it is not the importing country that should interfere in the policy of the exporting country to correct external effects that inflict losses in the exporting country. The main exception is the case of cross-boundary negative external effects, if the exporting country does export both the product and the external effects connected with its production. In the latter case, an international agreement—between neighboring countries in case of a regional cross-boundary problem, such as the pollution of a river, or a multilateral agreement as in the case of global commons—is called for.

Harmonization in order to take away regulatory barriers has often been slow because countries differ in their appreciation of external effects, both positive and negative. The latter category is the most relevant for this paper. Examples are chemicals for agricultural use, toxic waste, cars (with respect to the quality of exhaust gases) and packaging of products. As long as harmonization has not taken place, the regulatory diversity will give rise to trade barriers. However, strong forces are operating in favor of more harmonization. In some cases, harmonization has been speeded up by market forces. If large markets have high standards, it may be very profitable for exporters in low standard countries to meet the high standards in order to make larger quantities of an identical product. The relatively high U.S. standards for car emissions were adopted in the EU with the support of German car producers "*since they could then produce similar vehicles for both markets at lower cost.*"[19] The pull of green markets is also effective in North/South trade. It has been reported that Indian producers of clothing and shoes are preparing to meet high EU standards; this puts pressure on the Indian government to implement the EU standards in order to stimulate exports.[20] The proliferation of free trade arrangements between the EU and its neighboring countries shows a strong element of regulatory harmonization to the level of the EU.[21] The increasing openness of many economies implies a growing dependence on foreign markets and as such is a factor stimulating market driven harmonization. As small economies are generally more open than large economies, it is to be expected that smaller economies will adapt to the standards of the large economies as far as the latter's standards are higher. The relevant definition of the size of economies is the production capacity. As the USA and the EU are by far the largest economies in the world economy, attracting large shares of world exports and having high standards, most 'spontaneous' harmonization takes place in countries exporting to these large economies. Additionally, it is only natural that most of the conflicts over harmonization arise between the two largest economies, as these are used to set their own standards and be followed by most of their trading partners.

The case of cross-boundary external effects has to be solved by international agreements. Some progress has been made in this respect, but there are important subjects where progress is insufficient to stop the overexploitation of natural resources, such as the climate, fish, bio-diversity. Generally, the best approach is to introduce measures that address the external effect in a direct way, e.g. by limiting or forbidding certain emissions—the complete ban on CFCs is a good example—or the harvest of resources, such as fish. Product standards are a relatively inefficient way of addressing external effects, as they work with respect to the symptoms, not the source of the problem. Furthermore, such product norms run the risk of being used to enforce domestic policies in an extraterritorial way. For these reasons, the GATT/WTO dispute settlement mechanism has not approved unilateral product standards that were not backed by international agreements (the tuna-dolphin case). Under certain conditions, product standards may be acceptable under GATT/WTO law as a means

19. D. Vogel, *Trading Up* ...
20. J. Wiemann, "Green Protectionism: ...," pp. 91–120.
21. G. Faber, "Towards a Pan-European-Mediterranean ...," pp. 245–271.

to correct a 'policy failure' in a foreign country. Product standards will be a component of a set of trade policy measures, ranging from tariffs on selected products to complete boycotts of defecting countries. If a country defects from its obligations under an international treaty, sanctions are one of the few options. In some treaties trade sanctions have been included (e.g. in the international treaty to protect the ozone layer). But even if these sanctions have not been included, trade barriers seem justified if the defecting country inflicts losses on the other parties in the treaty.

It may be concluded that the harmonization of product norms is continuing, partly as a result of market forces. In order to address transboundary negative external effects product standards are not an efficient instrument. However, given the slow progress in directly addressing the problem by international agreements, the demand for product—and process—norms, and by implication for regulatory trade barriers will increase.

Transaction Cost

The second reason for introducing regulatory trade barriers is the lowering of transaction cost that may be high as a result of asymmetric information, high search cost, intransparency and the like. Third parties do not enter the picture in this category. By requiring suppliers to give information about their products, by setting more or less detailed standards or by prescribing prior approval the government tries to enable parties to conclude better contracts, or to lower the cost of gathering information about product qualities. The regulatory barriers that may be introduced are product and process standards. Most food standards are product standards as they prescribe the maximum acceptable levels of residues of chemicals used in agriculture and of additives in food products. In this category as well, process norms are used. Here the same problems as indicated in the last subsection arise if the physical qualities of the product do not show the properties of the production process. An important difference with external effects is that one is not allowed to ignore the issue as long as there is a legitimate transaction cost problem: the consumer or user should be allowed to buy safe products in a cost-effective way.

Regulatory diversity may be made less trade distorting in a relatively easy way for regulations that have been introduced to lower transaction cost. The more interventionist regulations (prior approval, detailed standards) could be replaced by less interventionist standards that leave more room for producers to design uniform products that meet the requirements of different countries. Labeling and target standards are cases in point. This should be considered in the following light. The capacity of governments to regulate product qualities effectively in order to lower transaction cost is falling. Technological development constantly gives rise to new products and many of them of a highly complex nature. Governments have increasing problems of keeping abreast of these developments. For that reason, in many countries public authorities limit themselves to issuing broad product requirements in the shape of target standards in stead of detailed standards. Furthermore it can be argued that consumers are increasingly capable of finding legitimate ways around government intervention. First, e-commerce is difficult to control and growing rapidly. As far as physical products are concerned, monitoring at the border remains an option. However, many products can nowadays be traded in electronic form: CDs, motion pictures, books, designs, professional advice, financial products. They are invisible to the public agents that want to make sure that standards are respected. Second, higher incomes enable people to go to foreign economies to buy goods and services (such as medical treatment) that are supplied beyond the control of their domestic public regulator. At the same time, it can be questioned whether there is still the usual necessity for the public regulator to decide for buyers which qualities of goods and services they should (not) buy. As a result of better education, higher levels of welfare and modern information technology, people are, or can be, better informed than they used to be. They are in a better position to make well-informed trade-offs between prices and qualities and the risks they are willing to carry. If regulators leave these trade-offs more to buyers, the condition of sufficient information should be fulfilled. Labeling and publication of product qualities in easily accessible forms by producers are such conditions. User groups, consumer organizations and other private organizations will be set up to further improve the level of information of potential buyers and users of products and services. However, for certain other kinds of products, the risks remain too high to leave the choice between products to potential buyers. This applies particularly to technical aspects of food safety, medicines and medical devices (e.g., heart valves).

Conclusions

On the one hand, several forces are at work to lower regulatory trade barriers in many areas and to deepen global integration. These forces include:

• market forces that induce producers and governments in small and poor economies to adopt the standards of large, high standard economies in order not to lose export markets;

• the diminishing capacity of governments to prescribe and maintain product standards as a result of the fact that consumers are richer and have the means to shop around the world;

• the trend of consumers becoming better informed in deciding what to buy; as a result of which there is less need for regulation;

• international agreements are coming about that address transboundary negative external effects; this pre-empts the use of product and process standards to prevent these effects.

Simultaneously, governments are under a mounting pressure to increase regulatory barriers in order to enforce domestic policies and principles on other countries. The same factors that make consumers better informed and enable them to buy goods and services beyond the reach of their regulatory authorities also inform them about production processes, labor and environmental standards in other countries and consequently to organize lobbies. As a result, consumer concerns are becoming a sometimes powerful force, which overrides scientific proof and economic reasoning in some cases. The arguments of the international trading order are that scientific arguments and international agreements and mutually recognized instruments should be used—such as the International Labor Organization for labor standards and international environmental agreements to protect the global environment. However, science cannot exclude all side effects of new substances, and negotiations on international instruments to ensure labor and environmental protection take much time. Perhaps it has to be acknowledged that in certain areas, countries have policy preferences that differ to such an extent, that harmonization is impossible at the moment or only at a very high cost. If large sections of the population of a country lose faith in the international trading order, it may be a better option not to try to harmonize product standards themselves but to make them as transparent as possible. This road has been taken in the Cartagena Protocol on Biosafety with respect to GMOs. However, this is no solution for the wish of NGOs to enforce the environmental and social policies of industrialized countries in poor nations. In order to realize more of their objectives, these groups should pressure their governments to conclude international agreements that enable poor countries to use cleaner and safer technologies and to export more to industrialized countries in order to improve the living standards of workers.

THE EU'S NEW STRATEGIES TOWARDS EMERGING ASIA AND LATIN AMERICA

Pitou van Dijck

Introduction

The position of the EU in the world economy has become less dominant with the emergence of new centers of gravity since the 1970s. Moreover, the strong orientation of the countries of the Union towards the regional economy decreased and consequently they have become more dependent for their economic prosperity on the rest of the world, as has been the case in all regions in the world economy. The growing significance of trade and direct investment linkages with countries outside the EU and the dynamism of newly industrializing countries in Central and Eastern Europe, Asia and Latin America have contributed to the urgency of reforming the external economic policy of the EU.

This study focuses on the new initiatives taken by the EU to foster its trade and direct investment relations with emerging economies in Asia and Latin America. More specifically, the study deals with three strategic options available to the EU. First, the Union may establish or restructure preferential trade areas (PTAs) to create a preferential margin for its producers over producers who are treated according to the most-favored-nation (MFN) principle in the export market. Second, the Union may take initiatives to facilitate trade and direct investment by the private sector in a coordinated manner with selected trade partners outside the framework of a PTA. Third,

---

This article is based on the results of a research project on the external economic policies of the EU, the full results of which are presented in P. van Dijck and G. Faber, eds., *The External Economic Dimension of the European Union.*

the Union may take initiatives to accelerate the multilateral process of trade liberalization and strengthen the multilateral trade regime as formalized in the principles and rules of the WTO.

The section 'The EU and the emerging economies' presents in a stylized fashion the most significant recent shifts in the trade orientation of the EU and the dynamics in the relationship between the Union and the emerging economies in Asia and Latin America. The section 'The Regional Dimension of the EU's External Economic Policy' investigates the regional dimension of the external economic strategy of the EU and presents the most significant recent initiatives of the Union to establish different types of special relationships with countries and groups of countries all around the world. As shown, in a fairly short time span the Union has developed an extremely complex strategy based on special relations with its neighbors in the east and in the south, its former colonies, its major trade partner in the Atlantic Basin and the emerging economies. The section 'The New Regionalism in Asia and Latin America' focuses on the new strategies of the emerging countries to support their insertion in world markets by the establishment of PTAs and other forms of special linkages. Asia and Latin America show contrasting experiences and Latin American countries particularly have created spiderwebs of PTAs to support their open, export-orientated growth strategy introduced since the second half of the 1980s. The sections 'Linking the EU with Asia' and 'New Linkages between the EU and Latin America' show the different strategies of the EU to foster its relations with Asia and Latin America. Clearly, the EU strategy towards emerging Asia differs fundamentally from the way the EU traditionally tends to frame its external economic relations. The section 'The EU Agenda for the Millennium Round' focuses on the new initiatives of the Union to strengthen the multilateral trade regime through its support for a new round of trade negotiations in the WTO. The section focuses particularly on the EU priorities and on the potential benefits of deeper multilateral integration for the EU and the emerging economies. In the final section some critical reflections are made on the complexities, controversies and contradictions involved when launching such a wide range of trade-related initiatives with a large number of partners.

The EU and the Emerging Economies

At the end of the millennium, the EU stands out as an economic union of fifteen member countries with a combined gross national product (GNP) measured at purchasing power parity (PPP) of 7.7 trillion U.S. dollar in 1998, slightly smaller than the U.S. economy and the equivalent of nearly 21 percent of overall world income, as illustrated in Figure 4.1. Over the last three decades, however, the size of the Union's economy relative to the world economy has shrunk, which in itself in no way implies that the EU is losing its economic strength or competitiveness but does imply that its gravity in world trade and direct investment flows has reduced.

Figure 4.1. Regions and Countries in the World Economy, GNPs Measured at PPP, in Trillions of US Dollar, 1998

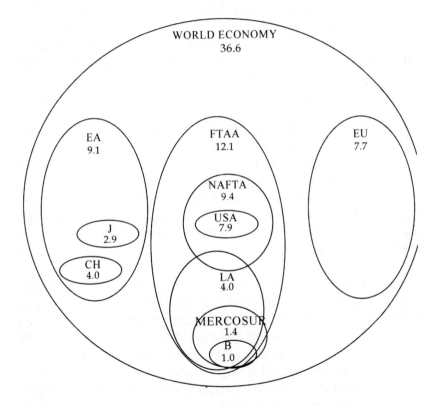

Note:, EA = East Asia, J = Japan, CH = China, LA = Latin America, B = Brazil. For all other abbreviations see list of abbr.

Source: Based on The World Bank, *World Development Report 1999-2000*, Oxford University Press, Oxford, 2000, Table 1.

At the same time, the countries in East and Southeast Asia were exceptionally successful in terms of overall long-term real economic growth over a period of more than three decades. The exception has been Japan that experienced a sharp decline in its growth rate during the 1990s. This truly East Asian miracle resulted in a significant shift in the center of gravity in the world economy from the Atlantic Basin towards the Pacific Basin.[1] The dynamic Asian economies have greatly improved their competitiveness in world markets and have rapidly reduced the income gap with the high-income countries during the last three decades. Growth rates declined sharply in 1997 and 1998, but by the very end of the millennium the region was heading for renewed growth.

The growth performance of the Latin American countries was much less impressive and much more volatile over the longer term. The region witnessed great dynamism in the 1960s and early 1970s when the Brazilian miracle astonished the world, but in the so-called lost decade of the 1980s the economies in the Southern Hemisphere stagnated. Finally, the 1990s showed renewed growth, but at moderate rates and interrupted by setbacks and crises.

When seen in a longer-term perspective, the role of the EU in the world trade system has declined significantly. Between 1975 and 1997, the share of the fifteen actual member countries of the EU in world exports (including intra-EU trade) declined from 42 percent to nearly 36 percent, and the share of the EU countries in world imports was reduced from over 41 percent to nearly 35 percent. This rather abrupt decline, which took place particularly in the 1990s, resulted from a strong expansion of world trade combined with stagnation in the EU trade performance in the early 1990s.

Notwithstanding the great progress made in integrating European markets, the share of intra-EU trade in total EU trade shrunk in the period 1990–98 from 66 to 60 percent and consequently the Union has become increasingly oriented towards the rest of the world economy. The changing trade orientation of the EU (excluding intra-EU trade) is shown in Table 4.1. The traditional strong orientation of the EU towards the markets of industrialized countries—inside and outside the EU—declined. Put together, the share of EU exports to industrialized countries outside the EU itself declined from 46 percent in 1990 to nearly 39 percent in

---

1. The World Bank, *The East Asian Miracle—Economic Growth and Public Policy.*

Table 4.1. Exports of the EU to Selected Regions, in Percentages (Excluding Intra-EU Exports), 1990–98

	1990	1991	1992	1993	1994	1995	1996	1997	1998
Industrial countries (excl. EU)	46.40	44.22	43.46	40.42	41.05	39.49	38.87	38.92	44.82
USA	20.59	19.20	19.71	19.16	19.42	17.82	18.10	19.20	20.05
Japan	6.10	5.96	5.47	5.20	5.47	5.67	5.63	4.90	3.97
Developing regions									
Africa	8.56	8.34	8.33	6.99	6.44	6.66	6.15	5.65	5.85
Asia	13.04	13.98	14.75	16.32	17.05	17.97	17.71	17.03	12.67
China (incl. Hong Kong)	3.20	3.52	3.98	5.09	5.22	5.28	5.07	5.03	4.50
Europe	14.46	14.44	13.70	15.18	15.19	17.24	18.78	20.78	20.03
Middle East	9.31	10.64	10.92	9.72	8.52	7.90	7.88	8.12	7.31
Latin America and Caribbean	5.34	5.98	6.55	6.61	6.64	6.75	6.68	6.54	6.74
Mercosur	1.44	1.64	1.80	2.13	2.53	2.93	2.91	3.19	3.16

Source: Based on IMF, *Direction of Trade Statistics Yearbook* (Washington, D.C.), several issues.

1997, but shot up to nearly 45 percent in 1998 during the Asian crisis. However, it is to be expected that the quick recovery of the Asian economies will stimulate trade with the region in the years to come and that the pre-crisis trend will be resumed.

Exports to the emerging economies in East and Southeast Asia expanded at a high rate. China (including Hong Kong) has been the single most important destination of EU exports to the region, and in 1997 and 1998 even more significant than Japan. The Asian tiger economies such as South Korea, Singapore, Taiwan, Malaysia, Indonesia as well as India have become important trade partners, albeit that trade flows have declined sharply during the Asian crisis. Trade relations with Latin America have been intensified, particularly with Mercosur/l and Mexico. Nevertheless, trade with Latin America is still of minor importance: by 1998, the shares of EU exports to Latin America, Mercosur/l and Brazil in overall EU exports excluding intra-EU trade were only 6.74, 3.16 and 2.04 percent respectively. Finally, it may be observed that the transition in the Central and Eastern European Countries (CEEC) has boosted trade and financial relations with the EU and the region has become an important trade partner of the EU within a short period of time.

Altogether, the USA, developing Europe and developing Asia have become three major trade partners of the EU of more or less equal size when measured according to EU exports. It is true that the Asian crisis sharply reduced European exports to the region, but in view of the region's great dynamism over a long period of time, it is to be expected that its role as trading partner will increase again after the crisis is over. The combined value of EU exports to Latin America and developing Asia now equals the combined EU exports to the Triad powers, the USA and Japan. So, not only has the EU become more dependent on world markets, but its orientation has shifted towards the newly industrializing countries of Europe, Asia and America, which has created an entirely new context for the design and execution of the common external economic policy of the Union. In this new context it is noteworthy that the share of the EU in imports in all regions in the world economy was reduced in the 1990s and particularly so in Africa, South America and in the market of the EU itself.

Although to some extent a loss of market share for a traditional supplier with a dominant market position is inevitable in a period of globalization and export-orientated industrialization in newly industrializing countries, the decline of the EU's import market shares contrasts sharply with the

Figure 4.2. The proliferation of preferential trade areas and special trade arrangements in the world economy

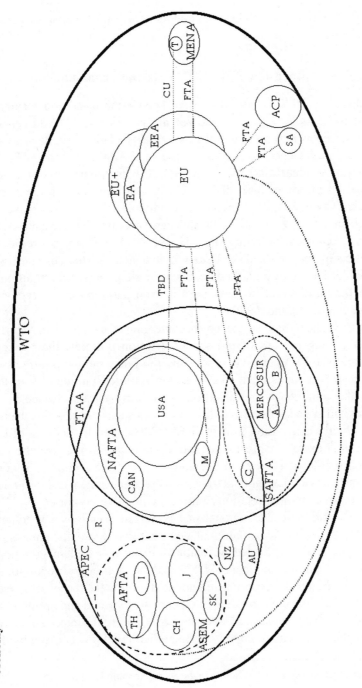

Note: A = Argentina, AU = Australia, B = Brazil, C = Chile, CAN = Canada, CH = China, I = Indonesia, J = Japan, M = Mexico, NZ = New Zealand, SA = South Africa, SK = South Korea, T = Turkey, TH = Thailand. For all other abbreviations see list of abbr.

growing share in supply of the USA and the more or less constant market share of Japan.[2]

The Regional Dimension of the EU's External Economic Policy

Since the early 1990s, new PTAs have been established and formerly established PTAs have been revitalized all over the world. All over the world, over ninety new preferential arrangements relating to trade in goods and services have been notified since the establishment of the WTO in 1995. By now, nearly all of the WTO's 136 members have notified participation in one or more PTAs and the share of world trade under PTA rules has increased strongly. As compared to the earlier wave of regionalism in the 1950s and 1960s, this new wave involves a much larger group of countries including the EU, the USA and several regional economic superpowers such as Brazil, Indonesia and Mexico. The USA in particular has made a marked change in trade policy as its traditional support for multilateralism prevented it from participating in regional trade areas until the late 1980s.

Contrary to the initiatives taken by the emerging economies to participate in PTAs during the era of import-substitution policies, their recent participation in PTAs aims at supporting the fairly radical programs of trade and direct investment liberalization initiated unilaterally in the context of comprehensive stabilization and reform programs. Hence, these countries had already liberalized their economies to a considerable degree prior to their participation in these PTAs. Moreover, the agenda of the new PTAs is more comprehensive aiming not only at the reduction of tariff and non-tariff barriers at the border, but at the abolition of non-border obstacles to international trade and direct investment and the active facilitation of economic relations among the member countries.

The worldwide spread of regionalism has created an entirely new context for the design and implementation of a new external economic dimension of the EU and has complicated the relationship between trade-negotiations that take place among members of PTAs and the multilateral negotiations in the WTO. Figure 4.2 positions in a stylized fashion the recent initiatives of the EU regarding the formation or extension of special and preferential trade relations with countries all over the world, amidst the major initiatives taken by the EU's main competitors, the other Triad powers, and by the

2. P. van Dijck and G. Faber, "The EU in the World Economy ...", pp. 8–15.

emerging economies in Asia and Latin America to create PTAs and other forms of special economic relations.

The Union has extended recently a large part of its *acquis communautaire* to its neighboring countries in the context of the European Economic Area (EEA) and a bilateral preferential trade agreement with Switzerland. The enlargement of the Union to the east and the intensification of the special relationship with the Central and Eastern European Countries (CEEC), as laid down in the Europe Agreements (EAs), dominate the policy agenda of the EU and require substantial adjustment in its common external economic policies including the Common Agricultural Policy (CAP).

It is not unlikely that the accession of the CEEC will have an impact on the positions the EU may take in regional and multilateral trade negotiations in the future as it may be expected that the new members will attempt to make the EU more protectionist regarding sunset industries such as clothing, shipbuilding and steel, which still play a significant role in their industrial structures. The protectionist pressures by the new members in the post-enlargement period will be concentrated in sub-sectors and product groups that are not produced by the present members of the EU and are highly protected in the CEEC against competition from third countries.

Also, the Union has been preparing a special Transatlantic relationship with the USA, by far its major trade and direct investment partner. There have always been strong doubts about the cohesion of Euro-American relations and the recent conflicts over the use of hormones in meat production and genetically modified plant varieties are part of a long list of conflicts over nearly everything that has been traded across the Atlantic since the very establishment of the EU and the creation of the CAP. However, the cohesion in the Transatlantic relationship has been more seriously at risk since the fundamental change in strategic setting with the end of the Cold War, the alleged reorientation of the USA from the Atlantic Basin towards the Pacific Basin, and the shift in U.S. strategy from multilateralism towards multilateralism *cum* regionalism.[3] The proposal for a Transatlantic Free Trade Area (TAFTA) appeared to be overambitious and was subsequently replaced by proposals for more modest mechanisms to support cooperation between these two megapoles. For the time being, a Transatlantic Business Dialogue (TBD) seems to be the only feasible result that has come out of these efforts.

---

3. J. Rood, "Transatlantic Economic Relations in a New Era", pp. 178–185.

The Union has intensified its relationship with its neighbors to the south by creating a customs union with Turkey and by establishing a special relationship with the Middle Eastern and North African (MENA) countries. Finally, the EU has recently established a new PTA with South Africa and is in the process of transforming the initial cornerstone of its external economic dimension—the non-reciprocal preferential trade arrangement with the group of seventy-one countries in Sub-Saharan Africa, the Caribbean and the Pacific, known collectively as the ACP— into one or more WTO-consistent preferential arrangements.

The New Regionalism in Asia and Latin America

To support their world-market orientation, the emerging countries in Asia and Latin America have taken a range of policy initiatives at the multilateral and regional levels. To start with, nearly all countries in the two regions have by now become members of the WTO and the fairly comprehensive binding of their trade barriers is among the major achievements of the Uruguay Round. The deepening of their integration in world markets is among the major objectives of the Millennium Round, at least from the perspective of the EU. Also, these emerging countries and their trade partners have taken initiatives to intensify their relations in a more selective manner. By now, many of the emerging countries participate in one or more PTAs with countries in their region or with trade partners in other continents.

In East Asia, economic links among the countries in the region have intensified because of high overall economic growth and a process of relatively early and gradual trade liberalization. Intra-regional trade has been stimulated by the complementarity between economies in resource endowments and comparative advantages. Informal networks and family ties rather than formal PTAs have contributed significantly to the formation of these regional linkages.[4] In this region, PTAs had only a limited role to play in stimulating trade and direct investment but this may change in the future, depending on the prospects of two regional initiatives. Since its establishment in 1967 until the early 1990s, ASEAN functioned particularly as a political mechanism. Hence, the promulgation of the establishment of an ASEAN Free Trade Area (AFTA) in January 1992 reflects a major change in direction. The initiative aims at reducing intra-

---

4. M. Noland, *Pacific Basin Developing Countries, Prospects for the Future.*

group tariffs to 5 percent within a period of fifteen years. The ambition is to have all ten countries in Southeast Asia included in the arrangement and to liberalize trade in manufactures, agricultural products and financial services. Moreover, the countries aim at the creation of an ASEAN Direct Investment Area (AIA) to stimulate FDI in the region.

Probably more significant for the region and the rest of the world economy may be the future implications of the initiatives announced by the APEC. The creation of APEC in 1989 was prompted by the continuous integration process in Western Europe and the shift in U.S. trade policy as reflected by the establishment of the Canada-US Free Trade Agreement (CUSFTA) of 1989 and the steps towards the NAFTA in 1993. Initially, APEC aimed at the facilitation of policy-coordination, not so much the coordination of trade liberalization, let alone the creation of a FTA. It has functioned as an open economic association among an increasing number of countries and with a broadening agenda. At the Summit in Bogor in November 1994 the plan was launched to turn APEC into a region of free trade and the USA in particular pushed hard for having the objective of free trade by 2010 for the industrialized APEC countries and by 2020 for the other members accepted and included in the Bogor Declaration.

So far, open regionalism has been the predominant approach towards trade liberalization in the region, indicating that the process of regional cooperation not only results in the reduction of intra-regional barriers to trade but at the same time in the reduction of trade barriers towards countries not participating in the coordinated endeavor to liberalize trade. Thus, open regionalism is characterized by concerted unilateral trade liberalization on an MFN basis, which has distinguished APEC from the PTAs in Europe and the Americas.[5] However, APEC countries differ in their appreciation of the implications of open regionalism for non-members, which reflects in part differences in trade interest and strategic objectives. Japan and the Asian emerging economies take the view that unconditional and non-discriminatory treatment of outsiders is preferable and this preference for MFN- tariff liberalization was confirmed at the APEC Osaka Summit in November 1995. However, the USA, Canada and Australia prefer extension of concessions to outsiders on a reciprocal basis to avoid giving the Europeans a free ride in the region. In case, however, extension of benefits to non-members were to be made

---

5. APEC, *Achieving the APEC Vision ...*, p. 2, and P. Drysdale, A. Elek and B. House, "Europe and East Asia: A Shared Global Agenda?" p. 6.

conditional to their trade liberalization, Article I of the GATT on the principle of MFN treatment is violated since such a measure would discriminate among non-members.

The intensity of the trade links among the countries in East and Southeast Asia and the APEC region exceeds levels expected on the basis of gravity models, suggesting that an implicit Asian or Pacific trade bloc favors trade in a discriminatory fashion. Brown, Deardorf and Stern find that outsiders may gain from an East Asian PTA due to scale economies and increased product varieties, but the CGE model of Lewis, Robinson and Wang shows that the significant trade-creation effects of a potential APEC PTA is accompanied by trade diversion for the EU.[6]

Although APEC is not meant to become a closed block, the process of regional harmonization of trade and investment-related rules and standards may have significant consequences for the capability of outsiders to compete in the APEC region, even if free trade would be extended unconditionally to non-members. Regional or group-wise harmonization of standards may have an effect on allocation equivalent to the reduction of policy-induced market distortions at the border although it is not necessarily optimal from the perspective of the participating countries. Thus, harmonization may have trade-creation and diversion effects and may consequently be detrimental to outsiders. Moreover, were conditionality to be introduced, rules of origin may limit the option for outsiders to gain from trade liberalization.

Soon after the change of administration in Washington early 2001, Australia and the USA initiated discussions exploring the options for a preferential trade agreement. The USA also started talks with Singapore and Chile on bilateral trade agreements. Al together, a new web of bilateral and groupwise trade agreements in the Pacific area is in the making including the Singapore-New Zealand agreement and involving the so-called Pacific Five, Australia, New Zealand, the USA, Singapore and Chile. Finally, it may be observed in this context that the recent negotiations of Japan with South Korea and Singapore on bilateral PTAs or special trade arrangements may be an indication of a shift in Japan's stance regarding participation in PTAs. It cannot be excluded that such deals may function as a model for future trade-policy frameworks, notwithstanding Japan's apparent refusal to participate in a PTA with Mexico as was

6. J.A. Frankel, and S. Wei, "The New Regionalism and Asia: ...," pp. 94–104.

suggested by the Mexican government. Hence, there are good reasons for the EU to take complementary initiatives towards the APEC region.

In the Latin American context, regionalism has traditionally played a much more predominant role than in East and Southeast Asia, and since the early 1990s a complex spiderweb of overlapping PTAs has been created in the Southern Hemisphere. By now, nearly all Latin American countries have become member of at least one PTA. The establishment of such a large number of intra-regional and inter-regional PTAs makes the recent liberalization process in the region highly specific and adds to the complexity of Latin America's trade policies. However, the recently established PTAs not only create new opportunities and potential gains from trade, but may also involve additional risks for insiders and outsiders in terms of trade and direct investment diversion and higher transaction costs. In the 1990s, the Andean Community, the Caribbean Community and the Central American Common Market (CACM) have re-emerged from the past and adjusted and re-activated their programs.

The role of Mercosur/l in the process of designing and shaping the Latin American trade-policy setting of the future is crucial since this customs union involves two regional economic superpowers with a combined production of over 40 percent of the region-wide GNP measured at PPP. Moreover, Mercosur/l is actively involved in establishing special and preferential linkages with many countries inside and outside the continent and by doing so, it is becoming the center of a more comprehensive trade regime that may integrate a large part of the Latin American market in the future. The extension of Mercosur/l and its new linkages with the rest of the region may be considered stepping stones towards an integrated and open trading system between the Latin American countries and a contribution to the realization of one of Brazil's foreign-policy priorities, the South American Free Trade Area (SAFTA).

The new initiatives to establish preferential linkages between the USA and Latin America mark a major change in policy for all partners concerned. As noted earlier, the USA supported multilateralism and has only recently broadened its policy options by getting involved in the establishment of PTAs. Within a relatively short time span, CUSFTA and NAFTA have been established and the USA has started to promote free trade in the Pacific Basin among the countries associated in APEC and pushed for a FTAA among all countries in the Americas. At the Trade Ministerial meeting in Belo Horizonte in May 1997 it was decided that the FTAA can co-exist with the existing bilateral and subregional PTAs to the extent that the rights and obligations under the existing agreements are not covered by or go beyond the rights and obligations of the FTAA. In Quebec in 2001, all heads of states of the Americas with the exception of Cuba signed a draft agreement to establish a FTAA by the end of December 2005.

The EU must respond rapidly to the policy initiatives taken by its major competitors in global markets and by the new regional superpowers in Asia and Latin America in order to reduce the risk of becoming an outsider in these markets and to avoid the costs of trade and direct investment diversion.

Linking the EU with Asia

The rapidly changing economic setting in East Asia made a critical assessment by the EU of the adequacy and effectiveness of its traditional instruments to support its relations with that region urgent. In the context of the EU's special and differential relations with countries around the world, a lack of balance was noticeable between the economic importance of regions and the content and significance of the Union's formal relations with them.[7] In 1994 the EU launched its New Asia Strategy (NAS), which was endorsed by the European Council of Essen in December. However, the initiative to establish non-formal 'Pacific-style' ties between Asia and Europe had already come from the side of the ASEAN countries by the end of 1994 and the dialogue-based information-exchange system called Asia-Europe Meeting (ASEM) was started in Bangkok in March 1996.

ASEM is meant to function outside formal regional structures such as ASEAN and the EU, and involves meetings among members of the private sector to facilitate trade, direct investment, technical and economic cooperation between large and smaller firms in both regions. However, its agenda is not confined to economic affairs but encompasses exchanges of political and cultural views as well.[8] Clearly, neither the EU nor ASEAN is seeking to establish a PTA to link the two regions and in that respect, the NAS differs significantly from the initiatives the EU has taken towards other regions. Both sides have an interest in enjoying the gains from trade and avoiding the risks of trade and direct investment diversion. As

---

7. J. Pelkmans, "A Bond in Search of More Substance: ..."

8. P. van Dijck, "Meeting Asia and Latin America in a New Setting" and M. Kagami, "Europe and Asia: Too Faraway?"

indicated earlier, an APEC PTA may divert trade away from the EU while the former enlargement of the EU with Spain, Portugal and Greece diverted trade in labor-intensive manufactures away from Asia, and the enlargement with Sweden, Finland and Austria diverted trade in more skill-intensive manufactures away from Japan. A future enlargement with CEEC such as the Czech and Slovak Republics, Poland and Hungary may cause additional trade diversion for the Asian exporters. However, the longer-term dynamic effects of integration in Europe are expected to stimulate exports from Asia at rates that exceed trade diversion effects.[9]

Rather than aiming at preferential access to each other's market, both sides strive to achieve a liberalization of the multilateral trade regime. At the first ASEM Summit in 1994 Asian participants proposed trade liberalization in Europe parallel to that in APEC, and less than two weeks later Sir Leon Brittan referred to the combined Europe-Asia effort to save the multilateral negotiations on financial services. At the second ASEM Summit in London in April 1998 an Direct investment Promotion Action Plan and a Trade Facilitation Action Plan were proposed. Moreover, the Asia-Europe Vision Group recommended that ASEM partners set the eventual goal of free trade in goods and services by the year 2025 by adopting a strategic framework for progressive trade liberalization among themselves. In the view of the European Commission, an Asia-Europe Cooperation Framework is required to set the general parameters of the ASEM process and is indeed to be adopted at the third ASEM meeting in October 2000. According to a working document of the European Commission, facilitation of the launching of comprehensive trade negotiations in the WTO and the promotion of a wide-ranging public debate on the implications of globalization are among the priorities for this meeting.[10]

New Linkages between the EU and Latin America

A series of initiatives has been taken to re-arrange and intensify the relationship between the EU and Latin America. Among the most significant of these initiatives are the interregional economic and trade cooperation framework between the EU and Mercosur/l in December 1995

---

9. J.A. Frankel, and S. Wei, *The New Regionalism ...*, pp. 89–91.

10. Commission of the European Communities, *Perspectives and Priorities for the ASEM Process ...*, p. 12.

and the proposals to establish a PTA with Mercosur. The European Council of Luxembourg of June 1999 approved the mandate for negotiations on interregional associations and subsequently, on the occasion of the Summit of Heads of State and Government of the EU and Latin American and Caribbean Nations in Rio de Janeiro in June 1999, the negotiations were launched and it may be expected that negotiations on tariff reductions will start by mid-2001.[11]

Notwithstanding substantial reductions in external trade barriers and generally low common external tariff rates of Mercosur, there is concern about trade-diversion effects, particularly in some capital-intensive sectors such as capital goods and transport equipment, which are of major importance from the perspective of EU exporters and investors. At the same time, however, the lowering of these high external import tariff rates may reduce the attractiveness of the Mercosur/1 market to European investors and limit the diversion of direct investment towards Brazil. Besides this, the EU has a large interest in the liberalization of services in Mercosur, particularly in the sectors of transportation, telecommunications, banking and insurance. Finally, a PTA could prevent EU firms suffering from the potential trade-diversion effects of a future SAFTA and a FTAA. From the perspective of Mercosur/1, a PTA with the EU may help to improve market access in a range of non-tropical agricultural products and may, moreover, reduce disadvantageous trade-diversion effects caused by the PTAs between the EU and the CEEC and MENA countries that have or will have preferential access to the EU market in a range of predominantly primary products that are substitutes for the products produced by Mercosur.[12] So far, lack of reform of the CAP of the EU and reluctance on the part of Mercosur/1 partners to liberalize sensitive industrial and service sectors have retarded progress on the road toward an intercontinental PTA between the EU and Mercosur/1 as well as with Chile.

PTAs with other emerging economies in Latin America such as Mexico and Chile are also part of the new external economic agenda of the EU. The integration of Mexico in NAFTA, its participation in APEC and in several PTAs with Latin American countries, made the establishment of

11. IRELA, *Economic Relations between Mercosur and the EU: Prospects for the Lomé Decade*, p. 3.

12. P. van Dijck, "Meeting Asia and Latin America in a New Setting" and V. Ventura Dias, "Managing Access to Markets: The EU and Latin America."

a PTA with the second largest economy of Latin America a priority for the EU. The overriding objective of the EU in the negotiations for a PTA with Mexico is to reduce the preferential margin that Mexico's NAFTA partners have over EU exporters in the Mexican market, preferably from 2003 onwards, and to halt the further decline of its market share in Mexico's imports. Cogently a PTA with Mexico may provide EU investors in Mexico with a combination of relatively low Mexican wages and good access to the markets of Mexico, the USA and the EU. From the perspective of Mexico, a PTA with the EU would reduce its strong dependence on the U.S. market, which has increased even further since the ratification of the NAFTA. It will facilitate access to the second largest integrated market in the world economy and, moreover, could facilitate access to the markets of the CEEC and the MENA countries. Such a PTA is a significant addition to Mexico's strategy of creating a spiderweb of preferential linkages with countries in the Americas and to its initiatives to strengthen relations with the Pacific Basin, particularly by its participation in APEC and its attempt to establish a PTA with Japan. Quite distinct from the negotiation agenda between the Union and Mercosur/1 and Chile, trade in agricultural products was not among the disputed principal issues in the negotiations with Mexico which were finalized successfully and in a fairly short period of time by the end of 1999.

Finally, the EU is in the process of redefining its relationship with a large group of small Caribbean island economies. Traditionally, the special relationship between the two groups of countries was framed by the Lomé Conventions which are among the first special external linkages created by the EU. In this context, the Caribbean countries benefited from preferential access to the EU market on a non-reciprocal basis and from development aid. Some of them benefited particularly from the Sugar, Rum and Banana Protocols and subsequent arrangements that aimed at safeguarding their market shares in the European market. However, after the ruling of the WTO panel on the EU Banana Protocol in favor of other banana-exporting countries in Central and South America that suffer from discrimination in the EU banana market, future arrangements with the Caribbean countries will be less WTO-inconsistent. More generally, it seems likely that in the first decade of the twenty-first century, the preferential relationship between the EU and the Caribbean countries may take the shape of a WTO-consistent Economic Partnership Agreement on the basis of reciprocal trade liberalization.

The EU Agenda for the Millennium Round

Notwithstanding the wide range of special and preferential trade relations the EU has established with a large number of countries, further progress at the multilateral level has a crucial role to play in advancing welfare, not only in the EU but in all regions of the world. A clear set of generally applicable principles and rules, backed by an effective dispute settlement mechanism, provides a degree of predictability and transparency that cannot be realized by a set of partly overlapping preferential or special trade and direct investment agreements.

For over two years the EU has called for a new comprehensive multilateral round of negotiations based on the principle of a single undertaking. The Union has targeted at 'an aggressive agenda aimed at tackling remaining obstacles to trade and thus expanding our opportunities for exports and growth'.[13] From the perspective of the Union, a broad agenda covering areas of interest to all major members of the WTO may facilitate the negotiations on the reform and liberalization of the agricultural and service sectors that are part of the WTO's built-in agenda which emerged from the Uruguay Round. The agenda should tackle obstacles to trade in specific sectors including agriculture, services and manufactures, and contribute to a more transparent and less discriminatory playing field for traders and investors. The decisions of the European Council of 1999 on the reform of the CAP in the framework of Agenda 2000 would constitute the framework for the Union's position in future negotiations in the WTO. In view of the rapidly increasing significance of the service sector in the economies of the EU member states and the strong position of the Union in world trade in services, the EU favors an ambitious agenda to improve market access all over the world and reduce the risk of discrimination by means of commitments to national treatment. In the area of manufactures, the EU aims particularly to encourage a further reduction of tariff barriers and to harmonize tariffs by means of a tariff-band approach with a low, medium and high band within which all tariffs should fall. Facilitation of trade-related procedures is required to improve the accessibility to the international market place. Moreover, in the view of the EU the new WTO round should contribute to the establishment of a multilateral agreement on direct investment, after the failure to reach an

---

13. Commission of the European Communities, *The New WTO Round*, p. 1.

agreement in the framework of the OECD, and should establish a multilateral framework for competition rules. More generally, the EU aims at supporting a deeper integration of developing countries in the WTO and at making the WTO more supportive to development.

The initiative of the Commission in launching a new, broad WTO round will, if successful, reduce the preferential margins offered to insiders of PTAs and the role of regional 'level playing fields'. Such a comprehensive multilateral round may deepen the relationship between the Union and emerging economies and provide an effective strategy to reduce the trade-diversion effects of PTAs for outsiders.

At the same time, however, the EU must be prepared to work to make its own external economic policy contribute to the proper functioning of the multilateral trade and direct investment regime that it intends to broaden and strengthen in the years to come. In view of the initiatives the EU is taking at the regional and multilateral levels simultaneously, this will require at least that the PTAs in which the EU itself participates, comply fully with Article XXIV and the Understanding on the Interpretation of Article XXIV of the GATT 1994, and with Article V of the GATS. Additional initiatives may be required as well to increase the chances of success of a new WTO round.

To gain support, a new WTO round should yield substantial potential benefits to the main trade partners of the EU and to the world economy at large. According to a recent study by the European Commission, a 50 percent across-the-board reduction in applied rates of protection by all countries in the sectors of agriculture and services—the so-called built-in agenda of the WTO—and in manufactured commodities, combined with an agreement on trade facilitation involving a one percent cut in transaction costs of international trade, would generate annual potential welfare gains for the world economy of up to 385 billion U.S. dollar. Slightly less than half of this total welfare gain would benefit the Triad powers. In absolute terms, the EU would be by far the largest beneficiary of such concessions enjoying a welfare gain of 92 billion U.S. dollar, the equivalent of 1.4 percent of its GDP. To a substantial degree, these gains are related to the simulated liberalization of the CAP. In relative terms, welfare gains are the largest for the members of ASEAN and the countries in Latin America and the Caribbean, and to a lesser degree for India. For the world as a whole, the annual welfare gain is estimated at 1.4 percent of GDP.

Additional gains may be derived from the successful conclusion of negotiations in the area of trade and competition. Increased competition particularly may generate gains in countries where competition law is not yet well established as may be the case in ASEAN countries, Latin America and the Caribbean. A WTO agreement on direct investment may contribute further to the reduction of distortions in the international allocation of direct investment, thus stimulating growth of welfare.[14] As the study indicates, a new round of liberalization with a comprehensive agenda will generate large benefits for developed countries and particularly for emerging countries in East and Southeast Asia and Latin America.

Notwithstanding strong support from the EU and the other major trading nations for the launch of the Millennium Round, the Ministerial Meeting of the WTO, held in Seattle in November 1999, failed to decide on the agenda and timing of such a round. At this stage, the entire approach to multilateral trade liberalization as envisaged by the WTO, has become highly controversial. NGOs in developed and developing countries have radically and loudly criticized the perceived negative effects of globalization on developing countries and the global environment, and are urging the WTO to take the developmental, social and environmental dimensions of trade and direct investment into account. At their meetings last June, seventeen developing countries, grouped together in the G 15 and including seven Latin American countries and one country in the Pacific Rim, Malaysia, called for more attention to be paid to the detrimental effects of globalization for the poor. Their statements and accusations contrast strongly with a WTO study which postulates that there is no simple relationship between trade and poverty, but that trade liberalization generally contributes positively to poverty alleviation, although admittedly such reforms create some losers and may exacerbate poverty. Moreover, the positive effects of trade reform will not suffice to combat poverty in the medium term.[15]

Not only does the present dead-lock frustrate progress in the negotiations on trade liberalization in the sectors of agriculture and services and in many other areas where initiatives are required in addition to the achievements realized in the Uruguay Round, but the postponement of the Millennium Round may seriously jeopardize the schedule for the negotiations on the establishment of PTAs between the EU and emerging countries, specifically Mercosur/1 and Chile, and will in all likelihood prolong these negotiations. Obviously, this is one of the main risks involved

---

14. N. Nagarajan, *The Millennium Round: An Economic Appraisal.*
15. L.A. Winters, "Trade and Poverty: Is There a Connection?"

when all parties are participating simultaneously in regional and multilateral negotiations on concessions in essentially the same sectors and product groups. Clearly, in negotiations on PTAs the EU and its partners have preferred to take this approach to alternative avenues to intensify their relations. Since all sides involved have a major interest in an open and transparent multilateral trade regime and share an interest in containing the damage of failed inter-regional negotiations, they may probably share a preference for delay of their interregional negotiations on concessions that really count over conflict and failure.

After having put so much effort into promoting the launch of this round, the present situation is particularly troublesome to the EU now that the future of this crucial dimension of its external economic policy is in limbo. In the current situation the EU must be prepared to take initiatives to remove the obstacles to a successful new round of multilateral trade negotiations. Among the obvious bottlenecks are the conflicts between the EU and its trade partners over the CAP and over the use of hormones and genetically modified organisms, and the lack of respect for the authority of the multilateral rule system itself. Moreover, the EU as well as the WTO itself, must be prepared to improve communication with society at large as negotiations and future concessions in the new areas will result in a further extension of multilateral ruling and discipline into areas that were traditionally under the exclusive control of national authorities.

Concluding Observations

By way of conclusion some observations of a more general nature are in place pertaining to the interaction between the regional and multilateral dimensions of the economic strategy of the EU towards emerging economies. As shown, the EU has been extremely active at both policy levels, and provided some specific conditions are met, such interaction may be mutually supportive.[16] However, there may be trade-offs between making concessions in regional and multilateral negotiations were a multilateral arrangement to generate larger concessions from trade partners in exchange for the concessions offered by the EU. Hence, the prospect of a more favorable *quid pro quo* at the multilateral level may diminish

---

16. P. van Dijck and G. Faber, "Introduction" and J. Bhagwati, P. Krishna and A. Pangariya, eds., *Trading Blocs*.

the attractiveness of making significant concessions in the context of a PTA as may be the case in negotiations on the CAP between the EU, Mercosur/l and Chile.

It is also noteworthy that the EU, the USA and many emerging economies and developing countries have participated in a new wave of regionalism at the time that successful multilateral negotiations in the GATT/WTO have substantially reduced the margin available to offer discriminatory preferences. This holds particularly for the EU which has committed itself to an average Post-Uruguay bound import tariff rate of 3.2 percent and applies a rate of 2.8 percent, measured with 1988 import values as weights.[17] Such low MFN tariff rates reduce the effectiveness of PTAs as an instrument to link large numbers of countries to the EU and increase the need to develop alternative instruments and mechanisms to foster interregional relations in the future.

Moreover, it may be noted that so far, the Commission has made no proposals for the agenda of the Millennium Round which are related to the functioning of PTAs and their relationship with the multilateral trade regime, notwithstanding the strong increase in the number of PTAs notified to the WTO in the 1990s. The EU in particular has contributed strongly to the worldwide spread of preferential trade relations. The emergence of 'mega' PTAs in East Asia, the Americas and between the EU and South America, involving the Triad powers and newly industrializing economies, will require strict WTO rules and discipline to avoid the undermining of the multilateral trade regime. The Understanding on the Interpretation of Article XXIV of the GATT 1994 has contributed somewhat to the clarification of the GATT provisions with regard to free trade areas and customs unions and has to some extent bolstered multilateral discipline in this area.[18] The absence of a call from the EU for further steps to strengthen WTO discipline may indicate a satisfaction with the actual WTO rules as laid down in the Marrakesh Agreement, but may also be the expression of a strong preference for room to maneuver in the regional domain without being restricted too much by the overruling multilateral powers of the WTO.[19]

---

17. J. Finger, and L.A. Winters, "What Can the WTO Do for Developing Countries', Table 14.2, p. 370.

18. GATT, *The Results of the Uruguay...*, and P. van Dijck and G. Faber, eds., *Challenges to the New World...*

19. J. Mathis, "The Community's External Regional Policy in the WTO."

ASIAN PERSPECTIVES

THE POLITICAL ECONOMY OF 'EAST ASIAN' COOPERATION
TOWARDS BETTER REGIONAL AND GLOBAL GOVERNANCE

Tsutomu Kikuchi

Introduction

The purpose of my article is to examine the prospects for regional cooperation between the ASEAN countries, and China, Japan and South Korea known collectively as ASEAN Plus Three,[1] on 'East Asian' cooperation, from the perspectives of strengthening regional and global governance.[2] There are rising expectations concerning the future of this forum in various parts of the region. However, the future development of this forum is still uncertain. There are many factors that could both stimulate and obstruct the strengthening of an East Asian regional architecture. This article argues that for the time being there is little possibility for the ASEAN Plus Three to evolve into more institutionalized mechanism for cooperation. However, it would contribute to enhancing regional and global governance, if it is more tightly linked to existing regional and global institutions. That is, the ASEAN Plus Three might play an important role in forging multi-layered governance structure. The progress of economic globalization and interdependence among nations has promoted moves towards multi-layered governance, where regulatory competence tends to be dispersed across global and regional institutions.

---

1. It should be emphasized that the ASEAN Plus Three framework is totally different from Malaysia's EAEC proposal in its origins and modalities.
2. For a more comprehensive analysis of the ASEAN Plus Three , see Tsutomu Kikuchi, "Plus Three: Backgrounds and Tasks" (in Japanese).

'East Asian' cooperation must be a part of this complex governance structure that is gradually emerging in contemporary international relations.

Challenges and Tasks

What challenges are we facing today? We are in particular faced with new challenges arising from various sources including globalization and political-economic changes in the region. The tasks facing Asia are huge. Addressing them requires increasing efforts at both regional and global levels.

Post-Cold War Issues

Asia is now in a transitional era. The distribution of power is unstable as industrialization changes relative capabilities among countries. The relationships among the major powers are still unstable and uncertain. Most of the states have territorial and/or historical disputes with their neighbors. There are still differences in basic values, although many countries have been moving towards democratic and market-oriented regimes. Korea and China (Taiwan) present the legacy of the Cold War, and are the focus of armed confrontation. The status of Taiwan is posing a serious challenge for the region in organizing regional governance structures that will include Taiwan as a constructive partner in the region.

Post-Colonial Issues

The nation-building process is still underway in this region. Most Asian nations are still affected by their colonial past. Many countries in the region have made great efforts to enhance state institutions and national cohesion among the peoples, but countries that face internal instability still remain. Their weakness causes many regional problems.

In the post-colonial modernization process, 'national autonomy' and 'national independence' are highly valued by political leadership. Many Asians still stick to a quite traditional or 'collectively-(mis?)conceived' concept of national sovereignty and the principle of non-intervention in internal affairs. They still have strong concerns about ceding national sovereignty in the name of integration and cooperation.

Post-Imperial Issues

China occupies a special place in Asian international relations, given its historical record and today's status as a rising power. We can distinguish various tiers of historical problems coexisting in today's international relations in Asia, which are a legacy of its 'Imperial Past'. By 'Imperial Past' I mean problems originating from, or accompanied with, the breakdown of a China-centered imperial system that began in the middle of the last century with the arrival of the Western powers. Most of today's 'hot spots' in Asia, actual or potential, are located along the periphery of the old China centered system. This fact attests the longevity what we call the 'post-imperial' problems. These are not necessarily memories of the past. The geopolitical reality still remains basically unchanged as far as China is concerned.

Post-Authoritarian Regime (1): Democratic Transition

Many Asian countries are facing the challenges in transforming their political regimes. Some ASEAN countries are confronted internally with unstable regimes. For many countries in Asia, political legitimacy has been based upon an implicit social contract by which the general public support their governments in exchange for a steadily growing prosperity. Economic hardship and uncertainty concerning the economic future have destabilized the domestic political situation and make it difficult to work towards a smooth transfer of power.

The extent to which regional cooperation can develop is likely to depend very heavily on the coherence and viability of the states and state structures within a given region. The absence of viable states (both in terms of effective state apparatus and mutually accepted territorial boundaries) makes the process of region-building difficult, if not impossible. The instability of political regimes, their intolerance of all opposition, and the erosion of state-led economic projects work to undermine sustained interstate cooperation. States remain the essential building blocks on which regional cooperative exercises are built.[3]

A new factor is introduced in the process of tackling the political transformation. Although governments and states remain, of course,

---

3. Andrew Hurrell, "Regionalism in Theoretical Perspective," in Louise Fawcett and Andrew Hurrell, eds., *Regionalism in World Politics*, pp. 67–68.

powerful actors in the efforts of enhancing governance, they are now sharing the national, regional and global arenas with an array of other agencies and organizations. Non-state actors or transnational bodies such as multinational corporations, transnational groups and social movements also provide governance services. Past experience demonstrate that cooperation between governmental and non-governmental actors has been vital in tackling various 'human security' issues such as landmines, environmental degradation and the need for humanitarian assistance.

Today, political authority and sources of political actions are widely diffused. This concept challenges the conventional Westphalian, state-based characterization of the global political order. If social movements, non-governmental organizations and regional political associations are excluded from the notion of governance, its form and dynamics will not be properly understood. In this context, it is a promising to see the emergence of civil society movements in various parts of East Asia.

Post-Authoritarian Regime (2): Democratization and Deeper Integration Issues

Political liberalization is important in forging a regional cooperative framework. New regionalism is no longer defined as simple mutual liberalization of trade but as harmonization and possibly coordination of domestic law (regulatory systems) and institutions.

The complexity of modern economy requires a detailed set of common laws and regulations for global markets. This is clearly illustrated by the extensive legal frameworks for regional markets such as the Single European Market and NAFTA. The focus of activities of the WTO and OECD has shifted towards the harmonization of domestic competition and business rules in so far as these are perceived as the major barriers to the smooth functioning of the global market.

Achieving common rules of conduct and entering into reciprocal commitments and obligations requires some degree of 'like-mindedness' on the part of the states concerned. Convergence of political institutions makes it easier to accept necessary levels of intrusive management, in terms of both standard setting and regulation, as well as effective implementation. East Asia is left far behind in this regard.

THE POLITICAL ECONOMY   101

Post-Territorial Issues: Economic Globalization

Economic globalization is posing serious challenges to nation states, especially to developing states in East Asia. Many countries in the region are clearly in the modernizing stage of development, which is defined by strong government control over society and restrictive attitudes toward openness and pluralist concepts of the world, despite the recent emergence of various civil society movements.

In the past the major foci of the international agenda were measures at the border and rules of interstate relations such as the principles of non-intervention in internal affairs, MFN and national treatment. The international community is increasingly concerned about what is taking place within borders in terms of competition and industrial policy, human right and 'human security', all of which are closely related to the governing structures of the countries concerned. Discussion is now taking place about creating a 'level playing field'.

Globalization is transforming states, markets, and social values, and requires new ways of organizing our lives to harness the benefit of, and limit the risks of globalization. In a global economy where there is a surplus of labor, the need to large territories and populations can be more of a burden than an asset. The impact of globalization has revealed the importance of reforming systems of governance in East Asia as well as in global institutions. Globalization also demands the establishment of more integrated regulatory mechanisms (harmonization and, if possibly, coordination of policies, domestic laws and institutions at the national, regional and global level) in order to govern the regional and global flows of goods, services and capital.

East Asia is now expected to make more substantial contributions to enhancing global governance. Global politics is confronted not only with traditional geopolitical concerns such as the spread of the weapons of mass-destruction, but with a large variety of economic, social and ecological questions. Terrorism, pollution, drugs, human rights are among the increasing number of transnational policy issues cutting across territorial jurisdictions. Meeting the challenges of globalization at various levels of governance requires forging new coalitions to achieve the necessary reforms of various international institutions of governance such as the UN, WTO and IMF. The aims are to enable them to maximize the benefits and reduce the costs of globalization to their citizen. There is a vital need to establish rule-based, tightly regulated governance structures at both regional and global levels.

Post-'Asian Miracle': A New North-South Divide in East Asia

Because of the huge differences in institutional capabilities of countries in the region in responding to the challenges of globalization, East Asia has been witnessing a 'North-South divide'. The emergence of a two-tier ASEAN is just one example. Political instability, economic disarray, human right abuses and environmental degradation are seriously affecting several countries in the region. Other countries with full capability to adjust themselves to globalization processes are looking for new coalitions with distant countries and regions to protect their prosperity and peace. In fact, the recent willingness of Singapore to conclude a series of bilateral FTAs with non-ASEAN countries demonstrates how seriously Singapore takes current political and economic difficulties in fellow ASEAN member states. This new initiative clearly demonstrates that Singaporeans are seriously concerned about being identified as part of an unstable Southeast Asia.

This quite legitimate Singaporean concern has caused a lot of suspicion and antipathy against Singapore among its ASEAN neighbors.[4] Japan, one of the few economies not involved in any discriminatory regional trading arrangements, has already began to change its trade policy and started formal negotiation with Singapore to conclude a bilateral FTA. This causes some concerns about trade and investment diversion in the region. Meanwhile, ASEAN's movement towards more liberal trade and investment arrangement through AFTA and AICO has been lagging far behind the expectations of foreign investors. There has also been a relocation of manufacturing sites from Southeast Asia to more promising countries such as China and India.

Post-'Flying Geese' Pattern of Development: Economic Competition among East Asian Economies

It has been argued that East Asia developed a regional, mutually complementary economic structure. A so-called theory of 'flying geese pattern of regional economic development' was advocated by many economists. However, the regional economic structure has recently become more competitive. China and ASEAN (and India) are competing for foreign

---

4. Thailand also expresses its strong interest in concluding FTAs with non-ASEAN economies.

direct investment and searching for new markets. In order to protect their respective agricultural sectors, Japan and South Korea recently decided to resort to the GATT/WTO safeguard measures, indicating the emergence of sharpening trade disputes among East Asian nations.

Given the increased economic competition among East Asian economies, it will not be so easy to agree to a region-wide industrial policy in East Asia and realize regional trading arrangements such as an 'East Asian Free Trade Agreement' within the ASEAN Plus Three framework. An 'East Asian FTA' may serve to strengthen political unity, but is not a policy that will be implemented in the near future.

ASEAN Plus Three and the Region

Rising Expectations

The governments of East Asia have been eager to promote regional cooperation within the ASEAN Plus Three framework. Japan has played a critical role in forging an East Asian framework of cooperation, especially in the field of building a regional financial architecture. South Korea and China expressed their willingness to support East Asian cooperation, although their respective motives differ considerably. The ASEAN Plus Three formula is expected to strengthen ASEAN by providing new cohesion through a process of 're-engineering'.

The 'Joint Statement on East Asian Cooperation' issued by the ASEAN Plus Three Summit in 1999 covered a wide range of possible regional cooperation. Following the 'Chaing Mai Initiative', in May 2001 ASEAN Plus Three successfully concluded bilateral currency swap agreements that are expected to make a substantial contribution to the currency stability in the region. The ASEAN Plus Three Summit held in 2000 had agreed to explore the possibility of concluding an 'East Asian Free Trade Agreement' and holding an 'East Asian Summit'. The leaders also agreed to set up an 'East Asian Study Group' (EASG) consisting of senior government officials to explore possible areas for cooperation in East Asia. The ASEAN Plus Three group also has provided a venue for the leaders of the three Northeast Asian countries (Japan, China and South Korea) to conduct informal trilateral consultation on issues of common concern. The agenda of this forum may be expanded to include issues not directly related to ASEAN such as tension on the Korean Peninsula.

Prospects for the future of the ASEAN Plus Three group

What are the future prospects East Asian regionalism or regional cooperation? There are numerous global and regional factors (both structural and ideational) that may contribute to consolidating East Asian cooperation.

Global Factors

Globalization of the World Economy: Increasing Global Competition
The so-called mega-competition, a result of the deepening globalization of the world economy has also promoted East Asian regionalism. This forced private enterprises have to re-organize their production networks as efficiently as possible. Since the 1980s East Asian enterprises had developed regional production networks, and thus facilitated regional division of labor. East Asian regionalism will further consolidate regional networks of production in order to enhance international competitiveness.

The Strategic Rationale
East Asian regionalism is also affected by moves towards regionalism elsewhere. Regionalism may be primarily understood as a strategy designed to enhance the power and influence of its members in the international political economy, strengthening their position vis-à-vis rivals in other regions. The strategy of regionalism (as a way to expand the size of the home market base) is seen as an instrument for asserting the strategic trade interests of states.[5] Following this line of thought it is argued that if NAFTA, EU and FTAA prove successful, this will invigorate the tendency towards regionalism in East Asia.[6]

Regional Factors in East Asia

Recognition of Regional Interconnectedness
The Asian financial crisis has underlined the interdependence of financial institutions in East Asia as well interdependence between Asian and the

---

5. It is argued that re-launching European integration in the single European Market program gave the greatest impetus towards North American integration in the 1980s. Following this argument, East Asian regionalism will be consolidated in line with those in other parts of the world.
6. R. Palam and J. Abbot, *State Strategies in the Global Political Economy*.

global financial systems, and assisted the negotiations towards the currency swap agreements in East Asia. There has also been a rise of awareness of regional interdependence in the areas of politics and security, as shown by the increased attention paid by ASEAN countries to Northeast Asian security issues.

Shared Feeling of 'Humiliation'
The Asian financial crisis was one of the key factors contributing to the consolidating of the ASEAN Plus Three framework, due to the awareness of interdependence, and the inadequacy of contingency plans in the face of a major economic crisis, most notably the absence of the facility of a lender of last resort in the case of a liquidity crisis.

In Search of a Collective Instrument to Defend National Autonomy and Development
East Asian regionalism has become a useful instrument in particular for developing countries to pursue the two basic national goals simultaneously: economic development through participation in the world economy and pursuing a policy independence/autonomy in the face of the merciless power of international capital. Given the fact that many countries still cling to a quite traditional concept of national sovereignty, regionalism as a means to protect national sovereignty certainly appeals to most East Asian countries.

Emerging New Coalitions in the Domestic Politics
The convergence of domestic policy preferences of the countries in the region has strengthened the dynamics of East Asian regional cooperation.[7] The active participation of state and private actors in the economic globalization process has had a grave impact on power allocation among domestic interest groups in East Asian countries. Globalization has been a major influence leading to the emergence of liberalizing (internationalist) coalitions favoring integration with the international economy, and influenced domestic decision-making processes.

Domestic factors offer an explanation of how and why members of a region may adopt more cooperative approaches to economic management.[8]

7. Stephan Haggard, *Developing Nations and the Politics of Global Integration.*
8. Etol Solingen, "Economic Liberalization, Political Coalitions, and Emerging Regional Orders," David A. Lake and Patrick M. Morgan, *Regional Orders: Building Security in a New World*, pp. 68–100.

In brief, if a coalition in power opts for vigorous participation in the liberal international economic exchanges, it will be amenable to cooperative regional arrangements as well. For those liberalizing coalitions regional cooperation may be more efficient for both its domestic political and global implications. New regional cooperative regimes in East Asia serve both the purpose of strengthening the liberalizing model at home, and of lubricating external ties to the global economy.[9] Indeed, regional cooperative schemes can be an effective tool for integration into the world economy while strengthening the domestic constituencies that support liberal reforms.

Lock-in Effects of Regionalism: Embedding Domestic Reforms into External Mechanisms

Some governments that encountered domestic opposition when introducing liberal economic reform measures used regional arrangements as an instrument to bind themselves to these reforms.[10] Also, locking the liberal reforms in through external arrangements is useful in terms of obtaining international credibility for reform efforts, thus contributing to attracting foreign investment. Given the fact that it is quite difficult to achieve economy growth without foreign investment, increasing international confidence is vital for East Asian countries.

Fear of 'Economic Marginalization'

For many of East Asian countries regional arrangements have been useful instruments for overcoming economic marginalization in the international economy.[11] For many ASEAN countries, economic marginalization presents a greater threat than security marginalization. ASEAN countries have to compete with newly emerging states, especially China, over foreign direct investment that promoted the economic development of the region during the last decades. In this context, regional cooperation is an effective path for securing access to foreign markets, capital, investment and technology.[12]

---

9. Etel Solingen, "Economic Liberalization ..."

10. Actually, this is one of the main motives for Japan to start the FTA negotiation with Singapore.

11. Louise Fawcett, *Regionalism* ..., p. 22.

12. Solingen points out; cooperative arrangements erode risk considerations and enable foreign investment, avoid potential sanctions and penalties from international private and public sectors. Solingen, "Economic Liberalization ..."

Regional and Global Governance: Interlocking Institutions

How should we evaluate this development of a new East Asian regional architecture for cooperation in terms of enhancing regional and global governance? In order to answer this question we will also have to consider various factors that stand in the way of developing East Asian cooperation.

Most of these regional mechanisms do not necessarily constitute legally binding reciprocal commitments, or instruments for their enforcement. Exceptions are cases in which the enforceable rules of international institutions are identical with those of regional agreements. It is to be expected that institutions in the region will remain relatively weak. ASEAN Plus Three will not be an exception given the exiting differences in national interest and the limits to the institutional capability of the countries in the region.

Despite such criticism a regional forum has the potential to play an important role in enhancing regional and global governance, especially when embedded within an emerging multi-layered regional and global governance structure. Institutions do not function themselves, they interact. East Asian regionalism may be strengthened by linking it to other existing other regional and global regimes. Global institutions may provide East Asia with appropriate 'focal points' on which the expectations of Asian countries converge. In turn, East Asian regionalism may contribute to extending the global norms and rules on the regional basis. In fact, countries in the Asia-Pacific have tried to enhance regional governance mechanisms through nesting/interlocking with various regional and global institutions, even if a overall structure still remain weak.

At this point, I should like to review some recent developments in the area of regional cooperation/governance.

First, Asia-Pacific trans-regional institutions such as APEC and Asian Regional Forum (ARF) were devised from the beginning to function in cooperation with global institutions such as the United Nations, WTO, IMF and NPT/IAEA. By harmonizing and coordinating its activities with GATT/WTO, APEC has developed a concept of 'Open regionalism' that encouraged member economies to comply with existing global trading norms and rules embodied in the GATT/WTO. In this way APEC has been contributing to enhancing global and regional economic governance, extending the application of global economic rules such as those of GATT/WTO into the region through intensive dialogue, and in addition providing various forms of economic and technical assistance. The ARF also has made strenuous efforts to link itself with the existing global institutions such as the UN, NPT, CTBT, MTCR, and UNCLOS. In turn, these global institutions have provided ARF with various norms and rules to strengthen regional politico-security cooperation.

The bilateral swap agreements concluded in May 2001 that followed ASEAN Plus Three's 'Chiang Mai Initiative' were coordinated with the IMF, in this way contributing to both regional and global currency stability. In fact, the bilateral agreements between Japan and Asian countries that took part in the initiative assume that 90% of the committed currency swap would be activated with the financial support of the IMF under conditionalities imposed by the IMF. In this regard, the new regional financial architecture in East Asia, supported by a network of bilateral swap agreements, is complementary to the role of the IMF. Although some Asian leaders such as Dr. Mahathir of Malaysia have consistently resisted the idea of the continuing influence of non-Asian institutions in Asian financial affairs, eventually they accepted the financial arrangements including cooperation with the IMF.[13] I have already referred to the nesting function of APEC and ARF. In Northeast Asia, KEDO, provides a basic framework to prevent the proliferation of weapons of mass-destruction in the Korean Peninsula. It incorporates global rules and norms derived from the NPT/IAEA regime. In Southeast Asia, ASEAN has contributed to stabilizing inter-state relations among its members by introducing the principles and norms embedded in the UN charter, especially the principle of peaceful resolution of conflicts. ASEAN succeeded in concluding the South East Asia Nuclear Weapon Free Zone (SEANWFZ) by nesting itself within the global non-proliferation regimes. In such a way global institutions could provide a 'focal point' as the basis for consensus building among the countries of the region.

In this regard, it should be noted that regional institutions such as ASEAN Plus Three could serve as an additional instrument to provide various forms of technical/economic assistance such as human resources and capital to its members that face difficulties in adjusting themselves to global norms and rules. Given the fact that most global institutions such as GATT/WTO and NPT/IAEA do not have instruments to provide such assistance for the members to promote their adjustment to the global rules,

---

13. Not only Japan but also South Korea and China strongly insisted that the emergency currency under the swap agreements should be provided together with that of the IMF.

the regional institutions could play a more constructive role in providing such assistance. This is another area where ASEAN Plus Three can make a contribution.

Second, the interaction between regional institutions in the Asia-Pacific has enhanced regional and global governance by linking various regional institutions, expanding their agenda and widening their functions. For example, through its linkage with NAFTA and ANZCER, APEC has developed trade and investment liberalization as one of the three major pillars of cooperation. APEC is also unique in making economic and technical cooperation one of the priority areas of cooperation, through its institutional coordination with ASEAN. A series of informal South China Sea workshops initiated and guided by Indonesia were supported by both ASEAN and ARF Ministerial meetings, thereby constraining countries from breaching regionally endorsed norms, rules and codes of conduct, although this may not be enough to fully prevent this. The basic principles, rules of conduct and activities of KEDO, an Asia-Pacific institution with exceptionally hard (i.e., binding) rules, have received strong support from such other regional institutions as ASEAN and ARF.

Third, inter-regional dialogues and cooperation between East Asia and other regions may also contribute to further enhancing regional and global governance. East Asia has recently engaged in developing inter-regional dialogues and cooperation with Europe, North America and South America through forums such as ASEM, APEC (ARF) and East Asia-Latin America Forum (EALAF). These forums have been and will continue to play an important role in encouraging mutual policy adjustment to enhance not only trade and investment relations, but also to help promote the spread of democracy, good governance and the rule of law across the region, and to promote consensus building between the regions.[14]

In Need of More Tightly Regularized Regionalisms

Coalitions of the Willing

Responding to the pressing regional and global issues, East Asian cooperation has to move towards establishing regional arrangements that entail the imposition of common rules of conduct and a set of legally-

---

14. On inter-regional relations, see Bart Kerremans and Bob Switky, eds., *The Political Importance of Regional Trading Blocs.*

binding reciprocal commitments and obligations, together with joint efforts to enhance overall regional structure through linking various regional and global institutions. Achieving common rules of conduct and entering into reciprocal commitments and obligations requires some degree of 'like-mindedness' among the participating governments. Given the diversity of the region, new coalitions should be explored for dealing with pressing issues. A suitable framework to do this is that of gathering like-minded countries within a group such as the ASEAN Plus Three. The recently concluded agreement on establishing a bilateral FTA between Japan and Singapore should be considered in this context.

Towards a Definition of 'East Asia'

It is common to define regions geographically. However, a region can be defined in other ways, for instance in terms of functions. Regions may be defined by interactions among their components. Interaction is usually the key to identifying what distinguishes a region from the rest of the international system. To constitute a region, it needs to display an intensity of interactions sufficient to mark it as a distinctive subsystem. Barry Buzan describes a regional security complex as a set of states with significant and distinctive networks of security relations that ensure that the members have a high level of interdependence in the area of security: an example is a group of states whose primary security concerns link them together sufficiently closely so that their individual national security cannot realistically be considered apart from one another.[15]

If we follow this functional definition of regions, the geographical scope of 'East Asia' may be expanded or narrowed, depending upon the intensity of interactions in a specific issue area. For example, the USA, Europe and Australia take part in 'East Asian financial interactions'. The USA is an essential part of East Asian security complex. In trade, virtually most states in the world are parts of 'East Asian economic complex', given a East Asian export-led economic development strategies. This argument implies that 'East Asian' cooperation should not be confined to the members of the 'ASEAN Plus Three' group, and should include other non-ASEAN Plus Three actors.

---

15. Barry Buzan, *People, States, and Fear: An Agenda for International Security Studies in the Post-Cold War Era*. See also various articles included in David A. Lake and Patrick Morgan, eds., *Regional Orders: ...*

Community- and Confidence-Building

The diversity of the economies in East Asia requires additional mechanisms to promote confidence and community building. In this context, the roles of institutions such as APEC, ARF and ASEAN Plus Three as frameworks for regional cooperation are essential. These forums can serve to create patterns of dialogue and cooperation, and thus promote mutual confidence building through intergovernmental networks within the region. Efforts to promote community building in the region are critically important given the diversity of the countries in the region, and are also essential to avoid creating a North-South divide within East Asia. In this process, non-state actors or transnational bodies such as multinational corporations, transnational groups and social movements also contribute to good governance, and their active participation in efforts towards community building is essential.

Conclusion

Although the institutional framework of individual institutions in the region remains relatively weak, the Asia-Pacific has tried to enhance it's regional governance mechanism through nesting and interlocking with various global institutions. In the light of this experience, East Asian regionalism could be developed and strengthened if they are connected, especially with the existing global regimes, thereby extending the global norms and rules on the regional basis. Thus, ASEAN Plus Three could serve as an additional regional mechanism in fostering the emerging multi-layered regional and global governance structure.

Also, nesting itself with other regional and global institutions, ASEAN Plus Three could also contribute to dealing with one of the pressing regional issues: how an emerging China can be accommodated into regional and global governance mechanisms. Our goal is to have a prosperous, stable and constructive China with fully integrated into regional and global governance mechanisms. The prospective Chinese membership into WTO is an important step in terms of accommodating China into rule-based international regimes. Through the ASEAN Plus Three, East Asian countries could individually and collectively make their best efforts to have China play a more constructive role to enhance regional and global governance.

Given the impressive progress of globalization and the accompanying pressing requirement of establishing a more regulated rule-based international order, the adequacy of the contemporary understanding of the principle of non-intervention in internal affairs have to be reconsidered. Today, domestic institutions and internal developments have enormous regional and global ramifications. In this context, an East Asian framework of consultation may provide more comfortable (non-hostile) environment to discuss such politically sensitive issues as human rights and human security, given the deep-seated concern of East Asians to 'intervention' of foreign powers into their policy management.

JAPAN AND LATIN AMERICA

Mitsuhiro Kagami

Introduction

The relationship between Japan and Latin America is strong in blood but weak in business. There are around 1.3 million *nikkei-jin* people of Japanese origin in Latin America, the largest population outside Japan. Recently these people have filled the demand for hardworking manual labor in Japan (called *dekasegi*). Around 200,000 are said to be living in Japan at present. This is a new phenomenon which has given rise to economic, social, cultural and even psychological problems.

Business relations with Latin America for the last ten to fifteen years were slender. Japan's exports to Latin America to total exports accounted for only 4.4 percent and imports 3.3 percent in 1996. Latin America accounted for 12 percent of outstanding FDI in 1994 and around 12 percent in total bilateral ODA in 1996. Japan's business interests have been principally preoccupied with the East Asia region. However, business relations with Latin America have shown a strong upward tendency in the late 1990s and this trend may well continue, owing to the extreme economic difficulties facing East Asian economies compared to the relative stability of the Latin American economies at the present time.

This article examines recent characteristics of and new factors in Japan's trade, FDI, and ODA with Latin America. And a possible new role for Japan including a new move of bilateral free trade arrangements in relation to Latin America is discussed.

A Brief History

Ethnic Ties

The first diplomatic treaty with Latin America was signed with Peru after the Meiji Restoration. The Peruvian ship the *Maria Luz*, heading for Peru, anchored in Yokohama in 1872 carrying Chinese laborers (coolies). The new government of Japan liberated the laborers and returned them to China on humanitarian grounds. The incident resulted in a diplomatic dispute between Japan and Peru, but it was finally resolved and a provisional treaty of amity, commerce and navigation was signed between the two countries in 1873.

Unlike the unequal treaty of amity and commerce between Japan and the USA, signed in 1858, which denied Japan tariff autonomy rights and included extra-territoriality (consular jurisdiction rights), the first treaty of amity, commerce and navigation signed with a Latin American country—Mexico in 1888—was an equal treaty. Similar treaties were subsequently signed with Brazil in 1895, Chile in 1897, Argentina in 1898 and Colombia in 1908. Following the signing of these treaties, diplomatic relations were opened and embassies set up between Japan and the various Latin American countries. At present Japan is busy celebrating the centenary of these treaties with the relevant countries.

The first Japanese emigrant to Latin America was said to have landed in Argentina in 1887. However, the first documented arrival was a group of people organized by T. Enomoto—a Dutch-educated Tokugawa government admiral who had been defeated by Meiji forces at Hakodate Castle, and then became an important member of the new Meiji government, and favored the development of Hokkaido and Japanese emigration to the Americas—who arrived in Mexico in 1897. Two years later, the first emigrants to Peru arrived, and in 1908, a ship called the *Kasato-maru*, disembarked a group of emigrants at Santos, starting large-scale emigration to Brazil. Usually, these new immigrants were first employed as indentured labor on coffee plantations and the like, but they gradually moved to the urban areas after their contracts expired and engaged in small business—running laundries, barber shops, flower shops and other such enterprises.

During the hostilities of the World War II period, diplomatic relations between Japan and major Latin American countries were suspended, but were re-opened in 1952 and emigration to Latin America also resumed, mainly to Brazil. The COTIA agricultural cooperative in Brazil began to accept young Japanese in 1955. This cooperative was founded by *nikkei* people in 1927 and contributed substantially to Brazilian agriculture by supplying fresh vegetables and fruits, mainly to the São Paulo region (COTIA was dissolved in 1994).

Because of the change in industrial structure ushered in by the shift from coal to petroleum, many coal miners in Japan lost their livelihoods and emigrated overseas. At the same time, Japanese who had businesses in Latin America began to settle in the region as trade and investment increased. By 1986, it was estimated that around 1.3 million *nikkei-jin* were living in Latin America: approximately 1.2 million in Brazil; 52,300 in Peru; 17,800 in Argentina; 10,500 in Mexico; 5,700 in Bolivia; 2,300 in Paraguay; and 1,900 in Chile. In addition, the number of business-related Japanese residents was estimated at around 124,000 in 1995.

The nikkei have contributed to Latin American society in various fields, not only agriculture but also the arts, engineering, and politics. Several nikkei have risen to high positions in their new countries such as S. Ueki (Brazil's minister for energy and mines during the 1970s) and C. Ominami (Chile's minister for economy during the early 1990s). A. Fujimori was the first *nikkei-jin* to reach the position of president being elected Peru's president in 1990, re-elected in 1995, and again in 2000 (but fled to Japan in November and resigned in exile).

During the late 1980s and early 1990s when Japan experienced a bubble boom economy, which created an acute shortage of labor, many nikkei temporarily returned to Japan from Latin America—mainly Brazil and Peru—to supplement the demand-supply gap, engaging mostly in hard manual labor. Such workers are called *dekasegi* in Japanese (literally meaning "go abroad and earn"). With the aid of a special legal status granted by the Japanese government—up to the third-generation of Japanese origin and their spouses could obtain work permits for Japan— around 200,000 nikkei had come to Japan by the mid-1990s.

Business Ties

Since the end of World War II, there have been three manufacturing investment booms emanating from Japan to Latin America: the late 1950s, the early 1970s, and the late 1980s. However, Japanese business interest in Latin America generally remained low during the 1980s and the first half of the 1990s because (a) external debt problems created a negative image of the region; (b) East Asia was booming; (c) guerrilla and narcotic activities posed security concerns.

In recent years, Japan has recorded a trade surplus with Latin America, with the exception of 1983. Japan's foreign direct investment (FDI) in Latin America between 1951 and 1994 accumulated to $55.1 billion. While Latin America's share of bilateral ODA had increased to around 12 percent in 1996, amounting to $986 million. It is expected that business relations between Japan and Latin America will be strengthened in the late 1990s and the twenty-first century. In the following sections, these relations will be surveyed, taking into consideration new factors, especially recent economic developments.

Trade between Japan and Latin America

Characteristics

After World War II, Japan began to export light-industry products to Latin America. Because the region had escaped the devastation of the War, markets were receptive to manufactured products. Following this, Japan slowly began to export plant-related machines and equipment. The construction of the USIMINAS iron and steel plant in Brazil, which the Japanese government and business circles were deeply involved with in the late 1950s, especially boosted these exports. At the same time, Japan imported primary products and minerals such as cotton, sugar, wool, and iron ore from the region. As Japan gradually succeeded in rebuilding its economy and re-industrializing, she began to export transport equipment and electric and electronics products to the region.

Several distinguishing features observed in trade between Japan and Latin America are as follows.

In terms of exports:

(i) The share of exports to Latin America to the total of Japan's exports was less than 10 percent (4–7 percent in the early 1980s and around 4 percent in the 1990s, actually, 4.4 percent in 1996). Between 1980 and 1996 Japan's exports exceeded imports (trade surplus for Japan) except 1983 ($–481 million). The surplus increased during the 1990s (the peaks being, $8,485 million in 1994 and $5,610 million in 1996), which reflected on the rapid liberalization processes of the region (see Figure 6.1).

(ii) Japan's exports of manufacturing products such as transport

Figure 6. 1. Japan: Exports and Imports with Latin America

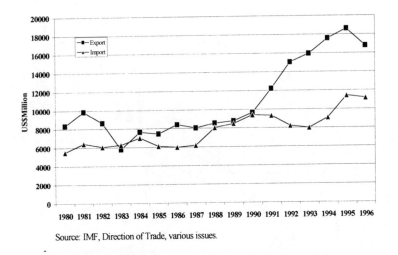

Source: IMF, Direction of Trade, various issues.

equipment, electric and electronics machines, and general machinery, accounted for almost 80 percent of total exports to Latin America (77 percent in 1983 and 82 percent in 1996) (see Figure 6.2).

(iii) The export of ships accounted for the largest share. Because Panama offered tax incentives to shipping companies, Japanese ships were sold to Panama to obtain the Panamanian flag (flag-of-convenience vessels). Ship exports share was 33 percent in 1983 and 34 percent in 1996, respectively (see again Figure 6.2).

(iv) Reflecting ship exports, Panama had the largest share (34 percent in 1983 and 33 percent in 1996), followed by either Mexico (9 percent in 1983 and 20 percent in 1996) or Brazil (12 percent in 1983 and 12 percent in 1996).

In terms of imports:

(i) The share of imports from Latin America to total Japanese imports was also less than 10 percent (4–5 percent in the early 1980s and around 3 percent in the 1990s, actually 3.3 percent in 1996).

(ii) In the early 1980s, Japan imported mainly primary products such as fuel, raw materials and food (in 1983, these three items accounted for 77 percent), while during the 1990s, their share declined (63 percent in 1996) and imports of manufacturing products such as metal products, chemical products and machines increased (30 percent in 1996). Fuel was the most important item (29 percent in

118

Figure 6.2. Japan: Exports to Latin America

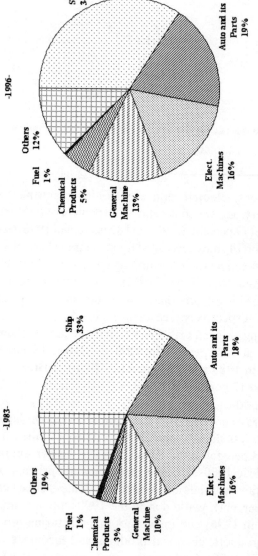

-1983-

-1996-

Source: MITI, *White Paper on International Trade*, 1984 and 1997.

1983) but its share drastically shrunk in the 1990s (7 percent in 1996), and mineral products replaced fuel (see Figure 6.3).

(iii) The major exporters were Mexico and Brazil in the early 1980s (for example, Mexico 29 percent and Brazil 26 percent in 1983). Mexico supplied petroleum and Brazil minerals such as iron ore. Chile overtook Mexico in the 1990s and Brazil moved clear at the top (Brazil 33 percent, Chile 24 percent, and Mexico 16 percent in 1996). Japan buys principally fish, wood and copper products from Chile and aluminum products and iron ore from Brazil.

New Factors

In the 1990s several new factors which affected trade and investment between Japan and Latin America emerged. First of all, the re-establishment of macroeconomic stability was a major factor in dramatically decelerating inflation, and progress in economic liberalization encouraged trade and investment to return to the region. Secondly, movements toward regional integration provided new opportunities and new markets. Thirdly, on the other hand, financial globalization created instant and volatile monetary crises in the region.

Liberalization and Macroeconomic Stability

After experiencing agonizing external debt crises in the 1980s, Latin American countries shifted their policies from government intervention to free market economies under what is called the Washington consensus. Together with the establishment of the World Trade Organization (WTO) in 1995, free trade and investment and small government became the new mode of the world. Latin American countries adopted free trade policies by lowering tariffs, abolishing import controls, and deregulating investments.

Success in bringing hyperinflation under control in Argentina and Brazil by fixing their currencies at per value to the U.S. dollar (Argentina in 1991 and Brazil in 1994), and the achievement of macroeconomic stability brought about recovery in Latin America. Growth returned after the lost decade of the 1980s. According to ECLAC,[1] the average annual inflation rate in Latin America dropped from 877 percent in 1993 to around 10

---

1. Economic Commission for Latin America and the Caribbean (ECLAC), *Preliminary Overview of the Economies of Latin America and the Caribbean 1999.*

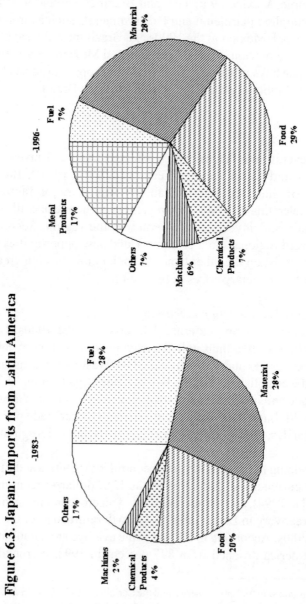

Figure 6.3. Japan: Imports from Latin America

Source: MITI, *White Paper on International Trade*, 1984 and 1997

percent in 1999. The average annual rate of per capita GDP of the region was –1.0 percent in 1981–1990 as against 1.4 percent in 1991–1999 (The year 1999 turned to have a negative growth of 1.6 percent).

Reflecting these economic climate changes, exports of goods from Latin America doubled between 1990 and 1997, while imports of goods to the region expanded 2.8 times in the same period. Net FDI to the region increased by four times between 1991 and 1997 ($10.7 million in 1991 and $44.0 million in 1997).

Regional Integration
Another movement, closely related to liberalization, which has had an important impact has been a surge toward the formation of regional trade blocs such as NAFTA and Mercosur/1. These subregions function not only as a new market but also as a new investment site. Within the integrated subregion new demand is created in the wake of trade and investment liberalization. Trade creation affects the trade of non-member countries, too, as the subregion grows (although trade diversion is also the case if non-member products are competing ones). It is said that Mercosur/1 has a large potential for new markets in the near future, particularly, for high-tech products from the East Asian manufacturing countries. Moreover, in the case of FDI, regional integration is an excellent opportunity to enjoy preferential treatment in the subregion because it will promote FDI inflows.

NAFTA, a free trade agreement between Canada, Mexico and the USA, became effective as of 1994. FDI into the NAFTA region has been increasing because FDI can enjoy preferences as well as utilize the booming U.S. market, although NAFTA has exclusive clauses for non-members such as rules of origin which include local content or compulsory use of locally produced cotton, mother boards and color tubes and so forth. The recent brisk showing of the U.S. economy has seen intra-NAFTA trade increase, with both European and Japanese FDI using Mexico as an export platform for the USA. For example, it is estimated that Japan's FDI to Mexico shot up ten times compared to the previous year to $3.16 billion in 1997.

Mercosur/1, a customs union between Argentina, Brazil, Paraguay and Uruguay, started in 1991, but it actually only began to function recently after the macroeconomic conditions of Argentina and Brazil stabilized. Reflecting stable exchange rates and the economic recovery of the two major countries (GDP growth in 1997: Argentina 8.0 percent and Brazil

3.5 percent), intra-Mercosur/l exports increased by nearly 20 percent in 1997, exceeding $20 billion for the first time.[2] In the last few years GDP growth has slowed down. Argentina is now (2001) in the negative.

Financial Crises and Their Impacts
The Mexican monetary crisis in 1995, caused by the over-issuance of short-term dollar-denominated government bonds (*Tesobonos*), ended up with the floating of the Mexican peso and its sharp devaluation and ensuing negative growth (-6.6 percent in 1995). Contagion effects (called *tequila* effects) hit Argentina heavily resulting in wild fluctuations on the stock market and negative growth (-5.0 percent in 1995). Financial globalization brought volatility to financial markets inducing a heavy dependence on short-term capital and portfolio investments, which supplement a large part of current account deficits. Violent inflows and outflows of short-term capital caused exchange rate control difficulties and resulted in shortages of foreign reserves when there were abrupt outflows of such capital. Coupled with immature domestic financial markets, these developments highlighted how the real economies of developing countries could be easily damaged.

In the case of Mexico, recovery was driven by the trade sector because the buoyant U.S. economy absorbed Mexican products through NAFTA. NAFTA (and the existing *maquiladora* system) did indeed help Mexico. U.S. imports from Mexico increased from $40.4 billion in 1993 to $110.7 billion in 1999 (2.74 times, see Figure 6.4). Consequently, Mexico regained its momentum to grow (5.2 percent in 1996, 6.8 percent in 1997, 4.9 percent in 1998 and 3.5 percent in 1999).

The East Asian monetary turmoil in 1997 also contaminated Latin American stock and currency markets directly but its influence was short-lived. In the mid- and long-run impacts are twofold: the one in financial and the other in the real sectors. Short-term capital which fled East Asia is looking for other prosperous markets and Latin America fits the bill. Voluminous inflows can be expected in the near future which will again destabilize money markets if not properly handled. Other possible impacts will be an export surge from East Asia to Latin America and fierce competition in the world market because the East Asian currencies have depreciated radically and, hence, their export competitiveness augmented.

---

2. Inter-American Development Bank (IDB), *Integration and Trade in the Americas*, Periodic Note, December (1997).

For example, the Thai *baht* depreciated from 25 to 54 to the dollar in the last six months of 1997, the Indonesian *rupiah* from 2,400 to 13,250; and the Korean *won* from 800 to 1,757 (end-January 1998).

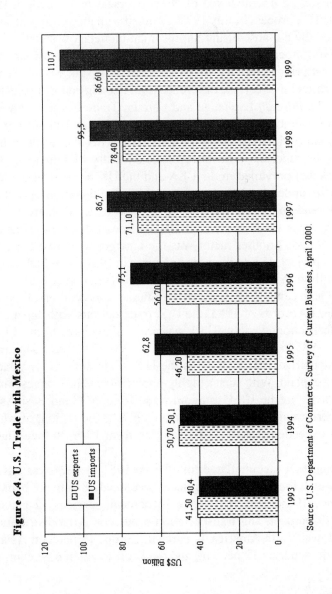

Figure 6.4. U.S. Trade with Mexico

Source: U.S. Department of Commerce, Survey of Current Business, April 2000.

Japan's Investment

Characteristics

Japan's FDI shows three peak years, 1973, 1981 and 1989. The 1973 peak was influenced by liberalization and yen appreciation. The Japanese government started liberalization of direct overseas investment in 1969 and expanded the process in July 1972. Coupled with the yen appreciation that followed the collapse of the Smithsonian monetary system in 1971 (called "Nixon shock"), Japan's FDI expanded four times between 1971 and 1973, just prior to the first oil crisis. The 1981 peak was caused by full liberalization, interest rate differences and two big energy projects in Indonesia. The Foreign Exchange and Foreign Trade Control Law was amended in December 1980 to open up payments below 100 million yen fully, that is approximately $830 thousand, (payments above 100 million yen have to be reported in advance to the Ministry of Finance). High interest rates that prevailed in the USA and the UK because of the tight money policies under the Reagan and Thatcher administrations, produced a large difference between internal (Japan) and external interest rates. Japanese overseas firms shifted funding sources from New York and London to Tokyo. Another factor was the emergence of two big LNG development projects ($1.8 billion) in Indonesia in 1981. Total FDI jumped from $4.7 billion in 1980 to $8.9 billion in 1981 (see Figure 6.5).

The 1989 leap came in the wake of continuous appreciation of the yen after the Plaza Accords of 1985, the U.S. trade deficits with Japan, and the East Asia economic boom. The yen sharply appreciated from 240 yen per dollar in 1985 to 140 yen in 1989. The "trade war" between Japan and the USA intensified year by year as the U.S. trade deficits with Japan continued to expand. With such a highly-appreciated yen, Japanese firms invested heavily in the USA to avoid trade friction. Good East Asian economic performance also invited Japan's FDI to the region, of which the amount exceeded that of Latin America from 1989 on (see Figure 6.5).

Outstanding FDI (accumulated total) from 1951 to 1994 was $463.6 billion, of which the manufacturing sector occupied 28 percent, banking and insurance 19 percent, real estate 15 percent, services 12 percent, commerce 11 percent, and transportation 6 percent. Area distributions were as follows: North America 44 percent; Europe 19 percent; Asia 16 percent; Latin America 12 percent; and the Pacific region 6 percent.

Figure 6.5. Japan: FDI from Japan (1969-94)

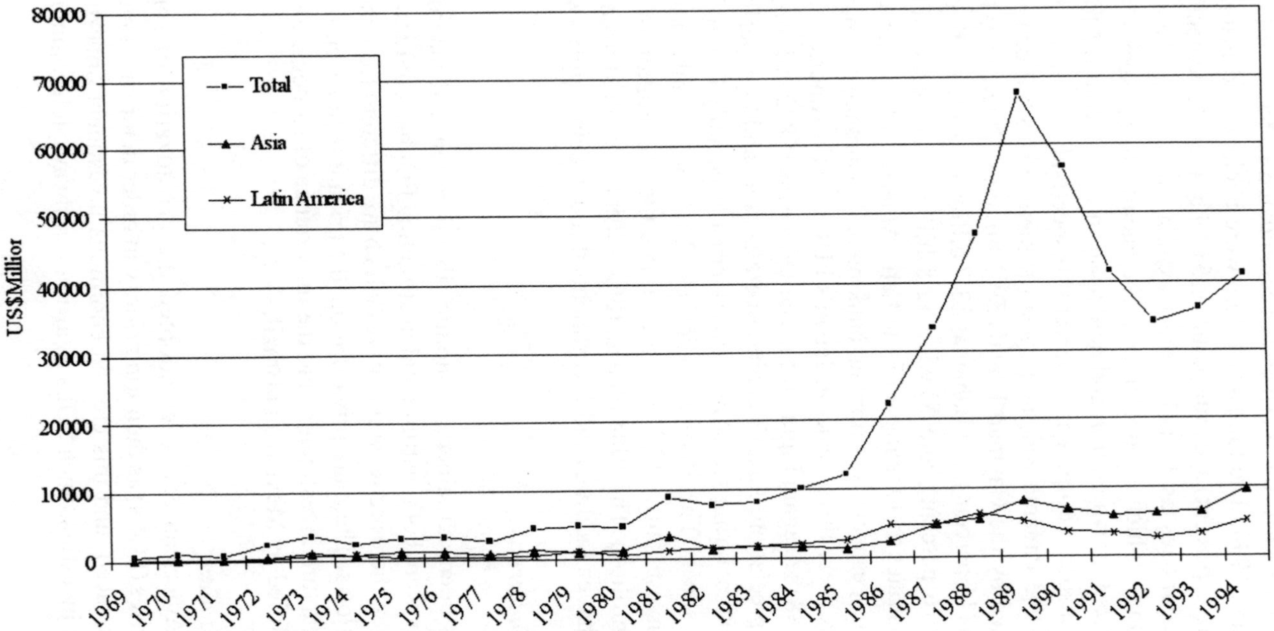
80000
70000
60000
50000
40000
30000
20000
10000
0
US$Millior
Total
Asia
Latin America
1969
1970
1971
1972
1973
1974
1975
1976
1977
1978
1979
1980
1981
1982
1983
1984
1985
1986
1987
1988
1989
1990
1991
1992
1993
1994

Source: Ministry of Finance, Monthly Statistics on Finance and Money, various issues.

Japan's FDI to Latin America accumulated to $55.1 billion between 1951 and 1994. The top two sectors were banking and insurance $18.4 billion (33 percent) and transportation $17.4 billion (32 percent), reflecting such countries as Panama, the Cayman Islands, the Bahamas, and Bermuda—which are tax havens. The manufacturing sector's share was 15 percent, of which iron and nonferrous metals accounted for 4 percent and transport equipment 4 percent, respectively. Country distribution shows that Panama was the largest recipient, $21.8 billion (40 percent), followed by the Cayman Islands $9.2 billion (17 percent), Brazil $8.8 billion (16 percent), the Bahamas $3.7 billion (7 percent), Bermuda $3.6 billion (6 percent), and Mexico $2.8 billion (5 percent). This clearly demonstrates that Japanese FDI to Latin America fully utilized tax haven measures, especially, shipping, banking and insurance companies.

There were three peaks in Japan's FDI to Latin America: 1973, 1979 and 1988 (see again Figure 6.5). The 1973 peak ($822 million), reflected yen appreciation, Japan's capital liberalization, and high performance in the manufacturing sector in Latin America, especially Brazil, just before the oil shock. The 1979 elevation ($1.2 billion), mainly represented a large investment in PEMEX to facilitate the importation of petroleum ($500 million). The 1988 plateau ($6.4 billion), resulted from active use of tax haven facilities and investments through debt-equity swaps.

New Factors

As has been explained, economic liberalization and macroeconomic stability were both instrumental in attracting FDI back to Latin America. However, there are several features which are different from those in past FDI inflows. These are privatization, the private sector's participation in infrastructure investments, and the importance of strategic location—as exemplified by Mexico and Brazil.

Privatization

Latin American countries adopted the privatization of state-owned enterprises (SOEs) as their top priority in order that market mechanisms be introduced, and this created enormous investment opportunities for foreign investors. Such SOEs as airlines, railways, telecommunications, power companies, petroleum-related activities, mining, and several government services were opened to the private sectors.[3]

It is estimated that 800 Latin American SOEs were privatized between 1988–95 and their sales realized $60–70 billion. For example, the sale of the Rio Doce Valley company (CVRD) in Brazil in 1997 springs to mind because a Japanese consortium's tender failed. A Brazilian consortium (CSN steel corporation with pension funds and the like) obtained it for $3.1 billion. Brazil has another round of SOE privatization programs looming and Peru is also accelerating its privatization plans. Thus, future investment opportunities are anticipated in the region.[4]

Private initiatives in infrastructure
Another innovation has been the introduction of the private sector into infrastructure investments. It was traditionally believed that infrastructure was a public good which only governments could build and operate for reasons of social cost. However, it has now been realized that the private sector can provide better services in some infrastructure projects such as toll roads and electricity services. Through ODA, the private sector now participates in infrastructure building.[5] Such new words as BOT (Build, Operate, and Transfer), BOO (Build, Own, and Operate), BLT (Build, Lease, and Transfer), and PFI (Private Finance Initiative) are now included in the infrastructure jargon.

International financial organizations such as the World Bank and the Inter-American Development Bank (IDB) are promoting private initiatives in this field. For example, the IDB is offering loans to projects such as: an electricity project in Colombia, a natural gas pipeline project in Mexico and an electricity project in Argentina, using BOO methods.

In the field of electricity services, private companies participate in generation and distribution as independent power producers (IPPs), breaking existing area monopolies. This is a new approach which was first seen in the USA following that country's deregulation of power utilities. A recent example of this new approach involved a Japanese trading firm with U.S. capital participates which won an IPP project tender in the Yucatan Peninsula to supply electricity to a local region.

---

3. Mitsuhiro Kagami, "Europe and Asia: Too Faraway?"
4. ECLAC, *Foreign Investment in Latin America and the Caribbean 1998*, and *1999*.
5. Masatsugu Tsuji, Sanford Berg and Michael Pollitt, *Private Initiatives in Infrastructure: Priorities, Incentives and Performance*.

Mexico and Brazil as strategic locations
Regional integration has brought about strategic considerations from the
commercial point of view. NAFTA has propelled Mexico into the position
of a strategic location or gateway to the U.S. market as well as to other
Latin American markets. Because of the strong U.S. economy, demand
for imports continues to be active, and European as well as Asian capital
has been using Mexico as an export platform to the USA and Canada. For
similar reasons, Brazil has emerged as a strategic location, because of its
important position at the core of Mercosur/l—which now covers Argentina,
Paraguay, Uruguay and associates, Bolivia and Chile. Brazil represents a
large domestic market, and following its successful stabilization of
macroeconomic conditions, has re-emerged as a highly-anticipated
investment country.

Indeed, a recent survey of Japanese manufacturing firms with more
than three overseas operations, covering projections for the next ten-year
period, conducted by the Research Institute for International Investment
and Development of the Export-Import Bank of Japan, shows that Brazil

**Table 6.1. Japan: Top-ten Promising Investment Countries over the
Next Ten Years**

Order	1997 Survey	Firms	1996 Survey	Firms
		269		264
1	China	196	China	195
2	India	98	India	103
3	USA	83	Vietnam	87
4	Vietnam	64	USA	81
5	Indonesia	57	Indonesia	64
6	Thailand	44	Thailand	63
7	Brazil	30	Malaysia	31
8	Philippines	29	Myanmar	29
9	Malaysia	25	Philippines	28
10	Myanmar	14	Mexico	16

Source: Research Institute for International Investment and Development,
Questionnaire Survey on Foreign Direct Investment, 1997 and 1996.

was the seventh most promising investment country in the 1997 Survey, while Mexico was placed tenth in the 1996 Survey (see Table 6.1).

Official Development Assistance (ODA)

In 1992, the Japanese government adopted the ODA Charter which is based on four philosophical considerations: (i) humanitarian aspects; (ii) recognition of interdependence among nations of the international community; (iii) environmental conservation; and (iv) support for self-help efforts of recipient countries. Along this line, the following four principles were set forth:

(a) Environmental conservation and development should be pursued in tandem.

(b) Any use of ODA for military purposes or for aggravation or international conflicts should be avoided.

(c) Full attention should be paid to trends in recipient countries military expenditure, their development and production of weapons and missiles of mass-destruction, their export and import of arms and suchlike, so as to maintain and strengthen international peace and stability, and from the viewpoint that developing countries should place appropriate priorities in the allocation of their resources on their own economic and social development.

(d) Full attention should be paid to efforts made to promote democratization regarding the securing of basic human rights and freedoms in the recipient country.

Japan has been the largest ODA donor-country in the world since 1991, reaching a peak of $14.5 billion in 1995 but falling back to $9.4 billion in 1996. Along the line of the above-mentioned principles, the share of environmental ODA to Japan's total ODA, for instance, increased from 12.8 percent in 1993 to 27.0 percent in 1996. Between 1995 and February 1997, Japan suspended grant-type aid to China in order to protest against its nuclear testing program. And following undemocratic measures taken by the Nigerian military government which was established in November 1993, Japan's ODA was suspended from 1994, except for emergency and humanitarian aid. It was reopened in May 1999 when a civilian government was established.

Bilateral ODA increased from $2.0 billion in 1980 to a peak of $10.6 billion in 1995, but shrank to $8.4 billion in 1996. Area distribution of Japan's ODA shows that Latin America's share increased from 6.0 percent

($118 million) in 1980 to 11.8 percent ($986 million) in 1996, while Asia's share diminished from 70.5 percent to 49.6 percent during the same period (see Figure 6.6).

Figure 6.6. Japan: Bilateral ODA, 1980, 1990, and 1993–1996

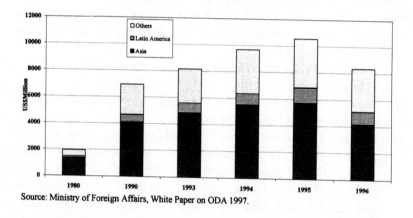

Source: Ministry of Foreign Affairs, White Paper on ODA 1997.

During the external debt crisis, Japan's ODA played a vital role easing its effects. For example, Japan's ODA occupied 68 percent of net inflows of total ODA by DAC/OECD countries to Mexico in 1988–91 to relieve the Mexican external debt under the Brady Plan.[6]

In the case of Peru, Japan's ODA accounted for 39 percent of net inflows of the total DAC's ODA between 1991 and 1994, becoming top donor country under the Fujimori administration. The relationship was marred when three technical experts from Japan's International Cooperation Agency were killed by a guerrilla group in 1991. This led to a withdrawal from Peru of such experts and of Japan's Overseas Cooperation Volunteers because of safety concerns. The unhappy incident of a hostage standoff at the Japanese Ambassador's residence in December 1996, and the rescue raid in April 1997, also delayed technical assistance and the dispatch of related experts to Peru.

---

6. Akio Hosono, "Ratenamerika Chiiki to ..."

Since Fujimori's flight to Japan, the corruption scandal surrounding his second-in-command Montesinos, a newly elected President in Peru, Alejandro Toledo, in June 2001, with closer links to the USA, it is difficult to predict if the strengthened association between the two countries will remain the same. However, if the Japanese government refuses to extradite Fujimori to Peru, as the Peruvian government has requested, it might not be likely.

New Factors

DAC/OECD released new approaches for assistance in 1996 called New DAC Development Strategies, which emphasize poverty alleviation, social development—education, health services, women—and environmental considerations. Under the pressure of liberalization and free market mechanisms, the poor and the weak are left behind. Therefore, this group in the population has become a new priority. One of the targets of the new strategies states that the proportion of the world's extremely poor will be halved by 2015.

When Prime Minister Hashimoto visited Peru in 1996 this was seen as an opportunity for the Japanese government to designate Peru an annual-based loan recipient. Furthermore, it was agreed that the New DAC Development Strategies would be applied first to Peru. (The overall aid plan for Peru has not yet been finalized because of the delays mentioned above.) Nonetheless, it proves that such considerations have become more important than before in assisting developing countries.

Recent movements toward governmental and administrative reforms in Japan have also had an affect on ODA discussions. Taxpayers are now keen to know about the effectiveness of ODA. The ODA budget has long been treated as a sacred cow because it was recognized as the country's most important contribution to world development. An average of $10 billion was channeled to ODA activities in each year during the 1990s, but for fiscal reform reasons the Hashimoto government has decided to cut the nation's contribution by 10 percent for three years starting in fiscal 1998. Moreover, owing to the recent yen depreciation trend, Japan's dollar-denominated ODA will fall further and the USA is likely to regain the position as top donor.

For Japanese people, security concerns have only recently become a major issue. However, this preoccupation is on the increase, as Japanese citizens have been taken hostage, kidnapped, and murdered in various politically unstable countries in the developing world. (For example, Japanese tourists were killed by Islamic extremists in Luxor, Egypt, and two university students were murdered in the Peruvian Amazon). These incidents and others like them have raised serious concerns in business as well as government circles and could ultimately have a negative effect on Japan's FDI and ODA mind-set.

New Relations in the New Era

Complementarity between East Asia and Latin America will be enhanced in the twenty-first century because of food and energy considerations. As has been shown, Japan depends greatly upon Latin America for food, raw materials and fuel, while Latin America imports manufactured products from Japan. Such a basic relationship is unlikely to change for the worse in the future, but is instead more likely to be strengthened. The *dekasegi* tie is another factor which can further strengthen this relationship as it contributes to technology transfer if properly handled. The fly in the ointment is that the monsoon spate of monetary crises which have shaken East Asia represents a new and major concern. Therefore, control mechanisms to exercise some control over world capital movements which cause sudden turmoil in financial markets are essential. And finally, Japan's role in the new era must also be taken into consideration.

Complementarity

Food
As Asian economies grow, demand for food increases, especially, consumption of animal protein as standards of living improve owing to increased incomes. Demand for feed such as corn and soybean also increases. Heavily populated countries like India and China may face food shortages in the future, so the potential demand for food is enormous. For example, China will be confronted by serious food shortages in the twenty-first century as several projections have pointed out.[7] Japan faces the same deficiency. Japan's self-sufficiency in food is now 62 percent (of total food in 1994). Japan is one of the largest food consumers per head of population in the world and import demand for foodstuffs such as meat, fish, fruits, and coffee as well as soybean is enormous.

---

7. Kazuya Fujime, *Long-term Outlook of Energy Supply and Demand in East Asia.*

This is very cogent when it is recalled that countries such as Argentina, Brazil, and Paraguay still have sufficient virgin land for agricultural development. It is said that China and Korea are trying to enclose land for food production purposes in these countries. Brazil's *cerrado* development proved that even acid soil could be transformed to arable land and that, provided it is allied to environmental considerations, vast agricultural potential remains to be developed.

Energy

By the same token, Asian energy supply is also insufficient to meet demand. China is already a net importer of petroleum and Indonesia is said to be set to become a net importer of oil. Here again, the Latin American region could greatly benefit, as it is often highlighted that the region has the potential to be a net exporter of energy if proper investments are implemented.

Notwithstanding recent financial disarray and consequent slow growth in East Asia, the region is expected to regain its momentum soon because of its high savings ratio, accumulated technologies, and well-trained human resources. Energy is said to be the greatest bottleneck facing Asian development. It is estimated that East Asia (China, Korea, Taiwan, Thailand, Indonesia, Malaysia, and Vietnam) will become a net primary energy importer of 422.2 million TOE by 2010 (foreign dependence: 17.8 percent) and its item-wise source will be coal 10.4 percent, oil 35.5 percent, and natural gas 17.1 percent, respectively.[8]

Therefore, Latin America has a good opportunity to increase its position as a major energy supplier. Promising projects abound, for example, the Camisea natural gas project in Peru, the Orinoco tar project in Venezuela, and the Cusiana oil project in Colombia. In addition, Latin America has great potential in hydroelectric power generation for domestic use.

Latin America as an U.S.-type exporter

So long as Latin America adopts free market capitalism, it has a comparative advantage in natural resources such as food, energy and raw materials. Japan and East Asia, especially Asian NIEs (Newly Industrialized Economies), can supply manufactured products. Therefore, there is a strong complementarity between the two regions.

---

8. e.g. Lester R. Brown, *Who Will Feed China?*

As industrialization advances in Latin America, the region can also supply high-tech manufactured products. And, here again, such a situation is widely expected to occur as Latin America is gradually expanding its manufacturing base. Taking the U.S. experience we can forecast one type of trade model between Japan and Latin America. The USA and Latin America share a great many similarities, especially, their size and relative under-population, natural resources and great agricultural potential. As has been described, the share of primary products (food, raw materials and fuel) imported from Latin America decreased from 77 percent in 1983 to 63 percent in 1996. This share is expected to decrease even more to around 50 percent (which is similar to the USA share in the 1980s). Between Japan and the USA, the share of the three primary items imported was 50 percent in 1983 and 31 percent in 1996 (see Figure 6.7).

It is surprising that Japan still depends so heavily on U.S. primary products. Therefore, Latin America can also enjoy a comparative advantage in primary products.

Dekasegi

The amended 1990 Law on Immigration Control and Recognition of Refugees permitted foreigners of Japanese descent (*nikkei-jin*) up to the third generation (and their spouses) to reside and work in Japan. The registered inflow of nikkei-jin jumped from 70,500 in 1990 to 151,800 in 1991 and reached 219,600 in 1995. These *dekasegi* people are employed in laborious manual occupations which normally Japanese do not want to do (known in Japan as "3 Ks jobs"-dirty, difficult and dangerous coming from their Japanese initials). From the statistics available, one in seven Brazilian nikkei has experience of *dekasegi* and one in five of Peruvian nikkei.

Dekasegi is a social and economic phenomenon. In Japan, an economic boom in the 1980s created a demand for unskilled labor tasks but the younger generation was reluctant to do such jobs and a labor shortage developed. Conversely, unemployment and hyperinflation in Latin America encouraged nikkei to head to Japan to earn higher wages. However, after the bubble economy burst, demand by "3 K" businesses for workers persisted and this demand enticed many nikkei to remain for extended periods. Usually, *dekasegi* workers, like any other people, want to return to their home country. However, as the length of their stay in

Figure 6.7. Japan: Imports from USA

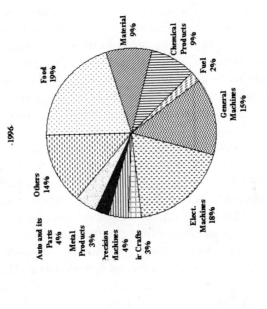

-1996-

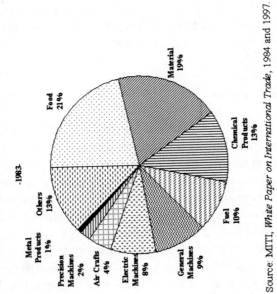

-1983-

Source: MITI, *White Paper on International Trade*, 1984 and 1997.

Japan has grown longer new needs and concerns have arisen, such as education for their children, social insurance and the like.

Furthermore, when nikkei return from Japan they do not necessarily obtain a job which utilizes their Japanese experience. And as *dekasegi* workers are said to be relatively highly educated—above high school graduate level—the jobs they do in Japan are not generally to their liking. As a consequence, in extreme cases, some returnees require psychiatric help to readjust to life in their own country. On the other hand, one of the positive aspects is that returnee nikkei can keep alive Japanese culture, language and tradition in their home countries and transmit this on to the next generation.

To utilize *dekasegi* experience in their own country, the job opportunities offered by Japan should be expanded more fully into the manufacturing sector. In Latin American countries, too, Japanese subsidiaries should employ *dekasegi* workers when they return. Another idea is that agencies should be established utilizing the returnees to run industrial estate management for Japanese affiliates, offering commissioned services such as negotiations with local governments, administration and labor management and import/export-related procedures. (This type of Japanese business has proven quite successful in industrial parks in China, for example, in Shenzhen Free Economic Zone). However, even more important than the above measures is the fact that Japan's FDI to Latin America should be increased. Thereby encouraging the *dekasegi* to play the role of a bridge between Japan and the region through technology and cultural transfer.

Financial Turmoil

There is a deep development gap in tradeables and non-tradeables in developing countries. Usually tradeables are developed because they are confronting world competition, while non-tradeables are not competitive because their markets are domestic and unaware of world competition. Liberalization and deregulation means that these non-tradeables are also thrust into world standards and quality levels. For example, utility services such as electricity and telecommunications are usually run by domestic monopolies or oligopolies and sometimes by government institutions. Privatization of these services, especially with foreign participation, brings about low prices and better services for end-users. Traditionally, another example is construction, where tenders are sometimes impinged upon by collusion or political interference, particularly, in the case of public investments.

The financial sector in many developing countries faces the same problems. Bankers are sometimes relatives of the prime minister or the president or have strong connection with members of the cabinet and other high political figures and are open to bribery. The banking system is often protected by the government through the Ministry of Finance (it is called a "convoy-of-ships method" in Japan). Monetary policies are sometimes executed not by regulations but by window guidance. Rules are ambiguous and lack transparency. Banking institutions themselves are weak and markets are not well facilitated.

Under these circumstances, it is quite natural that any abrupt introduction of market mechanisms to the financial sector results in confusions and turmoil or monetary crisis. For example, Thailand introduced its offshore market (Bangkok International Banking Facility) in 1993 to absorb foreign short-term capital. Multinational banks rushed to lend short-term money (for one month or three months) to Thai banks under a nearly fixed exchange rate against the U.S. dollar. According to the Bank for International Settlements, total international lending (majority is short-term lending) reached $736.6 billion for East Asian countries at the end of 1996, of which Thailand accounted for $70.2 billion. A major portion of this money went into real estate to boost land development and building prices. And when asset prices collapsed, total confusion followed in July 1997, with heavy depreciation of the Thai *baht*, large fluctuations of stock prices, speculative attacks, and a sudden shrinkage of foreign reserves, resulting in negative growth of the Thai economy, dropping from a growth of 6.4 percent in 1996. Furthermore, the collapse was contagious spreading to other East Asian countries and the ramifications still continue. Such a situation develops because there is no world central bank or world watchdog to control international financial flows.

A gradual approach to liberalization is needed in order not to create unnecessary social costs. Some controls on short-term capital are also to be recommended if confusion is to be avoided. Indeed, world financial money, especially that represented by mutual funds, is so enormous that the small amounts of foreign reserves held by developing countries cannot cope with abrupt and volatile in/out-flows of money. For example, Chile required prior deposits of an equivalent amount when short-term capital flowed into the country. In addition, facilities provided by international financial institutions such as the IMF, the WB, the IDB, and the Asian

Development Bank should be strengthened. Needless to say, self-help efforts such as prudent regulations, transparency in policy management, and fair business practices should be made in the financial sector of developing countries.

Japan's Role

Judging from this brief survey on trade, FDI and ODA, it is recommended that Japan strengthen the relationship with Latin America as follows:

(i) Regarding trade: Japan should make efforts to decrease trade surpluses by importing more Latin American products. Latin America should also expand commercialization efforts to sell their products to Japanese consumers.

(ii) FDI: There is an increasing tendency to direct this to the region, the fourth FDI boom, reflecting stable and prosperous economic activity in Latin America, while weak growth is seen in East Asia. However, Latin America has to facilitate basic infrastructure—including the use of private capital—and to deepen its industrial structure by fostering parts and component industries, what is called "supporting industries" and so forth. [9]

(iii) ODA: It is expected that the tendency here will be in decline over the next couple of years. Therefore, Japan has to enhance the effectiveness of its ODA under limited budgets. Japan's ODA can best be utilized in the two main areas mentioned above: infrastructure building and fostering supporting industries. Some measures should also be taken to better utilize *dekasegi* returnees.

(iv) In order to check and control international financial flows, Japan's multilateral assistance should be expanded. Coupled with policy-oriented leadership, financial aid for the IMF, the World Bank and the Inter-American Development Bank should be strengthened.

Liberalization has brought about changes in trade and investment policies. The success of the EU and NAFTA has prompted policy makers to rethink a complemetarity role of regional integration to multilateral trading systems. Among the top thirty GDP countries in the world only four countries/regions (Japan, South Korea, China and Taiwan) do not belong

---

9. Mitsuhiro Kagami, *The Voice of East Asia: ...*

to any type of regional integration or free trade agreements (FTAs). FTAs are increasingly being regarded as a pragmatic approach to achieving global liberalization. Recently trade policies seem to have changed toward regional integration, including bilateral FTAs in some Asian countries. South Korea under President Kim Dae-Jung is one of the most active countries in seeking FTAs. South Korea set up study teams for a Korea-Chile FTA and a Korea-Japan FTA in 1998. Japan has also formed study teams for a Japan-Mexico FTA and a Japan-Korea FTA and at present is doing a study on a Japan-Singapore FTA. The first study meeting was held in May 2000 in the Japan External Trade Organization (JETRO) for a Japan-Chile FTA.

The press conference held on April 3, 2000 by the Committee for Closer Economic Relations between Japan and Mexico in JETRO concluded as follows:

> *An initiative should be taken to promote a comprehensive agreement that liberalizes not only trade and investment, but also intellectual property rights, standards certification, government procurements and dispute settlement mechanisms. While giving adequate consideration to the agreement's possible effects on domestic industries, every effort should be made to create a basic framework for a FTA as soon as possible*

There is no doubt that FTAs will increase trade and investment between Japan and related Latin American countries.

AN ASSESSMENT OF THE IMPACT OF CHINA'S WTO ACCESSION
A COMPARATIVE PERSPECTIVE

Yang Zerui

Introduction

China is expected to have entered the WTO towards the end of 2001, 15 years after negotiations with other GATT/WTO members began in earnest. The international consensus seems to be that China's impact on the WTO will be comparable to that of Japan when it joined the GATT in 1955. With an eye to the possible consequences for the USA, members of the U.S. Congress have opposed China's WTO membership. This raises the need to reconsider the impact of China's entry into WTO on world markets. The major question is whether the rapid economic growth and high export growth rates that China achieved over the past 20 years will in fact accelerate even further, as was the case after Japan joined GATT. Is this a realistic assessment?

In order to answer this question we will examine several key factors underlying China's high economic growth and export growth rates, such as China's role in global markets, China's export merchandise structure, and the role of exports in China's economy as a whole.[1] This will be compared to the conditions of the Japanese economy at the time Japan joined GATT in 1955. We will conclude by venturing a prognosis of China's foreign trade in 2005 and 2010 and the possible impact on world markets following China's WTO membership.

---

1. Two recent papers discuss the question of reliability of Chinese statistics: Gerald Segal "Does China Matter?" *Foreign Affairs* 9/10, 1999, and Leslie Pappas and Lijia Macleod "The Numbers Game," *Newsweek*, 24 January 2000.

A Comparison of the Role of China's Foreign Trade in the Domestic Economy and in the World Market

Foreign trade grows as the economy grows—that has been the common experience of all developed countries. Large economic powers are invariably important foreign trade powers, such as USA, Japan and Germany. Yet the proportion of foreign trade in relation to the economy as a whole differs. In the case of large economies such as China, USA and Japan the role of foreign trade is somewhat different from that of smaller economies, such as Hong Kong, Singapore and Korea. For large countries exports should be a supplement and extension of their domestic economies.

The following two graphs show that China's export has increased quickly, and that the share of foreign trade of GDP reaches the average global level, yet nearly twice that of Japan and that of the USA. In the year of 2000, the trade share of GDP of China rose to as much as 44 percent, while the average share of the world and other big countries did not change conspicuously.[2] (Figure 7.1 and Figure 7.2)

China's trade and growing exports, and their share in China's GDP are obviously related to the strength of its economy, but this is not necessarily a simple proportional relationship.[3]

Table 7.1 shows that despite the high export growth rate and high trade share of GDP, China is still one of the poorest countries in the world. This forces us to ask the question why the economy has not benefited proportionately to the growth of trade and exports the way it did in the case of other countries. Looking for the reasons we may wonder whether there are some special features in China's economy and China's foreign trade. (Figure 7.3)

The figures in Table 7.3 show that China is already one of the biggest exporters in the world. The export merchandise gap between China and the other big countries shrank considerably during the past twenty 20 years, and China's ranking in world export merchandise rose from 32nd to 9th.[4] Without further comment these figures may give us a wrong image

---

2. In 2000, China's GDP was about 1.07 trillion (8.9 t RMB), foreign trade is 474.3 billion U.S. dollars. *People's Daily,* 17 January 2001.

3. The figures listed here were released by the Chinese government and quoted by the World Bank. The validity of these figures have been doubted by numerous scholars. See footnote 1.

Figure 7.1. Export and Foreign Trade Growth of China, 1981-2000, Millions of Dollars

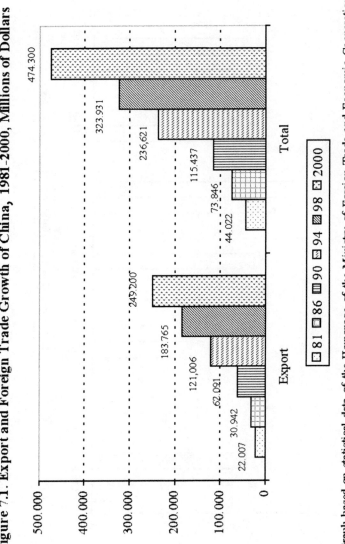

Graph based on statistical data of the Homepage of the Ministry of Foreign Trade and Economic Cooperation (MOFTEC), China.

Figure 7.2. Trade Share of GDP (%) in 1980, 1996, and 2000

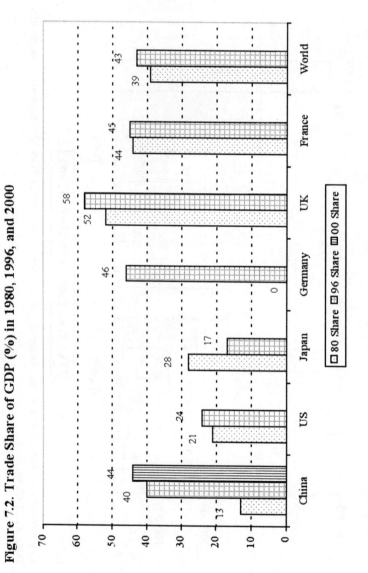

Graph based the *World Development Report 1998/99*, World Bank, p. 228–229.

145

Figure 7.3. China's Role in World Market 1999, 2000. Merchandise of Export, Millions of Dollars

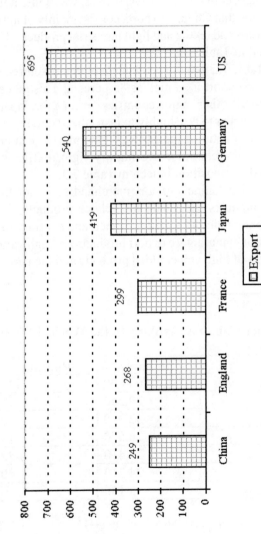

Graph based on World Trade Organization data. The data for China is that of 2000, for other countries are that of 1999.

of China's export economy. Despite its status as a huge exporter, in world markets China is mainly known for products such as slippers and umbrellas. This may sound slightly exaggerated, but does China export famous brands rivaling Mitsubishi, Toyota or Hyundai, Daewoo onto the world market? Which active Chinese entrepreneurs are widely known in today's global business community? Nevertheless, we should not jump to conclusions to assume that China's exports consist mainly of agricultural products, raw materials and textile and light industrial products. The actual situation is reflected in Table 7.2.

It appears from Table 7.2 that the percentage of manufactured goods in China's merchandise export is as high as 85 percent. This percentage is higher compared to all other major countries, except for Japan. These figures make China appear to be a highly industrialized country exporting the products of its manufacturing industries. Furthermore, we might expect that China's export merchandise are mainly light/textile industrial products. The actual composition is seen in Table 7.3.

Table 7.3 shows that China's export merchandise is not limited to manufactures, but includes chemicals and related products, machinery and transport equipment etc. As a matter of fact, and contrary to popular assumptions the main manufacture export products are high value-added products. The export of high value-added products and the percentage of

---

Table 7.1. GDP per Capita & Ranking in the World 1998, in Dollars

Countries	Dollars	Ranking
China	*760,000	145
US	29,240	10
Japan	32,350	7
Germany	26,570	13
UK	21,410	22
France	24,210	20
World Average	5,130	

Based on *2000 World Bank Atlas*, the World Bank, p. 14–15.

---

4. "Analysis report: foreign trade," China Statistic Bureau, available from http://www.stats.gov.cn/news/year50/year5013.htm.

high value-added products of China's export are top-ranking among major exporting countries.

With the level of China's industrialization rising, the export merchandise structure is improving quickly, and the high value-added product rises continuously. In 1998, the machinery and transport equipment export was 66.54 billion U.S. dollars, and it was the No. 1 export merchandise of China.[5]

Table 7.2. Structure of Merchandise Export, % of total, 1980 and 1997

	Food		A&R*		Fuels		Ores/Metals		Manufactures	
Year	80	97	80	97	80	97	80	97	80	97
China	...	7	...	1	...	4	...	2	...	85
US	18	9	5	3	4	2	5	2	66	81
Japan	1	1	1	1	0	1	2	1	95	95
Germany	5	5	1	1	4	1	3	2	85	83
UK	7	7	1	1	13	6	5	2	71	83
France	16	13	2	1	4	3	4	2	73	78
World	13	8	4	2	11	4	5	3	65	77

* agricultural and raw materials, figures not available.
Table based on *World Development Indicators 1999*, The World Bank, pp. 206–208.

Table 7.3. Structure of Manufactures in China's Export, 1998

Manufactures	Millions of dollars	% of total
Chemicals and related products	10,320	5.600
Manufactured goods and classified chiefly by materials	32,380	17.600
Machinery and transport equipment	*50,203	27.300
Miscellaneous manufactured articles	70,220	38.200
Commodities and transactions	100,000	0.056
Total manufactures	163,160	*88.800
Total export	183,760	100.000

* the percentage of 1999, 2000 is even higher than that of 1998.
Based on *Statistic data*, MOFTEC,
http://www.moftec.gov.cn/html/government/data_trade

5. See footnote 4.

In 2000, the export of machinery and transport equipment export reached $103.5 billion, confirming the No. 1 position of these exports in China's total export trade.[6]

Taken together, the figures quoted above seem to contradict the fact that average Chinese income is still very low, as apparent from Table 7.2. We also need to explain the fact that despite China's economic achievements it is hardly known for its brand products, and famous enterprises and entrepreneurs. Since the figures quoted above do not provide an answer, we will need a different approach to answer these questions.

The Structure of China's Exports

The economic history of developed countries such as USA, Japan, Korea shows that as the economy grows we witness an expansion in the number of national manufacturers and exporters rapidly entering the global market. The main actors of foreign trade are expected to be the major national companies both state and private, in particular for a large country like China. In fact, the opposite is true. In order to look for an explanation we have to turn to the role played by foreign direct investment (FDI). (see Figure 7.4 and Table 7.4)

Basically, FDI companies import raw materials and semi-products to China which are then processed in FDI companies within China. Subsequently, the finished products are exported to the countries where these FDI companies have their home base, or else to the global market. In China this practice is called "processing trade" (*jiagong maoyi*) or, "processing industry" (*jiagong chanye*). The figures presented here show that FDI import and export occupy the largest part of China's import and export. This amounts to 48.4 percent in 1999, 50 percent in 2000 as a percentage of China's foreign trade, compared to 0.1 percent in 1981. On the other hand, the share of China's state-owned enterprises in total export decreased from 99.9 percent in 1981 to 48.1 percent in 1999, 45 percent in 2000, and the share of the private sector and other is 3.5 percent in 2000.[7]

Though the processing industry and processing trade is very important for developing countries as part of their path towards modernization, its

---

6. See footnote 4. The number and percentage is higher than that of MOFTEC, see Table 7.3.

7. MOFTEC news, 19 February 19, 2001. In 2000, China's total trade was $474 billion, among which FDI trade was $237 billion, and the figures for state owned enterprises trade totaled $215 billion.

149

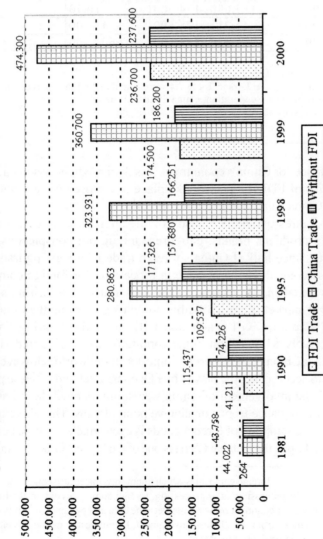

Figure 7.4. Foreign Direct Investment Companies (FDI) Trade in China's Import and Export, 1981–2000, Millions of Dollars, % of Total

Table 7.4. Growth Rate of FDI Trade in China's Export. Millions of Dollars, %

Year	Trade Growth	% of	Annual growth rate
1981–90	264,030-- 41,211	15608.00	75.0
1995–98	109,537--157,680	143.95	13.0
1998–99	157,680--174,500	10.70	*10.7
1990–99	41,211--174,500	424.00	17.5
1981–99	264,030--174,500	66091.00	43.0

* *People's Daily*, February 3, 2000. Beijing
The figures in Figure 7.4 and Table 7.4 were calculated on the basis of *Analysis Report*:
Foreign Economic Cooperation, China Statistic Bureau,
http://www.stats.gov.cn/news/year50/year5015.htm

---

importance for China's economy is less than might be assumed, since the activities of FDI companies take place in a closed circuit that does not affect China's national economy directly.

The figures quoted here also provide an answer to the question why China's products, brands, entrepreneurs are not conspicuous in world markets, since half of China's foreign trade is processing trade, even if Chinese companies that engage in processing for foreign companies as agents are taken into account.[8] This is the reason why China's presence in world market is hardly visible. China's government announced that China's import will reach one trillion in the coming five years, respectively $1.3 trillion in the coming 6 years.[9] This underlines once more that China is an important importer in the world. However once we take into account the role played by FDI companies and Chinese processing agents, the involvement of China's economy is much less than it might seem at first glance from a qualitative point of view. This also explains that China's consumption of foreign goods is even smaller than that of Korea or Taiwan, despite the fact that China is one of the biggest importers in the world.

---

8. This refers to foreign companies which import raw materials/semi-products to China's companies for processing; after processing, foreign companies export the finished product to the mother countries or world market. The data and percentage of this kind of trade are not available from the Chinese government. I would estimate the percentage to be in the range of 25 percent of total trade.

9. Announced by Minister of MOFTEC, 2 February 2000. Available from: http://www.chinamarket.com.cn/v.../?Mival=Newsdetail&ID=15599&Type_id=0 00/02/03.

We now wish to determine to what extent FDI relying on cheap Chinese labor and low wages contribute to China's economic progress, especially since China occupies the leading role as a global FDI processing base. If FDI is excluded the figures for China's total trade and trade growth are as follows (Table 7.5).

First of all, FDI trade is not only the biggest part of China's foreign trade, but also displays the highest growth rates in China's total trade. The average growth rate of FDI trade has been about 43 percent annually during the period 1981–1999. Excluding FDI trade, China's foreign trade

Table 7.5. China's Total Trade and Trade Growth Rate Excluded FDI, 1981-1999, Millions of Dollars

Year	Trade Growth	% of	Annual Growth Rate
1981–90	43,758-- 74,226	169.6	6.0
comparing:	total: 44,022--115,437	262.2	11.3
	FDI's: 264,030-- 41,211	15608.0	75.0
1990–99	74,226--186,200	250.9	11.0
comparing:	total: 115,437--360,700	312.4	13.2
	FDI's: 41,211--174,500	424.0	17.5
1981–99	43,758--186,200	425.5	7.5
comparing:	total: 44,022--360,700	819.4	15.7
	FDI's: 264,030--174,500	66091.0	43.0

Based on the sources used for Figure 7.4 and Table 7.4.

would decrease sharply to $186,200 million in 1999. In addition, the average growth rate of China foreign trade would also decrease sharply to a very modest 7.5 percent, compared to 15.7 percent of total trade growth trade in the period 1981–1999.

Moreover, in the past five years (1995–1999) the growth of China's trade excluding FDI trade has been 8.7 percent ($171,326 million to $186,200 million), the annual growth rate about 2.1 percent, compared to the growth rate of FDI trade of 59.4 percent ($109,500 million to $174,500 million), with an annual growth rate of 12.2 percent ,and total trade growing at 28.4 percent ($280,863 million to $360,700 million). The annual growth rate is 6.5 percent.

Here we can clearly see that when we exclude FDI trade, China's annual trade growth rate is about 7.5 percent in 1981–1999. This is a very normal trade growth rate, and should not be rated a particular achievement. In fact, there exists a dangerous trend since China's trade excluding FDI trade has been slowing down, especially during the past five years. It seems that excluded FDI trade China cannot even maintain the 7.5 percent of trade growth.

Taken at face value, the growth rate of China's foreign trade in 2000 was 31.5 percent. This is the highest growth rate of China's foreign trade recorded during the past 20 years. In order to interpret these figures correctly we have to take the following factors into account:

a) In that particular year, the global economy was in an excellent condition.
b) 2000 followed upon two years of low growth, low in 1999, and minus growth in 1998.
c) The increased role of FDI trade.

It follows that the growth rate of trade for 2000 cannot be used to extrapolate the growth of China's future trade. The figures for the second half year of 2000 are already indicating that the growth rate of China's foreign trade is sharply slowing down.[10]

During the past 20 years, the importance of FDI in China's economy and foreign trade has been growing fast. It is true that the role of China's state-owned enterprises in China's economy has been decreasing, but they continue to maintain a monopoly in main areas of industry and in foreign trade. China's infant private sector does not enjoy the right to engage in foreign trade. Today, China appears to open all industries and foreign trade to FDI and foreign enterprises, while restrictions on its own private sectors continue.

We have to conclude that China is the only case where FDI trade has acquired an overwhelmingly important role in foreign trade, compared to all other large countries. Although this deserves exploration and consideration with regard to the future development of the Chinese economy, this is beyond the task and theme of this article.

---

10. In December 2000, China's export increased 8.5%, in January 2001, the growth rate was 0.8%. What is worrying is that the total foreign trade in January 2001 fell by 25.2% compared to that of December 2000, from 43.4 b down to 32.5b (see *International Business Daily,* 15 February 2001).

The Historical Background of the Development of FDI in China

China began to accept FDI starting in 1981. The total figure of FDI units since then amounts to about 365,974. Total contracted capital is $681,575 million, and by the end of January 2001 the total of actually invested capital is $350,845 million.[11] During the past 15 years, average annual FDI growth rates have been about 32.9 percent. From 1993 China has been the No.1 FDI recipient among all developing countries, and in absolute terms is the No.2 FDI recipient next to the USA[12]

FDI trade occupies the largest share in China's total trade. If China's intake of FDI can maintain past rates, China's export may continue high growth. We need to add, though, that the benefits for China's economy as a whole are limited, a result of the weight of FDI playing a key role in China's trade.

Meanwhile, the percentage of FDI in China's total investment and FDI companies' output in China's total GDP is also growing quickly. Precise data and estimates are apparently not available; it is possible that the Chinese government does not keep such statistics.

Summing up we conclude that the structure of China's exporting actors is completely different from that in other large economies. FDI companies occupy the main position as importers and main exporters in China's total trade.

As mentioned above, there is an obvious need to question the positive role played by FDI in the development of China's economy. At the same time we must realize that now and in the foreseeable future FDI enterprises are and will be dominant exporters and importers in the Chinese economy. The role of China's state-owned companies, famous worldwide for their inefficiency, is decreasing rapidly in China's foreign trade. China's private sector which should shoulder the supplementary task of increasing China's competitiveness in world market is not allowed to have the right of import and export freely. This phenomenon takes place within the framework of a government policy that calls for the "establishment of a socialist foreign trade system and structure with Chinese characteristics."[13]

---

11. *Economic Daily,* 20 February 2000.
12. Analysis Report *Foreign Economic Cooperation*, China Statistic Bureau. See Figure 7.4 and Table 7.5.

Predicting the Possible Impact on World Markets of China's WTO Accession

As argued in the former section, quantitative projections of China's future foreign trade and its impact on world market tell us little about its qualitative impact, unless we take into account the role of FDI trade in China.

Extrapolating China's Export until 2005 and 2010

A review of the historic pattern and structure of growth of China's trade may assist us in predicting future patterns. Contrary to commonly held assumptions the rate of China's import and export was not exceptionally high in the years 1979 to1997 (Table 7.6).

These data show that the fastest growth period of China occurred in the period 1972–1978, a time of great political difficulties. I should like to add that the export growth rates for China as released by the World Bank differ. According to those figures the rate of growth was 11.5 percent for the years 1980–1990 and 15.8 percent in the period 1990–1997.[14]

As discussed before, the size of China's foreign trade is dominated by FDI trade. Whenever FDI to China slowed down in recent years, China's overall trade growth also slowed down.[15] It will be very hard for China to

---

Table 7.6. China's Import and Export Growth Rate, 1951–1999. Export and Import, %

Year	Export	Import
1951–59	17.0	15.8
1960–71	1.3	0.3
1972–78	20.5	25.6
1979–98	15.8	14.5
1995–99	*6.9	5.9

*See Table 7.5. Based on *Analysis Report: foreign trade*, China Statistic Bureau. See also footnote 4.

---

13. *China Foreign Trade Law*, available from MOFTEC homepage, Policy and Laws.
14. *World Development Report 1998/1999*, p. 210.

maintain the growth rate of incoming FDI as well as the size of FDI trade, even after China's entry into the WTO. One can hardly expect that China's foreign trade will achieve a big leap forward after joining the WTO. China already enjoys MFN treatment from all major countries, and the export to the world market relies on the competitiveness of the national products, and not on the FDI trade.[16]

As to predictions of China's growth of trade after joining the WTO, Mr. Shi Guangshen, Minister of MOFTEC estimates that China can maintain an 8 percent growth rate over the coming 6 years.[17] In my discussions with several Chinese economists specializing in China foreign trade the most optimistic guesses assumed that a growth rate of more than 10 percent would be difficult to achieve. Yet even assuming a growth rate of China's trade of 10 percent for the next 10 years our projection for China's total trade is as follows (Figure7.5).

According to this projection, in 2005 China may rank the No.6 among foreign traders in the world, after USA, Germany, Japan, France and UK;

Figure 7.5. The Total Trade of China in 2005, 2010, in Millions of Dollars

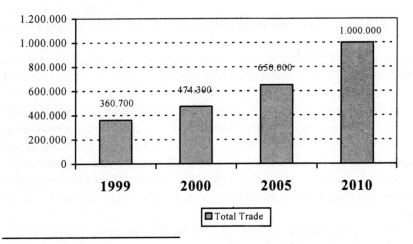

15. New FDI companies decreased 13.8% with the capital decreased 20.9% in 1999 to 1998. 1999 was the second year in a row the figures decreased. See *People's Daily*, 2 Feb. 2000.

16. See footnote 11.

17. *Economic and Trade News*, 2 Feb 2000. Available from: http://www.chinamarket.com.cn.

in 2010, China may be the No. 4, only surpassed by the USA, Germany and Japan.

FDI trade is likely to occupy an even more important position by 2005 and 2010. As the FDI trade growth in China's trade shows, the FDI trade percentage in total trade rises at least by 2 percent annually, resulting in a share of 60 percent in 2005 and 70 percent in 2010 (Figure 7.6).

FDI trade would occupy a dominant position in China's foreign trade in 2005 and 2010, as the present trend shows. In 2005, the size of FDI trade would reach $390,000 million against a total trade figure of $650,000 million, and trade excluding FDI trade will reach $260,000 million; in 2010 FDI trade would be $700,000 million, against a total trade to the tune of $1000,000 million, and trade excluding FDI trade reaching $300,000 million.

As discussed before, it is not appropriate to classify FDI trade as "China's trade", since FDI trade is in fact intra-company trade conducted by multinational companies. Their products should not be counted as China's products, and they do not constitute an essential contribution to China's economy.

Excluding FDI trade, China's foreign trade increases very slowly, lacking the ability to impact the world market.

The Effects of WTO Membership—Japan and China Compared

Japan joined GATT in 1955, and its membership had a sizeable impact on global trade. There is considerable concern about China's impact on world market after joining WTO (Figure 7.7).

In 1975, Japan exported 55,753 m, 28 times that of 1955's export, 2,010 m, and its annual export growth rate was 18 percent. As discussed above, China's foreign trade growth rate in 1979–1998 was 15.7 percent, lower than Japan's, even including China's FDI trade. The environment for China's exports will not completely change in the wake of joining WTO. Therefore growth rates cannot be expected to reach levels as high as those of Japan.

After joining GATT Japan's export structure changed heavily in 1955–1975, as shown in Table 7.7.

Table 7.7 shows that after joining GATT, Japan's export quickly shifted to heavy/chemical products, and the share of the textile industry in Japan's exports decreased. As discussed in Part I, current Chinese exports are already mainly in the area of high value-added products, and this

Figure 7.6. China's Trade, FDI Trade and Excluded FDI Trade, 1999, 2005, 2010, Millions of Dollars

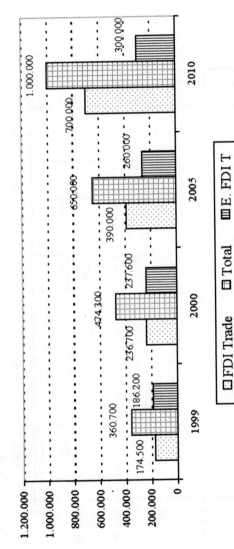

158

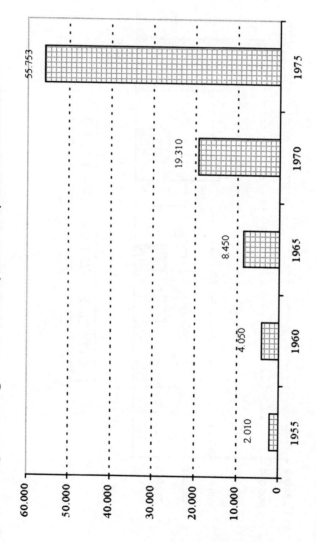

Figure 7.7. Japan's Foreign Trade Growth, 1955–1975, Millions of Dollars

Based on *Japan Trade White Book, 1955–1975*, Department of Trade and Industry, Japan.

Table 7.7. Japan's Export Structure Change, 1960–1975, % of Total

	Food	Textile	Ores/Metal	Heavy/Chemical Product	Others
1960	6.3	38.9	4.2	44	15.3
1965	4.1	22.3	3.1	62	12.1
1970	3.4	13.5	1.9	74	9.9
1975	1.4	7.2	1.3	83.2	7.3

Based on *Japan Trade White Book 1976*, Department of Trade and Industry, Japan.

---

development seems to have come to its conclusion. Summarizing the differences between Japan and China as a result of joining GATT and WTO respectively we may predict that

1. China can not catch up with Japan's export growth rate;
2. China's industrial upgrading will be different from that of Japan, since judging by the present composition of exports we must conclude that China is already "highly-industrialized" country, although its impact on world markets remains limited;
3. China's foreign trade relies on FDI trade, namely intra-company trade by multinational companies; Japan's foreign trade relied on national companies improving their competitiveness when moving into global markets. There were no FDI exporters in Japan's foreign trade at that time.

To sum up, there is little likelihood of China's membership of the WTO having an impact on world markets the way Japan did after entering GATT, this despite the fact that China may be the world's No.6 exporter by 2005 and No.4 exporter by 2010. The ability to impact the world market relies on industrial upgrading and improvement of competitiveness coupled with high economic growth.[18] It is not related to China having a huge national territory, a big population and a big potential market: if that were important, why did countries with huge population figures such as India, Pakistan,

---

18. As Mark Frazier pointed out, most predictions concerning China's impact on the world market take the continued growth of the Chinese economy for granted. Therefore, the real significance of China's WTO accession does not in its short-term benefits, but in the restructuring of China's economy over the next decade. *ChinaOnLine*, Feb.5, 2000.

Nigeria, Bangladesh not exercise a deep impact on world markets after they joined GATT?

Conclusion

Having assessed the nature of China's export growth and its important role in the world market, and having analyzed China's special export and exporters structure, I ventured a prediction of China's foreign trade by 2005 and by 2010. Based on these estimates I attempted a comparison of the effects of Japan's impact on global foreign trade after joining GATT, and the estimated effects of China's expected membership of the WTO. This leads me to the following final conclusion:

1. There are few reasons to expect that China's accession to the WTO will have a major impact on world trade. If any, it would be in minor areas such as slippers and umbrellas. Its impact on the world market can not be compared with that of Japan when it joined GATT;
2. The key to the impact on the world market lies in China's ability to achieve growth through enterprises owned by China/Chinese, and their competitiveness in world markets;
3. Under the current political/economic system called "socialism with Chinese characteristics" China's manufacturers and exporters structure can not be expected to achieve a big transformation after joining WTO. Also, restrictions and prohibitions related to activities by the private sector will continue;[19]
4. On the contrary, we must take into account another possibility, namely that imports will increase rapidly and export growth may be cut to zero, or at least come down to slow growth rates.[20] The reason is that China's WTO entry will favor the entrance of foreign

---

19. A Chinese scholar from Australia, Yang Xiaokai argues that China's Agreement for joining the WTO places China's private sector on a completely unequal footing. The private sector is not mentioned or considered by the Agreement. See "Two possible consequences after China joining WTO," Yang Xiaokai, 18 January 2000; 21 *Century News* (Chinese), Tokyo.

enterprises in the Chinese market, while it is impossible at this stage to provide an estimate for China's future exports based on improved competitiveness of China's state-owned enterprises and FDI investment. In that case it is easy to predict that China will respond to such a situation by putting a stop to further liberalization in accordance with WTO rules, in order to maintain a trade balance and protect its national industries. In addition, foreign exporters to the Chinese market may be "asked" to agree to voluntary export restrictions.

---

20. A paper in *ChinaOnLine* (no author indicated) discussed this possibility. The author expects that China's export may grow slowly, while import grows rapidly after China joining WTO, for it would be easier for the competitive multinational companies to enter the China market, while China's companies' competitiveness remains unchanged. See "Imports increase rapidly, export growth slows," 7 January 2000. Available from: http://www.chinaonline.com/issues/wto/currentnews/open/b200010520-SS.asp

LATIN AMERICAN
PERSPECTIVES

TRANSFORMATION IN LATIN AMERICA
INTEGRATION, COOPERATION AND REFORMS

Marianne L. Wiesebron

The buying and selling of Brazil Inc.
Latin America's largest economy is being transformed by a boom
in takeovers and joint ventures.

Let the party begin.
Brazil's privatization program is as complex as it is gigantic. But
it promises huge rewards to foreign investors ... [1]

In Latin America, import-substitution industrialization has been replaced by open economies; or rather trade liberalization, at a rapid pace, with sometimes dramatic consequences for the national industries and the labor market. At the same time, in that continent, where public enterprises represented a very substantial part of the economy, privatization is taking place on a large scale. It started in Chile in 1973 after the military take-over, a bit later in Argentina, after the coup of 1976. Mexico followed in the 1980s and Brazil joined the ranks in the1990s. In July 1998, Telebrás, the Brazilian telecommunications company, was put up for auction, the largest single privatization in any emerging market.[2] Furthermore, in a number of Latin American countries, the whole social security system is being revised, retirement and health schemes are being modified, mostly privatized, and job security for civil servants is being abolished.

---

1. *The Economist*, 9 November 1996, p.95; *Ibidem*, 26 April 1997, p. 63.
2. *International Herald Tribune*, "Brazil Braces for Phone Firm Sale," 27 July 1998, pp. 11, 13.

Unemployment, an increasing informal sector, growing poverty, increasing inequality and unrest are the results. For instance, the fortune of the richest Mexican was estimated at 6.6 billion dollars in 1995, equal to that of the earnings of the 17 million poorest of his country.[3] Inequality has only increased since, and not only in Latin America.

Besides the following of neo-liberal tenets at a national economic and social level, there have been important developments, such as the establishment of quite a number of bilateral and multilateral agreements, within Latin America and outside.

In this study, the changes at an international and national level in Latin America, with a focus on Mexico, as a member of NAFTA and the Mercosur/l countries will be analyzed. Special attention will be paid to Latin American relations with the United States of America, the European Union and, to some extent, to the recent relations with Asia, including the Asian crisis, and finally how all these developments affect that area.

Globalization and Regional Integration

In fact, there have been quite a number of attempts at integration in Latin America, in different forms, since independence in the first two decades of the nineteenth century. One more recent attempt, again not quite successful, was the creation of a Latin American Free Trade Area (LAFTA) in the 1960s. It seems that in the nineties, institutionalization of relations is finally taking off. The regional forms of cooperation on the American continent are considered limited in scope, as no supranational institutions were established such as exist within the European Union.[4] The rapid way integration is working may prove otherwise. Regional cooperation has been brought about because of a growing economic complementarity and a need to form alliances confronting other existing processes of

---

3. A. Gresh, "L'ombre des inégalités," *Le Monde Diplomatique*, Sept. 1997, p. 1. See also V. Bulmer-Thomas, ed., *The New Economic Model in Latin America and its Impact on Income Distribution and Poverty.* In particular see H. Pánuco-Laguette and M. Székely, "Income Distribution and Poverty in Mexico", in V. Bulmer-Thomas, ed., *The New Economic Model in Latin America* ..., pp. 185–222.

4. J.M. Grieco, "Systemic Sources of Variation...," in E.D. Mansfield,. and H.V. Milner, eds., *The Political Economy* ..., pp. 164-185. G. Kahle, "Grundprobleme der Integration ...," and H. Pietschmann, "Integration und Bürokratie", both in M. Mols, *Integration und Kooperation in Lateinamerika,* pp. 27–51 and 61–74.

integration, such as the European Union. Intraregional trade in Latin America has been growing at a fast rate.[5] The most important events have been the establishment of the Common Market of the South (Mercosur/l), in 1991, and the North American Free Trade Area (NAFTA), in 1994. The first represents the deepest form of integration after the European Union, forming a customs union in the Third World, and, since 1994, negotiating as one bloc with third countries. The second one is much more limited in scope; however, it is the first agreement between countries of such different economic development and power.

At an intercontinental level, APEC, with members in the American continent and in Asia, is an institution of growing importance. Maybe to offset this American-Asian cooperation, the EU launched a new forum with Asia, ASEM, which had its first meeting in April 1996. The idea is to strengthen the dialogue between the EU and ten (Southeast and East) Asian countries, on political, economic and cultural aspects. In the 1998, at the biennial government meeting, special attention has been paid to the Asian crisis. Alongside the public sector, the private sector has also been involved from the start, in particular the Asia-Europe Business Forum, which is very active in furthering cooperation between entrepreneurs from both continents. The Asia-Europe Foundation, set up for the involvement of civil society and for fostering cultural exchange, is much more low-key. The main focus is, without doubt, economic.[6]

The European Union has also paid special attention to Latin America. It is strengthening its ties with Mercosur/l, with a first important agreement being signed in December 1995. A new agreement was signed with Mexico in 1997. A Free Trade Agreement was finally signed and agreed by all parties in 2000. However, its policy seems more a reaction, after circa 40 percent loss in trade, than a really positive step. Negotiations are under way for free trade agreements with Mercosur/l and Chile, an associated member of Mercosur/l. But, they are progressing slowly as the European Union (EU) seems to have other priorities. The EU is more interested in its internal reorganization and enlargement to Central and Eastern Europe, which is also reflected in the decrease in preferential treatment given to their former colonies in Africa, Caribbean, Pacific, the ACP countries. The situation is clearly reflected in some statistics. According to figures

---

5. W. Karlsson and A. Malaki, *Growth, Trade and Integration in Latin America*, pp. 4–6.
6. I. d' Hooghe, "Het ASEM-forum ...," *Internationale Spectator*, 55, 6, 2001, pp. 324–328.

from 1999, intra-trade within the EU is 63.4 percent, in Western Europe, 69.1 percent (including Norway and Switzerland); with NAFTA 9.9 percent, of which the USA 8.9 percent; Asia, including Australia and New Zealand, 7.5 percent; Central and Eastern Europe 3.7 percent, with the Baltic States and the Russian Federation included, 5.1 percent. Africa represents 2.5 percent of the trade, and the Middle East and Latin America are trailing just behind with 2.4 percent. In 1997, Asia was the most important region outside the EU, followed by NAFTA. In its interaction with Latin America, there has been an increase since 1990, when trade was only 1.8 percent, which means a 25 percent growth rate.[7]

Regional Integration Within the Americas: From Traditional U.S. Monroeism Towards the Age of Globalization

This is a far cry from European domination of Latin America, which started, of course, in colonial times with Spain and Portugal and was practically taken over by Great Britain in the nineteenth century. Although the Monroe Doctrine dates from 1823, it was only in the twentieth century that the Americans really started to implement this view and its concomitant policies In fact, a radical change began in 1898, the year Spain lost Cuba and other colonies to the Americans. A couple of years later, T. Roosevelt added the 'big stick-policy" for good measure, which F.D. Roosevelt later tried to offset by speaking of the 'good neighbor' policy.[8]

The United States always saw Latin America as its back garden, fenced off to others. In the twentieth century, it was busy keeping out what it considered to be weeds, two in particular: communism and drugs. According to John Foster Dulles, communists were defined as those who appeal to *"the poor people* [who] *have always wanted to plunder the rich."*[9] In practice, communism was often alleged in order to have a stick to beat those whose policies went against American interests. Since the end of the Cold War its threat has receded and drugs have become the main issue. The crux of the matter is that these two alleged weeds

---

7. Figures based on the *Annual Report*, 2000 and 1997, of the World Trade Organization Secretariat, Geneva, 1997. See also table 4.1 in the chapter "the EU's new strategies towards emerging Asia and Latin America" by P. van Dijck, earlier in this work. N. Moussis, *Access to European Union, Laws, Economics, Policies*, pp. 513–556.

8. G. Kahle, "Grundprobleme ...," pp. 39–43. *The Economist*, "The War of 1898", 3 January 1998, pp. 48–50.

9. N. Chomsky, *Year 501: The Conquest Continues*, p. 158.

warranted direct intervention or the use of heavy duty material and the deployment of specialized personnel and armies to root them out and the implementation of a series of measures to try and break their resistance. In the process, it had the advantage of training Latin American personnel according to American standards, which also included lessons in techniques of torture, and stimulating the sale of weapons.[10] The recent Plan Colombia, introduced to combat drugs is a good example of these different aspects, with the sale of enormous quantities of weapons, the training of personnel and the presence of American experts on Colombian territory. There are about 300 to 400 military and civilian personnel present, and an American anti-narcotic brigade, although the fight seems to be directed more against the guerrillas.[11] Apart from this, the U.S. view of Latin American's role in the world after World War II was clearly expressed in Washington. It had "to sell its raw materials" to the USA and "to absorb surplus U.S. capital." Some industries might be developed as long as they did not become competitive with American industries.[12]

After the fall of the Wall in 1991, to be sure Latin America kept within its bounds of influence, President George Bush launched the Initiative for the America's. It is based on three ideas: trade, private investments and the reduction of debts. According to Bush, the prosperity of that continent depended on free trade not aid. The ultimate objective is to arrive at a Free Trade Area for the Americas (FTAA). Bush introduced the 'fast track' concept, so that agreements with other countries could be either accepted or rejected by Congress without being discussed clause by clause, but each has to be presented again for every new proposal. Congress accepted it in May 1991. Since this project commenced, quite a number of agreements have been signed, at bilateral and multilateral levels, between all kinds of different parties on that continent. In June 1991, three months after the establishment of Mercosur/l, an agreement was signed between the Member States of Mercosur/l and the American Government, known as the Rose Garden Agreement, to boost trade and investment. Meanwhile negotiations had started between the governments

---

10. Th.E. Skidmore and P.H. Smith, *Modern Latin America*, pp. 273, 355–358, 361–397. See also Stephen E. Ambrose, *Rise to Globalism, American Foreign Policy since 1938*.

11. M. Lemoine, "Au Coeur de la plus veille guerilla d'Amérique Latine ...," *Le Monde Diplomatique*, May 2000, pp. 18–19.

12. Chomsky, *Year 501: The Conquest Continues*, p. 156.

of Canada, the USA and Mexico to create a North American free trade area, NAFTA.[13]

NAFTA: Reshaping the Backyard of the USA

NAFTA represents the greatest economic bloc, in terms of GNP, in the world. It is a bloc joining developed and developing countries, with some very different characteristics: Canada, an enormous country with a small population; the USA, the world's unchallenged leading power since the fall of the Berlin Wall in 1989; and Mexico, a developing country, with a population of nearly 100 million. There had already been closer cooperation between two member states, Canada and the USA, who had signed a free trade agreement in 1988. This agreement did not cause much excitement as it was signed between two highly industrialized countries, with comparable economies and high standards of living, for most parts of the population. Some argued that this agreement was superfluous, in view of the existing long historic integration between the two countries, while others found it high time, forcing Canada to open up its economy more, and making a joint stance in trade problems possible. In 1990, negotiations started with Mexico, which would lead to its inclusion in the agreement, creating NAFTA. It required enormous negotiating efforts from the American Presidents Bush and his successor, Clinton, and President Salinas in Mexico. The text was ready early 1993, but the American Congress only approved it by October of that year. The objectives of NAFTA go further than that of a conventional free trade area, which abolishes tariffs and non-tariffs barriers. They include tracing joint trade policies, stimulating the liberalization of services, investments and intellectual property. Furthermore, the harmonization of national legislation on the environment, social welfare and workers' rights is foreseen. All this implies, in fact, Mexican adaptation to American demands so as to avoid 'unfair' competition.[14] In fact, free trade can be

---

13. J.-M. Caroit, "L'Initiative pour les Amériques fait des inquiets," *Manière de Voir* 36, Nov.–Dec. 1997, pp. 38–40. Acordo entre os Governos da República Argentina, da República Federativa do Brasil, da República do Paraguai, da República Oriental do Uruguai e o Governo dos Estados Unidos da América relativo a um Conselho sobre Comércio e Investimentos (19 June 1991), in *Mercosul: Legislação e Textos Básicos*, Brasília, pp. 123–128.

14. W.A. Orme, Jr., *Understanding NAFTA: Mexico, Free Trade and the New North America*, F.W. Mayer, *Interpreting NAFTA: the Science and Art of Political Analysis*, S. Abreu e L. Florêncio and E.H. Fraga Araújo, *Mercosul hoje*, pp. 88–89.

considered a misnomer, as the agreement is about free investment, that is American investment, in Mexico.[15]

Though these might be the avowed goals, there is also a clear political agenda, and the United States government hopes to solve or at least substantially reduce some problems through this agreement. The Americans have been preoccupied for a long time by the enormous influx of Mexicans, legal and many illegal, into United States territory. The Americans had a choice: either admit Mexican people or Mexican goods, to offset the stream of immigrants. By helping to develop the Mexican economy, there would be less reason for such large numbers of Mexicans to try and find some kind of future elsewhere. In the USA, meanwhile, trade unions, and also many farmers and other entrepreneurs, were afraid that cheap Mexican labor would create unfair competition for the Americans. Another alleged point of anxiety was less stringent legislation on protection of the environment, which would imply even more unfair competition. This explains the very extensive Treaty, with all its clauses designed to prevent Mexicans from having an unfair advantage.[16] Since the implementation of the agreement, on January 1, 1994, reality shows that the United States is doing quite well in Mexico and is reaping a higher return than the Mexicans do. Moreover, American industries can keep wages low in their own country by threatening to move their factory to the southern neighbor. In fact, the Mexicans had to overcome an enormous financial crisis, which started in the end of 1994 and continued for much of 1995. The country was also much affected by the prices of oil, which went down in 1998 and even more in 1999, while in 2000 things are looking up and are continuing to do so in 2001. While the economy seems to be doing better, with an annual increase in GDP since 1995, in the country over 50 percent of its population is poor and half of these live in abject poverty.[17]

In Mexico itself NAFTA has had different effects. The north has been growing most, expanding the already existing *maquiladora* [assembly plants] business. However, the *maquila* industry is also vulnerable, as it is immediately affected by any crisis in the USA. 90 percent of those

---

15. D. Green, *Silent Revolution. The Rise of Market Economics in Latin America,* pp. 146–150, Harry Browne, e.a., *For Richer, For Poorer. Shaping US-Mexican Integration.*

16. *Tratado de Libre Comercio de América del Norte,* Texto oficial.

17. F. Mestries, "Mexique," in *L'Etat du Monde,* 2000, pp. 377–383. *The Economist,* "Zedillo's legacy to Fox," 9 September 2000, pp. 71–72.

hired in 2000 were fired in the first four months of 2001. On the other hand, the *maquila* industry has become quite complex and is heterogeneous in nature: some of its sites are just simple assembly plants; while in other sectors technological advanced factories have been established.[18] The Mexican center is getting mixed blessings, while the south is showing no improvement at all, maybe even the reverse is true. That is why, and not by coincidence, a rebellion was launched in Chiapas, on the same day as NAFTA came into effect.[19]

Chiapas is the poorest state in Mexico, with huge inequalities. The state is rich in oil but has the worst schooling in Mexico. There has never been any attempt at agrarian reform there. Chiapas has the most archaic infrastructure in Mexico and most processes of modernization have passed it by. The revolutionary movement, *Ejercito Zapatista de Liberación Nacional* (Zapatista National Liberation Army, EZLN), is fighting for indigenous rights and better economic conditions. At the same time, and this makes it so difficult for the Mexican government to settle these issues, the EZLN wants democracy for Mexico, a step which the ruling party in Mexico, the *Partido Revolucionário Institucional* (Institutional Revolutionary Party, PRI), has been able to avoid taking for quite a number of decades.[20] Hundreds of insurgents have been killed, and occasional massacres occur, as the army and paramilitary are embroiled in conflicts with the *zapatistas*, and many people are being displaced, creating a situation in which there is no war and no peace. Even so, it seems probable that without NAFTA, the Mexican government and army would undoubtedly have acted with less 'restraint'. Investigations have been going on, high-ranking party officials have been dismissed, which is something new in Mexican politics. Meanwhile, the overall domination of the PRI has been waning and the two important opposition parties, the *Partido Revolucionário Democrático* (Democratic Revolutionary Party, PRD), a party to the left of the PRI, and the *Partido Acción Nacional* (Party of the National Action, PAN), a conservative party, consequently more to the right, have been winning some key posts at state and municipal level. A major victory for the opposition occurred in 1997, when the first direct elections, for mayor of the capital, Mexico D.F. were held. There were

---

18. K. Kopinak, *Desert Capitalism: what are the maquiladoras,* J. Carrillo, ed., *Mercados de trabajo en la industria maquiladora.*

19. Skidmore and Smith, *Modern Latin America,* p. 260.

20. M. Lemoine, *Les 100 Portes de l'Amérique Latine,* pp. 51–56, 287–288.

won by Cuauhtémoc Cardenas, of the PRD.[21] This led to changes within the PRI, with hard-liners getting the upper hand, thus helping a weak government Zedillo, which did not bode well either for the *zapatistas* and their sympathizers, or for further political openings. The American government, for its part, is more interested in stability than democracy.[22] In 2000, the long historical cycle, which started in 1929, was broken in Mexico: a candidate who was not from the PRI won the presidential elections. Vicente Fox, from the PAN, was the winner, thanks to the cooperation between the PRD voters and the PAN. A different situation is emerging in Mexico, although the PRI will still be playing a major role in Mexico, as many bureaucrats, key figures, political and otherwise, belong to that party and cannot be replaced overnight or dismissed out of hand. What the social consequences of this change will be has not yet clearly emerged. Fox, a former manager of an American multinational, is a firm believer in neo-liberal tenets, although he has also stated that he wanted to improve the situation in his country.[23] What that means in reality is another question. However, Fox, as he has promised, has defused the stalled situation in Chiapas. In March 2001 there was a march from Chiapas on the Mexican capital, meetings were held at the highest level with EZLN representatives. They went to Congress while *subcomandante* Marcos was received by the President. Indigenous rights were to be recognized specifically and something would be done about land reform in southern Mexico. The bill eventually voted in by Congress is a very watered-down version, to protect the interests of the southern landowners. The question is if the situation will remain defused.[24] In any case, the bill will not solve the problem of poverty of the many Mexican Indians.

While the Mexicans are trying to come to grips with economic problems and wonder what political changes will be introduced, illegal immigration is still going on. Such immigrants still constitute a cheap and badly treated pool of labor in the USA. At the beginning of his term, wanting to take advantage of the high demand on the labor market in the

---

21. G. Couffignal, "Mexique. L'heure du pluralisme," in *L'Etat du Monde, 1998. Annuaire économique et géopolitique mondial*, pp. 220–225.

22. J. Ward, *Latin America, Development and Conflict*, pp. 30, 43, 53, 55, 108–112.

23. *The Economist*, "Mexico's once-ruling party faces the shock of opposition," 15 July 2000, pp. 55–56.

24. *The Economist*, "Back to square one in Chiapas," 5 May 2001, p. 54.

USA, Fox suggested an increase in legal immigration.[25] If that will materialize is another matter, certainly as the American economy has been
slowing down recently, and workers have been fired rather than hired.

Strangely enough, while a continuously more sophisticated machinery
is put into place to keep illegal entrants from crossing the Mexican-Ameri-
can border, federal agents with tremendously modern equipment do not
seem capable of doing much about keeping illegal weapons from entering the Mexican border. Actually, the number of weapons arriving in
Mexico, legally and illegally, is increasing substantially, the result of the
growing importance of Mexico in the drugs trade, which will be dealt
with later. When the Mexican Ambassador protests in Washington, the
American government answers it is a question of demand, while for drugs
it is a question of supply.

However one looks at it, the Mexicans seem to be on the receiving end,
and, while trade has tripled, NAFTA has not made things better for most
Mexicans. The Americans have quite a number of ways to stop Mexican
goods from entering the American market. American states can often rely
on the 'grandfather' clause to support their constituencies against Mexican imports. The grandfather clause legislates that, should states or coun-
ties have regulations which precede the NAFTA agreement and diverge
from the Treaty, the older regulations apply.[26] If not, other methods are
introduced to limit the alleged advantages Mexicans might have. The
long dispute about tomatoes from Sinaloa, which were considered to be
competing with those grown in Florida, though absolutely correct according to NAFTA regulations, has led to new agreements and has been
resolved to Florida's advantage. Mexican tomato growers, afraid of all
kinds of proposed American measures, mostly non-tariff barriers, agreed
not to sell below a certain reference price, reducing the price advantage
they had. Thus, Florida growers do not have to become more competitive
or diversify, two watchwords others are repeatedly told to apply.[27]

---

25. *The Economist*, "Breaking foreign policy taboos," 26 August 2000, pp. 43–44.
   26. J. Witker, "Evaluación de los aspectos jurídicos ...," in R. Buve and M. Wiesebron,
eds., *Procesos de integración* ..., p. 81.
   27. A.B. Peschard-Sverdrup, "The U.S.–Mexico Fresh Winter Tomato Trade Dispute: ...,"
Entrecaminos, Vol. 2, Spring 1997, pp. 51–66.

From NAFTA to FTAA

The ultimate goal of the Americans does not stop at Mexico. The idea is to enclose the whole American continent. Following up on President Bush' Initiative for the Americas, from 1991, President Clinton started working on the enlargement of NAFTA, as the road, which would ultimately lead to the FTAA. Another option could have been bilateral agreements. At a meeting of the Organization of American States (OAS), in Miami, in December 1994, thirty-four countries decided that talks for a FTAA should be concluded by the end of 2005.[28] However, the enthusiasm for this plan was not as substantial as President Clinton would have liked. For the USA, the rest of the continent has become increasingly important. In 1996, it accounted for 40 percent of total U.S. foreign sales. This was equivalent to the combined markets of Japan, China and East Asia and nearly double that the EU. The former trade representative Barchefsky expected, that by 2010, Latin America would become a bigger market for the Americans than Japan and the EU together.[29]

In September 1997, the month preceding Clinton's first state-visit to South American countries, since he came into office in 1992, the president tried to get support in American Congress for the fast track procedure to enlarge NAFTA. When Clinton became aware he would not get enough congressional backing for his plan, he withdrew it, with the intention of trying it again at a later stage, which did not materialize during his presidency. The meeting in Santiago, on the 18 and 19 April 1998, the follow-up of Miami 1994, was relatively low-key. The issues addressed were important—improving education, human rights, better working conditions, combating poverty and social inequality—but are rarely political priorities, and no money was allocated for their realization. Trade aspects were to be worked out in different working groups.[30] The lack of the fast track had certainly not helped the Americans negotiators,[31] but it will buy time for those Latin American countries that want to take things more

---

28. The OAS includes all independent countries of the American continent minus Cuba, or rather the actual Cuban government was excluded from participation in 1962.

29. IRELA, "Constructing the Free Trade Area of the Americas: A European Perspective", p. 3.

30. Declaración de Santiago, 20 April 1998. Segunda Cumbre de las Américas [Santiago Statement. Second Summit of the America's], Santiago, Chile: 18–19 April 1998.

31. *NRC Handelsblad*, "Tanend enthousiasme voor Amerikaanse vrijhandel," 18 April 1998.

slowly and are not [yet] prepared to create a FTAA quickly or join NAFTA along the Mexican lines.

The two main players in the FTAA negotiations are the USA and Brazil, as leaders of the two main countries of the hemisphere, although evidently of a very different weight. The reluctance of Mercosur/l and, in particular of Brazil, to commence FTAA negotiations concerning tariffs reduction is the upshot of the fact that, while American tariff's are lower than those of Mercosur/l, the real problem lies in the non-tariff barriers. In fact, the USA is the country which imposes most non-tariff barriers to the entry of Brazilian products.[32] Other areas of concern are those of patents and intellectual property, the so-called TRIPs Agreement, with comprehensive rules for copyright, trademark and patent protection, based on the U.S. model, which all WTO members are bound to observe.[33] Brazil and other countries regularly experience problems with the U.S. government, which has begun legal proceedings against Brazil in the WTO, for instance, over the use of cheap generic medicines, instead of expensive American pharmaceutical products. However, in the matter of AIDS, the Brazilian government has finally won the battle with the American government, in 2001, after an enormous public outcry. But this is just one victory, related to the horrific AIDS problems in Africa.

The Argentineans can present quite different opinions. Sometimes they do agree with the Brazilians that while the Americans do not lift a number of trade barriers, it is useless to carry the FTAA discussions any further.[34] At other moments, especially since Domingo Cavallo is back in the saddle as Minister of Economy, he seems to hope that joining the FTAA might help solve the country's enormous economic problems, but other Argentineans are not quite so convinced, in particular not the business sector.

Since George W. Bush has become the 43rd American President, the situation has changed. Bush has made his first foreign visit to Mexico, to see his friend Fox and to underline the importance of Mexico, and this hemisphere for him. In fact, he proposed speeding up the FTAA and advancing the date to 2003, which was rejected by President Cardoso. In the meeting in Quebec in April 2001, it was decided that the agreement

---

32. IRELA, "Constructing the Free Trade Area of the Americas: A European Perspective," especially p. 6.

33. TRIPs: Agreement on Trade-related Aspects of Intellecual Property, within WTO. Steven Shrybman, *The World Trade Organization ...*, pp. 111–119.

34. Mercopress News Agency, 11 December 1997.

should be signed by the beginning of 2005 and be implemented by the beginning of 2006. This seems extremely fast, simply in view of all the technical aspects that have still to be agreed upon before that date, and without taking into account any political aspect. Moreover, the outcome of the 2002 presidential elections in Brazil might also change the equation.

Chile

While these multilateral negotiations are going on, one candidate for NAFTA enlargement, and which had been waiting for an invitation for a good number of years, had decided to not to wait any longer, as the fast track was not forthcoming: Chile. Until recently, the Chilean government had not made a very clear commitment either way, either in the direction of NAFTA, or in that of Mercosur/l, looking in both directions at the same time. Chileans consider themselves in a special position because of the country's geographical situation. The country has a very long coastline stretched out along the Pacific and has pretty inaccessible borders that isolate it from the rest of Latin America: in the north, the driest desert in the world, the Atacama Desert; in the south, inhospitable Patagonia; and the rugged Andes mountains all along the east. Chile has won itself a bit of a reputation as a free rider, using its relations with the Asian countries— it sees Asia as its natural vocation—and its membership of APEC, as a bargaining chip in Mercosur/l, of which Chile became an associated member, having signed an agreement with Mercosur/l, in 1996, to implement an area of free trade within ten years at the latest. That same year, a very comparable agreement has been signed between Mercosur/l and Bolivia.[35] During the Asian crisis, these close relations did not prove to be the asset the Chileans had hoped for.[36] Besides, it does not seem to have been as helpful within Mercosur/l as expected, even without the crisis. This is probably because of the fact that Chile has specialized in a number of markets different from those pursued by its Mercosur/l partners.[37] It seemed, for a while, that the Chilean government had decided to become a full member of Mercosur/l, and that a date had even been

---

35. "Acordo de complementação econômica Mercosul-Chile" (25 June 1996) and "Acordo de complementação econômica Mercosul-Bolivia" (25 June 1996), in *Mercosul: Legislação e Textos Básicos*, pp. 199–216, 219–234.

36. *The Economist*, "Chile. All Good Things Must Slow Down," 7 March 1998, pp. 71–72. *Ibidem*, "Chile. Battening down", 4 July 1998, p. 54.

37. G. Couffignal, ed., *Amérique Latine, tournant de siècle*, p. 48.

quoted, 1 January 2001. That date was a bit optimistic because of the requisite transition measures, as Chile has the lowest tariffs of the five. Some months before that date, the Chileans started looking to the north again, instead of to its neighbors in the south. The Argentinean crisis is having a negative impact on the Chilean economy. On the other hand, if Chile wants to maintain or strengthen its special ties with Europe, closer cooperation with Mercosur/l might still be a better bet. But the country seems to be sitting on the fence again.[38]

Mercosur/l: Latin America Gaining Greater Independence from U.S. Leadership?

Mercosur/l was established in 1991 as a common market between Argentina, Brazil, Paraguay and Uruguay. This is the fourth largest economic bloc in the world, in terms of GNP.[39] Contrary to expectations, Mercosur/l has been a success at most levels, integration between the four countries is progressing well and faster than foreseen, and intra-trade is growing at a much faster rate than expected.

This rapid development is surprising as these countries had little contact, having historically developed relationships with Europe and later with the United States of America rather than with each other. Furthermore, there is also rivalry between Argentina and Brazil going back a long way, to the colonial period, when a number of wars were fought over land between the Spaniards and Portuguese. Since the independence of both countries, in 1816 and 1822 respectively, although they were allies at times, as during the war against Paraguay (1864–1870), most of the time they were diametrically opposed, indeed even declared enemies. The enmity seems to have been fierce at times, resulting in an arms race between the two neighboring countries that at moments seemed to head toward the acquisition of a nuclear capability. Cooperation between them is a relatively recent phenomenon, a result of economic necessity in the present-day globalized and regionalized world. In fact, the *rapprochement*

---

38. N. Saavedra-Rivano, "Chile and Regional Integration," in S. Nishijima and P.H. Smith, ed., *Cooperation or Rivalry...*, pp. 97–109. *Gaceta Mercantil*, "Sul-americanos formam blocos para enfrentar Alca" [South-Americans form blocs to face the FTAA], 10 July 2001, pp. 1, 8.

39. *Relaciones America Latina-Union Europea: nuevas perspectivas. Documentación de base* [Latin America-European Union relations: new perspectives. Basic documentation], Santiago, CELARE, 1995, p. 206.

between the two countries already began under the military dictatorships, when both countries were suffering from grave economic problems. These were the outcome of enormous debts crises, and massive inflation, and while trying to tackle these, both countries were being confronted with protectionist measures from the USA and, to a lesser degree, from the European Economic Community (EEC). Argentina was in an even worse quandary, being isolated as a result of the Malvinas/Falkland War, by both the EEC, now the EU, and the American government, which supported the UK and did not show continental solidarity, not respecting its own Monroe Doctrine, proclaimed in 1823.[40] In fact, this war and the European and American actions helped to boost the cooperation between Argentina and Brazil and stimulated the search for economic independence from both these traditional partners. This bilateral cooperation, which led to the first formal bilateral agreement in 1985, resulted a bit later in the creation of the Mercosur/l.[41]

A great deal of water still has to flow under the bridge before Mercosur/l can be defined as a real common market, but many issues are being addressed, such as harmonization of legislation to promote integration.[42] Indubitably, if all is to work well, a better infrastructure is needed. This is an enormous task as internal contacts hardly existed for centuries and natural barriers abound, but such a step is essential to encourage trade within Mercosur/l. A number of projects are under way: one, a waterway linking the Tietê and Paraná Rivers, from São Paulo to the Rio de La Plata. Work is finished as far as the Itaipu dam, the last and biggest obstacle. Three locks will be built there, construction began in 1999, after which transport to Buenos Aires will be possible. Already, soya and corn are transported in huge quantities on the finished stretch, substantially lowering freight costs as well as reducing the fleets of trucks on the roads.[43] Another project is the construction of a bridge between Argentina and Uruguay, over the wide Mar de la Plata. Such a long bridge, over 40 kilometers, will have serious consequences for the environment. An even

---

40. *Europa-América Latina: 20 años de documentos oficiales (1976–1996)*, p. viii, K. Middlemas, *Orchestrating Europe. The Informal Politics of European Union 1973–1995*, pp. 126, 710 (note 48).

41. N. Moussis, *Access to European ...*, pp. 538–539, M. Bandeira, *O eixo Argentina-Brasil: o processo de integração da América Latina*, pp. 73–83.

42. Tratado de Assunção, 26 March 1991. *Mercosul: acordos e protocolos na área jurídica*, pp. 19, 21.

43. *ISTOÉ*, "Mississipi brasileiro," 5 August 1998, pp. 55–57.

more environmentally controversial project is a planned waterway through the Pantanal, an enormous unique wetland in Brazil, with a delicate eco-system, which would be heavily affected by this plan. It remains to be seen which will ultimately win, economic or environmental objectives. The fact that a protocol was added to the Agreement between Mercosur/l and Chile, specifically on the physical integration of Mercosur/l and Chile, does not bode well for the environment.[44] In the short run, the environment has had a reprieve because of the economic problems in that area. In the long run, the environment in these countries could benefit from a well-developed tourist industry, but that would need significant investments. In fact, problems are more severe in the huge urban areas than in tropical forests, though problems, such as pollution, access to drinking water, sewerage, waste disposal, receive less media attention.

Besides environmental problems, some other pressing matters, are the social aspects of integration. The preamble of the Treaty mentioned that social justice should go hand in hand with economic development.[45] There has been no further reference to social aspects in the Treaty, or a social charter. Among Mercosur/l institutions, one specific committee, consisting of civil servants, trade unionists and employers, discusses issues such as labor, employment and social security schemes, but these meetings have not made much progress. Therefore, trade unions, some government officials and others were stressing the importance of establishing a social charter and the need to do so fast. In June 2000, a Charter was established but it is so short and so vague, that not much can be expected from it.[46] The social issues seem to be the weakest part of Mercosur/l, and, so far have warranted the least interest from governments and administrations, which might not be totally surprising at this time of numerous neo-liberal reforms. In the member states, social security schemes, such as retirement schemes, health services have been reformed or are in the process of being reformed. Civil servants are losing their job security in countries where unemployment benefits, as far as they exist, are also being reduced,

---

44. "Protocolo sobre a integração física do acordo de complementação econômica Mercosul-Chile," in *Mercosul: Legislação e Textos Básicos*, pp. 216–218.

45. Tratado de Assunção, 26-3-1991. *Mercosul L: acordos e protocolos na área jurídica*, p. 19.

46. Carta de Buenos Aires sobre compromisso social en el Mercosur, Bolivia y Chile, XVIII Reunião do Conselho do Mercado Comum, 30-6-2000. Following this Charter, on 14 December 2000, an institutional meeting of ministers and authorities of social development was established. www.Mercosul.gov.br.

SEARCH ALL

simultaneously with a wave of privatizations. At the same time, national governments are reducing the financing of the administration at lower levels.[47] This has gone farthest in Argentina, where, under President Menem, the hard currency—a *peso* was made equal to a dollar in the Constitution in 1991—is affecting the population tremendously, mostly in the provinces, but poverty is also increasing in Buenos Aires at a tremendous rate. 56 percent of the Argentinean population is living in poverty, and 17 percent of them have problems getting one square meal a day. Lack of money at the provincial level, as the national government is reducing funding at lower levels, and the upshot is non-payment of salaries, which, in turn, is creating poverty and social unrest. Strikes and protest movements are frequent. Unemployment is rising. The hard currency is also very much affecting the economy as Argentinean products have great difficulty competing with that of other countries, all the more as the strong sector in Argentina is (still) agriculture. Industry, never its strong suit, was debilitated during the military dictatorship (1976–1983) and has been on a slippery slope ever since. Debt, national, provincial and private, on the other hand, has been rising, especially in recent years. This often-praised model of the IMF is in a profound crisis, after succeeding years of recession.[48] In a desperate gesture President De la Rua, who took office in 2000, after two Menem mandates in the nineties, appointed Cavallo as super minister of the economy in March of 2001, in the hope of rebuilding international confidence for the Argentinean economy.[49]

At the same time, when the *real* was introduced in 1994, the Brazilian currency was also linked to the dollar but in a much less stringent way, as the Brazilian Government has been able to observe the consequences of such a strict policy in the neighboring country. In the first years, after a period over overvaluation, the *real* has steadily been devalued until January 1999, when it suddenly lost nearly 50 percent of its value. The

47. D. Garcia Munhoz, "As reformas e as mudanças na Previdência Social," in R. Carrion and P. Vizentini, *Globalização, neoliberalismo ...*, pp. 241–253, J. Feghali, "Neoliberalismo no Brasil:" in *ibidem,* pp. 254–259.

48. C. Lozano, "Los efectos del ajuste neoliberal: ...," in R. Carrion and P. Vizentini, *Globalizaçãoo, neoliberalismo, privatizações ...*, pp. 148–169, J. Beinstein, "Entre dette et pillages, une économie à genoux," *Le Monde Diplomatique,* July 2001, pp. 12–13.

49. M. Chossudovsky, "Au Coeur de la crise, le pillage. Recolonisation programmée au Brésil," *Le Monde Diplomatique,* March 1999, p. 20. *The Economist,* "Argentina's economic crisis. Austerity, or bust", 21 July 2001, p. 43.

Argentinean crisis has had a negative impact on the *real*, and its value has declined even more, which in turn greatly affects Argentinean trade with Brazil, its most important trading partner. This is also affecting relations within Mercosur/l.[50] Differences in currency value have already led President Menem to suggest the creation of a single currency within Mercosur/l at a summit meeting in December 1997. If one currency does eventuate, the Brazilians would most probably reject the dollar. Meanwhile, in June 2001, the Argentinean Senate approved Cavallo's proposal to link the peso also to the euro each for 50 percent, in principle, when both currencies will have the same value.[51]

Such a gesture might be not only a financial signal, it could also send a political signal to both the USA and the EU. Following the 1995 agreement between Mercosur/l and the EU, the intention is to arrive at a free trade agreement between the two blocs, which would be something totally new, a free trade agreement between two blocs and over two continents. Former EU Commissioner Manuel Marin, responsible for Latin America, wanted to get this agreement signed by 1999, or 2000 at the latest. It suddenly became less urgent as plans for the FTAA were moving at a slower pace. More delays were caused because Marin's colleague in agriculture, Franz Fischler, was less enthusiastic, as Argentina and Brazil are considered too much as competitors of some EU countries. Most of their colleagues followed Marin's view and have given a the Council recommendation to commence negotiations, but it is not clear when they will be concluded. One positive element is that all member states have interests in Mercosur/l and associates, which is very rare.[52] However, two additional problems slowed down the negotiations. First, member states wanted to wait for the round of new negotiations for the WTO—which had not got off the ground since the Seattle debacle in November 1999—to avoid having to make concessions twice. Second, internal reforms and enlargement seem more pressing problems than furthering trade with Mercosur/l. Even so, talks are moving ahead slowly, and in July 2001, EU Commissioner of Trade, Pascal Lamy, during a visit to Brazil, presented the Mercosur/l

50. For instance, *O Estado de São Paulo*, 12 July 2001, pp. B 1, 3, 4, 5.
51. *Agence Europe*, "UE/Argentine/euro," 22 June 2001, p. 23.
52. Rumos *do desenvolvimento*, Entrevista [Interview]: V. Bulmer-Thomas, February 1998, p. 7. *Bulletin Quotidien Europe*, "(EU) EU/*Mercosur*/Chili", 6 June 1998, p. 9; *ibidem*, 9 July 1998, pp. 5–6; *ibidem*, EU/ *Mercosur*/Chili: Commission recommendation to Council for approval to negotiate association comprising free trade area, enhanced cooperation, political and security partnership," 23 July 1998, pp. 6–7.

member states with a ten-year liberalization proposal over 100 percent for industrial products and 90 percent of agriculture.[53] In fact, the EU is the first trading partner of Mercosur/l, and maybe it does not want to lose its advantage to the USA, which is pressing so aggressively for the FTAA.

From Mercosur/l to SAFTA

To counter that threat in some way, the Brazilian government wants to go beyond Mercosur/l and, if possible, create the South American Free Trade Area (SAFTA), but also strengthen its ties across the Atlantic, especially with South Africa, and with Asia. This last continent is becoming an ever more important trading area for Brazil, and more than a trading area, as agreements are being made to bolster technological cooperation, joint research projects and in other areas of mutual interest, even if there are some bumps along the road.[54] The creation of SAFTA would be a way to strengthen relations within South America, and be in a better negotiating position for the establishment of a FTAA.

Meanwhile, for Mercosur/l, the association with Chile and Bolivia, both in 1996, is already a start for SAFTA. In 1997, the Peruvian government asked to become associated. According to Article 20, of the Asuncion Treaty, all countries, members of the Latin American Integration Association (ALADI) may enter into negotiations to belong to Mercosur/l. These countries include all South American countries and Mexico.[55] A couple of months later, during the Iberio-American summit which was held in Venezuela in November 1997, the members of the Andean Community (also known as Andean Pact or Group), Colombia, Ecuador, Peru and Venezuela, decided they wanted to speed up the integration process

---

53. *Agence Europe*, "UE/ *Mercosur*: l'UE a presenté au Mercosur une offre pour la libéralisation do 90% de l'agriculture et 100% de l'industrie en dix ans," 5 July 2001. *Gaceta Mercantil*, 10 July 2001, p. 8.

54. IRELA, Dossier 61, "MERCOSUR: Prospects for an Emerging Bloc," pp. 30–33. P. Vizentini, "Mercosul: A Brazilian Strategy towards the World Reorganization," in M. Wiesebron, ed., *Mercosul: facing a New Millenium*, pp. 9–15.

55. *Carta Capital*, "*Mercosur*, un parceiro conveniente. A adesão do Peru traz novas oportunidades ao Brasil, apesar da turbulência política" 11 June 1997, Vol. II, n° 50, pp. 74–76. Tratado de Assunção, 26 March 1991, Capítulo IV, Adesão, art. 20, *Mercosul: acordos e protocolos na área jurídica*, p. 26. ALADI was created by the Montevideo Treaty of August 16, 1980. There are 11 member states. Besides these 7, they are Colombia, Ecuador, Mexico and Venezuela.

with Mercosur/l. The idea is to create a strong bloc, to have more influence on the ongoing negotiations, before entering FTAA. In a meeting of South American heads of states in Brasilia in August 2000, in the final *communiqué*, President Cardoso announced that the aim was to establish SAFTA by the end of 2002.

Talks seem to be progressing, although closer integration between the Andes Group and Mercosur/l could be hampered by the fact that there are quite still a number of very serious problems in the Andes countries. There are still guerrilla insurgencies, besides (para)military activities and disturbances choreographed by drugs cartels. Problems are worst in Colombia, where the state and the administration are falling apart undermined by the endemic violence, with tens of thousands of victims over quite a few years (for instance, 26,664 violent dead in 1996 according to the National Police, about 35,000 in 1997), and corruption, mostly as a result of drugs money. The problems in Colombia have deep political and economic roots that go back quite a number of decades and were not caused recently by drugs, (para)military and guerrilla activities, but may unavoidably be exacerbated by them. In the elections in 1997, numerous political candidates, national and local, were killed. Others, perhaps wisely, did not stand for election. Feuds are fought at the local level. Kidnapping for ransom has become an important industry. Colombian society seems to be falling apart. It is the most violent country after South Africa and El Salvador.[56] The question is if further integration may help Colombia become more stable. Integration can play a positive role, as the averted return to a military dictatorship in Paraguay in April 1996 has shown. Pressure from the Argentinean and Brazilian governments helped defuse the coup attempt.[57] Another problem facing Colombia is the negative grade the country gets from the American government, in the certification system in the fight against the drugs production and trade. This implies that trade preferences with the USA are abolished and that loans from international organizations, such as the International Monetary Fund or the Inter American Bank for Development, will not being granted. Colombia failed in 1996 and 1997, even though it has spent more on the battle against

---

56. M. Chernick, "The Crisis of Human Rights ..." *LASA Forum*, XXVIII, 3, 1997, pp. 20-23. M. Wouters, "De vermoorde Democratie ...," *ALERTA*, oktober 1997, pp. 11–12.

57. M. Pastore, "Democracy, Defense, Integration and Development ...," *LASA Forum*, XXVII, 3, 1996, pp. 4–6.

drugs than the USA, in relative terms. Mexico, another member state of NAFTA, just scraped through.[58]

All these problems seem to have led to aspirations for change amongst the various populations, which translated into votes for independent candidates, not linked to the traditional elite's of South America. In 1998, in Ecuador and Colombia, two outsiders won themselves quite a following. In Colombia, the winner was the candidate of the opposition, Andres Pastrana. President Pastrana wants to address a number of these issues, and, in first instance, did open negotiations with the two most important guerrilla groups, although his success seems limited. Meanwhile, Ecuador faces an enormous economic crisis, which led to huge popular protests and even a coup, toppling the newly elected president. These protests, mostly by the indigenous population and public-sector unions, were against the dollarization and privatisation processes. But Ecuador has gone even one step further than Argentina and the national currency, the *sucre,* has disappeared. The new President, Noboa faces some stiff opposition.[59] It is not yet entirely sure in which direction the country is going. Others who also seem to be regaining favor are military ex-dictators or would-be dictators. In Bolivia, ex-dictator Banzer was elected president. In Paraguay, it seems democracy is growing stronger. After the murder of the vice-president, in March 1999, and some days of unrest and violence, President Raúl Cubas left office. Cubas, a close friend of General Oviedo, had freed Oviedo, responsible for a failed *coup d'état* in 1996, against the wishes of the courts and of Congress. Oviedo was considered responsible for the assassination of the vice-president, and his men shot some demonstrators. Oviedo left the country and so did Cubas. The president of the Senate became the new president and formed a broad coalition. Economically, the country is suffering from the currency crisis of its neighbors.[60] In Venezuela, a former colonel, Hugo Chavez, who attempted a coup in 1992, was elected president on 6 December 1998. Venezuela, a rich country, has an enormous poor population. The government and elite never developed alternatives to its main export-product, oil, and have never invested enough in their own society. When oil prices were high—and Venezuela was one of the initiators of the Organization of Petroleum Exporting Countries (OPEC)—there was a well-off middle class.

---

58. *The Economist,* "To decertify, or not?" 21 February 1998, p. 14.
59. *The Economist,* "Ecuador, Still fragile," 2 September 2000, p. 52.
60. L. Costa Bonino, "Paraguay," *L'Etat du Monde, 2000,* pp. 446–447.

Corruption is rife, oil prices have plummeted and the fiscal deficit is enormous. Under such adverse conditions, the informal sector has been growing, as have the shantytowns and crime.[61] Chavez is tackling the enormous problems of the country in an original way, trying to dismantle the traditional elite structures, not an easy task, and to build new ones to take their place. The challenges Chavez faces in solving the economic and social problems of his country are enormous. High oil prices, stimulated by Chavez, are helping to generate income now, and the country has to start diversifying economically at a rapid pace. His unorthodox approach is viewed with mistrust, mostly outside the country, which might not be helpful in the long run.

The whole region received a boost with the summit meeting of all South American heads of states in Brasília in August 2000. Besides the discussion round SAFTA which, if it could be got off the ground, would theoretically boost cooperation throughout the whole continent, the development of a better infrastructure and the study of complementarity, which would certainly be helpful, the other issue addressed was the situation in Colombia, and foremost the American billion dollar 'aid' package in the form of weapons, as far as there consequences for other South American countries. Brazil, for one, does not want to involve itself in internal problems of other governments.[62] In July 2001, in spite of all the problems, and most recently, in July 2001, a high-level meeting was held to stimulate negotiations between Mercosur/l and the Andean Community.

Altogether Mercosur/l is doing quite well, and in spite of some major crises, of which the present one, seems the most important, it is moving forward.[63] An important factor may well be that all-powerful organizations, such as the São Paulo Federation of Industries (FIESP), serve to underline the importance of Mercosur/l, but also organizations such as the *Mercocidades* (Net of Mercotowns), an initiative developed at local level in 1995 to stimulate cooperation between municipalities at political, economic, social and cultural levels, want to strengthen Mercosur/l. There

61. *NRC Handelsblad*, "Latijns Amerika kiest voor onafhankelijkheid," 2 June 1998, p. 4. *The Economist*, "It's all Chavez," 4 July 1998, pp. 54–55; *ibidem*, "Ecuador, Now for the Hard Part," 18 July1998, pp. 54–55, *ibidem*, "Paraguay, Deadlock," and "A Message from the People," 12 December 1998, pp. 63–64.

62. *NRC Handelsblad*, "Zuid-Amerika boert nu achteruit," 4 September 2000; *The Economist*, "Brazil's Foreign Policy. Southern Crossroads," 26 August 2000, p. 44.

63. C. Banega e.a., "The New Regionalism in South America," in M. Schulz e.a., ed., *Regionalization in a Globalized World* ..., pp. 234–249.

are many more associations, from very different sectors of civil society, which have the same purpose.[64] Inevitably these associations prefer to increase cooperation with the EU, rather than with the USA, especially in the social field. The big question will be how the Argentinean crisis is to be solved.

Latin America—Asia

Meanwhile, a number of other developments are also taking place outside the American continent and with non-traditional partners. Asia in particular has become an interesting alternative, as relations between Latin American and Asian countries are devoid of the negative sentiments that are associated with the traditional partners. Among the Mercosur/l partners, Brazil has developed the strongest links to Asia. Governments and businesses are discovering mutual benefits.[65] Joint ventures are being set up, but also numerous projects involving technology and transfer of know-how. However, in the short term the Asian crisis may add a new perspective on these developments, and the recent nuclear tests in India and Pakistan have further complicated the situation.

Of course, Latin America's relations with Asia-Pacific did not commence just with the most recent phase of intensive globalization. These relations are much older. Some substantial immigration took place from East Asia to Latin America, and there have been other contacts. For instance, representatives of these countries would meet during conferences of the non-aligned nations. Furthermore, for a long time, these two areas have often been compared, especially the 'tigers' in both regions, and they were often seen and saw themselves as competitors. More recently, both sides have perceived the benefit of mutual cooperation, spurred on by economic necessity in a changing world. The expansion of relations between Asia and Latin America is also a strategy for diversifying long-standing relations. The Asian crisis, and its consequences, may have slowed the process somewhat.

---

64. *La Sociedad Civil del Mercosur y Chile en la Asociación con la Unión Europea*, Santiago, CELARE, 2000.

65. P. Vizentini, "A Ascenção da Ásia Oriental e sua Projeção Internacional: ...," *Ciências e Letras*, 1997, p. 133, IRELA, "*Mercosur*: Prospects for an Emerging Bloc," Dossier 61, 1997, p. 33.

Before the crisis, a fair number of new developments in the economic area had taken place over a number of years. In 1996, 20 percent of trade from Mercosur/l countries went to Asia, and only 18 percent to the USA. Mercosur/l and ASEAN (Association of Southeast Asian Nations) started a dialogue and are discussing trade issues.[66] The interests go further in areas such as joint projects in technology, sciences, education, communication and development of energy resources. These new international dimensions are the consequence of a changing world. At the same time, they often imply a number of fundamental reforms, which are being implemented nationally.

The Brazilian Government had established a special relationship with its Indian counterpart, that went beyond the pursuit of economic interest and technological cooperation. Both governments are supporting one another in a bid to win a seat on the Security Council, as permanent members, the consequence of regional backing that probably is not forthcoming.[67] After the nuclear tests of India, President Cardoso broke off the agreement existing between the two countries, but that may just be a temporary political gesture.

Technological cooperation between Latin American and Asian can be useful, in part because some of these countries do not have enough money to go it alone. The fields of cooperation can cover many aspects: space technology, in particular satellite industry, energy, which includes oil, and possibly nuclear industry, information technology, software, and also technical norms, which are becoming ever more important. The ability to participate in the international market with products that conform to safety, health and other regulations, will determine a country's ability to perform on the world market. It requires huge investments to produce these items according to international standards. Also important is membership in technical committees in the WTO. Therefore, cooperation can be very useful in this area.[68]

Economic interests between Latin American and Asian vary quite a bit. With Japan, most of these relations are quite traditional: the export of

---

66. IRELA, "Constructing the Free Trade Area of the Americas: ...," 1997, p. 5, "*Mercosur*: Prospects for an Emerging Bloc," IRELA, Dossier 61, 1997, p 33..

67. S. Pinheiro Guimarães, ed., *Estratégias Índia e Brasil,* This extensive publication covers political, economic and technological cooperation between both countries.

68. M. Lousada, "Normas e barreira técnicas: ..." in S.P. Guimarães, ed., *Estratégias Índia e Brasil ...*, pp. 555–561.

primary and agricultural products to Japan and the import of manufactured goods, such as cars, from Japan, though NAFTA seems to be slowing down Japanese car imports into Mexico. More recently Japanese migrants to Latin America contributed to the building of a special relationship with Japan. The largest amount of Japanese migrants world wide is found in Brazil. Their special know-how is used to boost Brazilian exports to Japan. The election of Fujimori contributed to the growth of Japanese-Peruvian relations, resulting amongst others in an increase of Japanese investments.[69] His effort to get a third term in office did not endear him, either nationally or internationally. His sudden departure in September 2000 left a number of questions marks, raising doubts about the future direction of Peruvian foreign (economic) policy, and the implications for Peru's relations with Japan, where Fujimori decided to take refuge as a Japanese citizen. The Japanese Government seems unlikely to extradite him.

Conversely, Brazil and other Latin American countries feel a greater political affinity with China. Japan belongs to the First World and is a very close ally of the Americans, while China is a large, promising developing country with a strongly independent attitude. Brazil also feels on a more equal footing with it economically. The Malaysian government has already offered to play a central role in the process of economic development between South American countries, especially Brazil, and Southeast Asia. Another country with 'new' interests in Latin America, mostly Brazil, is South Korea.[70]

In the wake of the Asian crisis, problems have been arising. Asian currencies have been devalued. In Indonesia, this was very substantial, making Latin American products which come from currencies which have been stable for a couple of years, often linked to the dollar, more expensive. Latin American products have more difficulty competing on third markets, or on the markets of their Asian counterparts, while Asian products are becoming even cheaper on the Latin American market. Economic growth in Latin America, which had been picking up after the shock of trade liberalization, is being affected and slowing down.[71] There are, of course, other important factors that also play a role, such as the movement of

---

69. P. Vizentini, "Brazil-Asia Relations …," *IIAS Newsletter*, 16, 1998, p. 4.

70. *Ibidem.*, P. Vizentini and G. Rodrigues, *O dragão chinês e os tigres asiaticos*, pp. 108–109.

71. *ISTOÉ*, "Um gosto amargo de saquê …," 1499, 1998, pp.108–110.

short-term flight capital. To give just one instance, flight capital in Brazil was being taken out at the tune of one billion dollar a day during the month of August 1998, a consequence of panic over the situation in Russia, although there is no real parallel between both countries. The presidential elections that were due in Brazil in October that year, may have had some influence too. The incumbent president, Cardoso, emerged as the winner. Meanwhile, Brazil's currency reserves were reduced to half. As was said before, Argentina has not yet recovered from its economics crisis, which is also affecting the other Mercosur/l countries, Chile and, up to a point, Mexico. All this is not helping to solve the problems of unemployment or unequal income distribution, both destabilizing factors.

Conclusion

Integration can have a positive effect on the stability of a region. Thanks to Mercosur/l, a military coup was prevented in Paraguay. Thanks to NAFTA, the situation in Chiapas seems relatively stable, although certainly far from being solved, especially at a social level. The question is, of course, how far the economic crisis will encourage integration. It could be seen as a way helping out of the crisis, but, actual trends give the impression that governments do not see it that way and that integration will proceed at a slower pace.

   It is vitally important that the relations within South America and those that have been developing between Asia and Latin America are nurtured further. This, in spite of, or even more because of, some uncertain factors within South America and the set-back because of the Asian flu and some strategic and political destabilization as a result of changes of governments and nuclear tests. In the short term, the situation is certainly not very conducive to such alliances, as competition is becoming fiercer, and governments will see it as their first priority to take care of the economy, to solve the actual problems and to take strong political stands. This will be the case in Asia as well as in Latin America. Furthermore, the need for help from institutions such as the IMF will not stimulate any alteration of existing international patterns or stimulate the use of different paths. However, in the long term, cooperation is the only way to prevent a new form of re-colonization, while, so far, neither Latin American governments nor their Asian counterparts seem capable of achieving greater independence from traditional systems, in spite of more intensive forms of regional integration.

Moreover, the social cost of integration should not be forgotten or shelved for too long, especially if it is being compounded by all kinds of social reforms. Nevertheless, reducing unemployment, investing in health and education, combating social inequality are necessities to be able to maintain a certain degree of autonomy.

If such steps are not taken, violence will become an ever more important problem. Urban violence will continue to increase as a consequence of social inequality, rural violence because landless peasants and forgotten Indians are fighting hugely unequal land distribution and the consequences of neo-liberal reforms. More violence is generated by drugs trafficking, by those involved in the drugs trade and those who are fighting it.[72] The activities of the Americans from the Drugs Enforcement Agency and direct military intervention in that area are certainly not becoming less important in the foreseeable future.[73] In fact, American action in Colombia shows quite the opposite trend.[74] The enormous influx of weapons into Latin America is certainly counterproductive to furthering stability, as are all the other forms of violence.

The effects of globalization magnify all this, with capital circulating freely, with all the consequences of this, certainly in the case of short-term invested capital. The free circulation of labor, meanwhile, is being ever more restricted. The role of trade unions is greatly being reduced. Another destabilizing factor is the result of new technological and scientific revolution which creates an increasingly bigger group of people who do not have the education, and therefore do not have the access to jobs, which would make them part of actual developments. They are no longer exploited but are simply excluded from this brave new world. Women are the greatest victims of these changes, as they are often less educated, have less job security, and have more family responsibilities. They look after the children, so investing in improving the future of women makes sense not only for them but also for the next generation.

---

72. H. Prolongeau, "Violences dans les rues et dans les têtes," *Manière de Voir* 36, Nov.–Dec 1997, pp. 68–70. H. Prolongeau et J.-Chr. Rampal, "En Amérique latine, l'industrie des enlèvements," *Le Monde Diplomatique*, Nov. 1997, p. 3. Ph. Revelli, "La résistance des 'sans-terre' du Brésil," *Le Monde Diplomatique*, Sept. 1997, pp. 14–15.

73. W.A. Orme, Jr., *Understanding NAFTA ...*, p. 97. M. Aguire, "Narcotrafic, l'alibi de Washington," *Manière de Voir* 36, Nov.–Dec 1997, pp. 71–72.

74. *The Economist*, "The Gringos Land in Colombia," 2 September 2000, pp. 51–52.

Some hope comes from actions at a municipal level in Latin America. To give one example, in 1989 Porto Alegre launched an experiment in participatory budget, with direct citizen participation. The inhabitants of the town decide what projects deserve priority and how money is going to be invested. This has been an increasing success and has become part and parcel of the running of the town. The participatory budget has also been introduced into quite a number of other towns and even at state level in Brazil, such as Rio Grande do Sul, of which Porto Alegre is the capital.[75] In January 2001, the first World Social Forum, a counterpart of the economic forum held at Davos, was held at Porto Alegre. This is proof of the dynamism which exists in Latin America and might, at least, help keep the situation in balance.

Of crucial importance to the development of Latin America and the way it will be transformed will be the course future integration will take, in particular if Mercosur/l succeeds in going forward, in spite of the actual crisis, and if SAFTA materializes by the end of 2002, as scheduled. In the great order of things, the roles of the USA and the EU will be paramount. The question is in how far the FTAA project will go ahead and in what form. This depends, in part, on the attitude and possibilities of South American countries but, also, on that of Europe. Will the EU let Monroe come out the winner or will it try to reclaim some of its former power on that continent? Its commitment in the coming years can be measured by the way it is forging ahead with its projects for Mercosur/l, Chile and Latin America, more generally and by its determination to strengthen Mercosur/l and other developments in that continent. This attitude can only be helpful if it is also reflected in multilateral forums. In that case, there is hope for some social improvement.

---

75. M. Wiesebron, "Brazilian Democracy at a Municipal Level," pp. 27–40.

MERCOSUR/L AT CROSSROADS
DIFFICULTIES IN THE INTEGRATION
PROCESS OR NEOLIBERALISM'S CRISIS?

Paulo G. F. Vizentini

In the context of the emerging global order, Mercosur/l is the first South American integration process to have produced concrete results and to have opened up regional alternatives to achieve a better international positioning for the countries of the Southern Cone. A study of the future of Mercosur/l in the light of its first most significant crisis raises several strategic issues. Does this crisis sound the death knell of this initiative or is it merely a passing storm? Which solution will be the most appropriate: a deepening of the process; the creation of supranational institutions and the widening of membership; or a slow down of objectives and timetables in a search for a more realistic approach? Whatever solution transpires, the creation of a system of structured relations between South American countries depends on it. And in order to analyze the problem of the prospects of Mercosur/l, it is essential to identify its formative elements, evolutionary trends and the international and domestic challenges with which it is faced at the turn of the century. The most important exercise is to point out which of Mercosur/l's dimensions were hit by the crisis.

The Historic Dimension: Brazil-Argentina Rapprochement

Historically, the matrix of South American regional integration has been the cooperation between the two most important countries of the area, Brazil and Argentina. The first systematic coming together of the two countries, that lasted from the 1950s to the end of the 1970s, which were then caught up in the throes of the changing populist and military regimes of anti-left National Security orientation, has to be counted a failure.

Neither the strategies devised by ECLA (1948), nor the first attempts to promote effective economic integration in the Americas such as the LAFTA, the Central American Common Market (CACM), the CARIFTA, later CARICOM, and the Andean Pact, were able to produce enduring solutions to the predicaments inherent in development.

The reasons that accounted for the relative failure of these experiences, judged in the light of their stated goals, are to be found in the structures of the import substitution economies that were not conducive to the opening up of markets, in the fact that the United States and the financial bodies under its influence tried to impose their own regulations on these institutions and, finally, in the implementation of the National Security Regimes in Latin America. Some of them tried to establish closer economic relations with the United States, while some others, such as that of Brazil, plunged deeper into industrialization and the process of import substitution. Inevitably the divergent geopolitical views espoused by the various countries led to the worsening of mutual distrust and rivalries.

At the beginning of the 1980s, the proximity of Brazil and Argentina would become the backbone of the regional integration process, consummated by the establishment of Mercosur/1 in 1991. Contrary to what is generally presented in some Latin American International Relations handbooks, this rapprochement was not an outcome of democratization, but a product of a much older, more complicated and deeper process of which democratization is only a part.

In the new adverse international scenario that had been emerging since the first oil crisis of 1973, but specially since the restructuring of the international capitalism that followed, Geisel's government (1974–1979) started to give priority to Latin America as a field of action for Brazilian foreign policy. Trying to extend our influence to small neighboring countries, which was the policy of the Médici government (1969–1974), was not enough: it was essential to improve relations with Argentina. Geisel set out to negotiate the dispute over the Itaipu hydroelectric dam with Buenos Aires, mainly after the beginning of the military takeover in Argentina in 1976. This initiative, as well as others in different fields of the bilateral relationship, was strengthened with the outbreak of the Falklands' War in 1982, at the height of the external debt crisis that was affecting Latin America and at the time of Reagan's reinvigorated Cold War. Not only did Brazil support Argentina during the conflict, this era also marked a period of a process of growing *convergence* between the two countries, even beginning to assume the shape of an *alliance*.[1]

Since, instead of accepting the negative impacts that the politico-economic reordering of the world was imposing, Geisel opted to strengthen the process of import substitution and to search for an even more autonomous foreign policy, the international pressures for the redemocratization of the country intensified. Our foreign policy and the national development project were the main targets of these new international pressures. Argentina experienced something similar during the Falklands War when the Western powers, specially the United States, made it clear that they did not need its military regime in the new global and regional context. The new international agenda was now emphasizing the opening up of the national economies of the peripheral countries and redemocratization.

Thus, the revival of democracy under Presidents Raúl Alfonsin (1983–1989) and José Sarney (1985-1990) emerged in a climate of adverse economic and diplomatic conditions. In a context of serious economic difficulties, the debt crisis has left Latin American countries extremely vulnerable to the pressures exerted by the International Monetary Fund and the World Bank. At the same time, the conflict in Central America, after the Sandinista victory in Nicaragua in 1979, helped Reagan's government to bring the Cold War into the hemisphere, which allowed for additional pressures to be exerted and the use of different diplomatic and military instruments in Latin America. Faced with this scenario, both countries joined the Contadora Support Group and instigated a systematic, institutionalized relationship in a group formed by Mexico, Panama, Colombia and Venezuela, thereby constituting a systematic and institutionalized relationship, with the objective of promoting a peaceful solution to the conflict in Central America, created after the American invasion of Granada.

In 1985, the Iguaçu Declaration, the result of the rapprochement between Argentina and Brazil, set up a commission to study the integration of the two countries and in 1986 the Integration and Economic Cooperation Proceeding, which forecast the intensification and diversification of trade contacts, was inaugurated. As a result of this effort, in 1988 the Brazil-Argentina Treaty of Integration, Cooperation and Development (*Protocolo de Integração e Cooperacão Econômica, PICE*), that presaged the creation

---

1. Sérgio Abreu e Lima Florêncio and Ernesto Henrique Fraga Araújo, *Mercosul Hoje*, pp. 34–40.

of a Common Market between the two countries within ten years, was established. Beyond the reasons already pointed out, this cooperation was also guided by the growing exclusion of Latin America from the world system—while at the same time the USA were trying to bring to an end to the development of the countries there and to stifle nationalist aspirations—and it represented an attempt to present common diplomatic answers to the international challenges, the search for trade complementarity, the creation of a regional trade influx and a common effort in the technological field and in specific projects. So, PICE, in the words of Samuel Pinheiro Guimarães, Ambassador and then Director of the Research Institute of International Relations of the Brazilian Ministry of Foreign Affairs,

> *had as its main strategy the purpose of overcoming with caution the historical economic and political rivalry between Brazil and Argentina by creating a gradual and balanced process of commercial openness and joint mechanisms of industrial and technological development among the two biggest countries of South America.*[2]

Mercosur/l as an Answer to the New World Order

The end of the 1980s witnessed the end of the Cold War, *Perestroika* and the collapse of the Soviet camp, which led to the acceleration of the globalization process, hastened the Scientific and Technological Revolution, encouraged technological and economic competition among the developed countries and led to the formation of economic blocs. In this scenario, the already precarious Latin American international situation was severely aggravated. The upshot was that Brazilian diplomacy went in search of a new model for its international positioning. During Collor's government (1990–1992), there was a small convergence with the American proposals for the creation of a New World Order that, in regard to Latin America, was expressed in the *Washington Consensus*, the Forum which defined the neoliberal agenda for Latin America at the beginning of the 1990s.[3] As with other opportunities which have arisen in the country's diplomatic history, the analysis elaborated by the neoliberal government of Brazil erred in believing that if Brazil offered a horde of concessions to the United States, much more would be received in exchange. This idea was supported by the old view of a privileged alliance with the White House and also by the fact that the United States had won

---

2. Samuel Pinheiro Guimarães, *Quinhentos anos de periferia*, p. 18.
3. Duncan Green, *Silent Revolution.* pp. 2–5.

the Cold War, and not by the emergence of a post-hegemonic world order, which was what was happening in reality.

In 1990, the American president, George Bush, launched the Enterprise for the Americas Initiative, proposing the creation of a free trade area extending from Alaska to *Tierra del Fuego*. It was a strategy designed to respond to the building of the European Union and the emergence of East Asia as an economic power to be reckoned with, and it was tailored to allow Washington to reassert its world hegemony in the post-Cold War world. To face these challenges, the United States needed to articulate an exclusive economic space in which to act and to improve its exports as an essential mechanism to recycle its productive and technological basis and to generate less expensive means to sustain its world hegemony. This process had already been initiated with the integration of North America: in 1988 cooperation treaties between the United States and Canada were signed and in 1990 the talks with Mexico began.

These initiatives would lead to the implementation of the North American Free Trade Agreement (NAFTA) on January 1, 1994. American policy was defined by Alfredo Valladão as the *Lobster Strategy*: NAFTA would be the head, the main center, Latin America, the tail, a protection and a markets and resources reserve; the claws project out over the Pacific and the Atlantic, supported by the military alliances in Asia and Europe. A U.S. presence in these regions would be designed to prevent the emergence of regional hegemonic powers and its actions (interventions) would be focused on unstable areas that stretched from Russia to the East Africa, cutting through the Middle East, as suggested by Henry Kissinger.[4]

The Brazilian response to these new challenges and to the negative effects produced by the neoliberal project of joining a U.S. led world order, implemented by the Collor government, while Itamaraty (the Brazilian Ministry of Foreign Affairs which played an important role), acted to compensate for the negative effects by accelerating and strengthening Brazil-Argentina co-operation towards integration. In March 1991, the Treaty of Asuncion was signed, creating the Southern Cone Common Market (Mercosur/l), joining Brazil, Argentina, Paraguay and Uruguay. The other countries already had some form of cooperation with their bigger neighbors. The Treaty implemented a tariff reduction for all products and set the date of 31 December 1994 for the definitive creation of a Common Market encompassing the four countries with the total

---

4. Alfredo Valladão, "Ordem Mundial: a estrátegia da lagosta," p. 22.

liberalization of inter-regional trade and the adoption of a common external tariff. It is noteworthy that the original timetable proposed by the Sarney-Alfonsin treaties was cut by almost half.

In this context, the objective of the Brazilian Minister of Finance, Zelia Cardoso de Mello, of the Collor Government, was to inject a new meaning into the cooperation between Brazil and Argentina, by making it an instrument to allow for faster tariff reductions, especially with the added participation of Uruguay and Paraguay. Thereby, an integration with a development profile was transformed into an instrument of neoliberal economic policy.

A change of track in foreign policy was natural as a consequence of the impeachment process of President Collor, his resignation and the passing of the mandate of Itamar Franco (1992–1995). This was being exacerbated by the mainly negative results and frustrations produced by the alliance with Washington, which Collor tried to set up as Brazilian elite's had done in the past, mistakenly hoping to receive favors in return for their positive attitude towards the USA. Moreover, it was aggravated by the neoliberal strategy of economic deregulation, privatization and the passive opening up of our markets (without compensations). The goal of the new diplomacy was to contain the disagreements with the United States at a low level, dealing only with the most immediate problems. In 1993, when he was Minister of Foreign Affairs, Fernando Henrique Cardoso stated that

> it is true that the United States is individually our major partner. But a privileged integration with this country would be impossible due to the dynamism and vitality of our own exports to the North American market where it is usual that our products suffer many restrictions. The United States does not open its markets to Brazil. Brazil does not have the keys to North America.[5]

Mercosur/l's Decision-Making Dimension and Mechanisms

Comprising an area of almost 12 million square kilometers, Mercosur/l is home to a population of 200 million inhabitants. Its GNP, although modest in comparison to those of the EU and NAFTA, has been growing faster than theirs and will achieve a significant weight in the next few decades. It should also be borne in mind that soon Chile and Bolivia, both of which have already joined Mercosur/l, should be added. Mercosur/l's definitive

---

5. Fernando Henrique Cardoso, *Política Externa em tempos de mudança*, Brásilia, p. 239.

institutional structure was established in the Ouro Preto Protocol of 17 December 1994 which also represented the closure of the transitional period of the agreement. Here, the decision-making mechanisms that are contained in this structure are analyzed in the context of their technico-administrative and politico-diplomatic dimensions. The specific characteristics of these mechanisms set them apart from those present in the EU and also in NAFTA, since they correspond to the political and historical peculiarities inherent in the process of integration in the Southern Cone.

Mercosur/l, which was launched by the Treaty of Asuncion of March 1991, gained its own juridical international identity in December 1994 as stated in the Ouro Preto Protocol. Since 1 January 1995 it has constituted a Customs Union, the only one in operation in the developing world, as noted by Florêncio and Araújo (the inter-zone trade liberalization was complemented by the creation of a Common External Tariff). This means that the Common Market Council has the mandate to sign agreements with other regional integration poles or countries. However, this does not make the Council a supranational institution.

Most of the decision-making institutions that were present in the transitional period of Mercosur/l (1991–1994) were preserved in its definitive structure. The highest level of decision making, the Common Market Council, which is composed of the Ministries of Foreign Relations and Ministries of Economics or Treasuries, of each of the four countries, comes together twice a year. Although the Presidents of the members of Mercosur/l are, informally, the supreme power of the decision-making process, the decisions are officially implemented by the Council in order to avoid the political burden which might be incurred by certain deliberations. These decisions, in turn, are the result of a *consensus*. It is the Council's function to define the general guidelines of the integration process in a broad sense as well as to articulate the political efforts essential to develop them.

Sometimes, Mercosur/l's decision-making institutions are regarded as 'inferior' and 'less developed' than those of the EU, a fact that, hypothetically, could be characterized as an inherent weakness in the integration process of the countries of the Southern Cone. However, as I will try to argue by comparing the contexts of each of the two processes and their institutions, this is an erroneous impression. Three issues are usually pointed out: the absence of a Communal Parliament, of a Court of Justice and of supranational institutions.

Regarding the first issue, Mercosur/l's member countries do not view the creation of a Communal Parliament, like the European one, as being in their interest and would not even be able to establish such an institution, simply because all the power of decision making in Mercosur/l is located at the intergovernmental level. In the same sense, the need for a supranational Court of Justice also do not apply, since all the rules are reached by consensus and are compulsorily adopted in the national legislations. *Ad hoc* supranational courts are established to deal with specific problems since Mercosur/l has conflict-resolution mechanisms.

In any discussion of the lack of supranational institutions, besides the already mentioned fact that the decision-making process is reached by consensus, it is important to remember that Latin American countries, and those of Mercosur/l in particular, have a very strong and traditional presidential political culture. So, the separation of state and governmental functions is practically non-existent in South American countries. The state apparatus is permanent and, in the Brazilian case, is linked to the national development project, while a government is a more coinstantaneous administration of a temporary team. In the diplomatic arena, despite the integrationist rhetoric that dates back to the independence movement era, it is essential to identify a certain individualist tradition. Supranational institutions in Mercosur/l would be perceived as an insidious back door to giving up sovereignty, a thing that the member states are not willing to accept. Brazil, when supporting the intergovernmental mechanisms of decision, also tries to achieve a considerable improvement in its international performance. Apart from acting as a regional bloc, the member states continue to speak with their own voices (inside a common political policy). In the case of Uruguay, Paraguay and Argentina, it is important to recall that the intergovernmental decision-making practices make them feel safer, secure in Brazil's stronger relative weight.

It should also be noted that a *spirit of community* is still missing, although it is now slowly taking shape. So far, since the integration process has been very recent, the bloc is only composed of four countries and there are no workers within them who share such a spirit (that goes beyond national preferences). Finally, it must pointed out that the existence of intergovernmental decision-making instruments, instead of rigid supranational institutions, is allowing a more rapid advance of the integration process. In this sense, these more flexible mechanisms are leading to the better exploitation of a favorable common reality.

However, it should never be lost sight of that the undeniable efficiency of the decision-making institutions of intergovernmental character would not have been achieved without the adoption of consensual mechanisms. Although decisions reached by consensus initially demand a significant effort that takes more time, they have an important advantage. During the negotiations, all the actors feel safer and when, after great effort, a consensus is reached, all have a feeling of commitment towards its implementation (which does not produce resentful minorities). Obviously, a strategy of consensus demands a permanent negotiating creativity, but this is exactly what generates the *process* and that represents a much richer exercise than voting pure and simple. In this sense, the consensual system emerges as a natural mechanism for aggregating all. As stated by two Brazilian diplomats, *"consensus produces tensions, which translate into energy."*[6]

Yet, the lack of supranational institutions also represents certain problems. In the context of the Latin American tradition of self-centered countries, the absence of supranational institutions may leave the whole more vulnerable to external pressures, a matter which is turning out to be a fundamental issue. In a certain way, so far, this represents a problem with no solution, since these institutions need time to be implemented. Mercosur/l cannot copy the European model because both realities are extremely different but, indubitably, it can rely upon the experiences of its institutions. Besides, while facing the neoliberal ideology of the 'minimal State' which is the heritage of the Anglo-Saxon countries as a role model for the South, Mercosur/l, as a project in development, should fight for the survival of the State as an entity capable of articulating and leading the economic development and the regional integration processes.

Mercosur/l as a Platform for International Projection

Since the beginning of the 1990s, Brazilian diplomacy has had to abandon the third-world rhetoric of solidarity among developing countries, focusing its efforts on the open questioning of international rules that are regarded as unfair and obstacles to the development of peripheral countries. Consequently a great variety of issues linked to the former foreign policy matrix were eliminated from our international agenda, to be replaced by new ones such as human rights, the environment, the nuclear

---

6. Florêncio e Araújo, *Mercosul Hoje*, p. 70.

program, intellectual property rights and the end of market quotas for the national computer industry. The adoption of several international regimes, the search to establish satisfactory relations with the United States and the opening of the Brazilian internal market, plus the recent implementation of the Monetary Stabilization Plan (the *Real* Plan of July 1994), have all been attempts to re-establish the external investors' confidence in Brazil and to adapt the country to the new realities. In spite of these policies that indicate an acceptance of international rules, Brazil has abandoned neither its diverse partnerships nor its characteristics of a global trader.

How has it been possible to combine these two levels? As the external conditions for Brazil's international projection deteriorated in the 1980s, Brazilian diplomacy was not able to sustain its relations with the most important regions of the world in the same way as it had done in the past. The growing protectionism and the new international realities made relations with the European Community and Japan more difficult. At the same time, the crisis in the Soviet camp and the Third World crisis have made privileged links with these areas unfeasible, at least for the present. Equally, the regional order that emerged in the Middle East after the Second Gulf War has not been conducive to the establishment of strategic relationships with this area.

Therefore, the worse international conditions grew, the harder Brazilian foreign policy had to try to create a new regional reality. It was postulated that through the integration with neighboring countries, Brazil would enjoy not only more immediate economic benefits, but would also strengthen its regional platform, improving its participation (and that of its southern partners) on the world stage. In this sense, Mercosur/l, despite the official rhetoric, would represent neither an end in itself nor would its commercial aspects be its main objective, but it would be part of a more comprehensive project. When the United States announced the creation of NAFTA, Brazil reacted by launching SAFTA in 1993 and establishing the Zone of Peace and Cooperation in the South Atlantic (ZPCSA) with South American and African countries, in a strategy which was designed to build a series of concentric circles radiating from Mercosur/l.

The first of these initiatives attracted other South American nations to join Mercosur/l through a process of negotiating free trade agreements. Within this framework, Venezuela, Bolivia and Chile had already negotiated cooperation agreements with Mercosur/l in 1995 and 1996. The creation of a South American area of integration, with Mercosur/l as its hard core, would broaden the alternatives and the means of resistance

Fig. 9.1. Concentric Circles

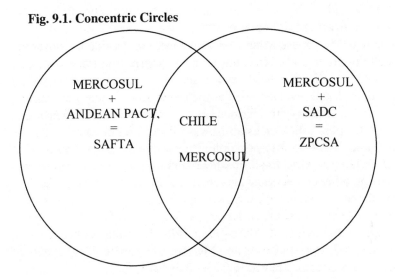

MERCOSUL + Andean Pact, Chile = SAFTA
MERCOSUL + Southern Africa Development Community (SADC) =
Zone of Peace And Cooperation in the South Atlantic (ZPCSA)

open to individual countries such as Chile, which are confronted with
NAFTA's power of attraction. Pertinently, the opportunity for regional
integration on a larger scale creates alternatives for the continental
countries making them much less vulnerable to external pressures to adopt
orthodox liberal programs of adjustment that would be needed to sustain
privileged relations with the developed countries or to be in proper shape
to join NAFTA. NAFTA itself had turned out to be an authentic 'siren
song' for some Latin American nations.

In the second case, the idea was to create a concentric circle encompassing all the South Atlantic, establishing cooperative links among
Mercosur/l, post-Apartheid South Africa and some newly emerging countries in Southern Africa. This new space would convert itself into an area
of economic growth, gaining from the existing and potential
complementarities already present. True to the spirit of the times, this
initiative would broaden the framework of South-South cooperation and
also open a permanent route to the Indian and Pacific Oceans, leading to
strategic alliances with the medium powers and/or emerging markets of

the Third World. This latest aspect seems to be specially important in mapping out Brazilian diplomacy.[7]

December 1994, at the Miami Summit Meeting, President Clinton re-launched the proposal for creating an hemispheric free trade zone that later would be called the Free Trade Area of the Americas (FTAA). At this meeting, Brazil revealed itself as the proponent of the future convergence and cooperation of the various already existent integration projects, rejecting the possibility of establishing bilateral agreements with the United States. True to this principle, Itamaraty (Brazilian Ministry of Foreign Affairs) worked to secure the assurance that even with this rapprochement, other contacts and agreements with additional areas, such as those with the European Union, would not be dismissed. In this sense, in response to American strategic advances, Mercosur/l launched negotiations with the EU that led to the signing of the first inter-bloc economic agreement, the European Union and Mercosur/l Inter-Regional Treaty of Cooperation, signed in Madrid in December 1995.

As expected, Mercosur/l's fairly positive results in the economic field and its cooperation with other poles of integration in the context of growing economic and technological competition in the North are leading to growing divergences with the United States. Not only is the permanent broadening of trade relations inside Mercosur/l an issue, but other elements are also leading to friction. This integration is expanding geographically, strengthening and is keeping to the projected timetable. At the same time, it is broadening socially. Today, we are able to observe an integration from below, characterized by the interaction of new social and political agents, such as the Net of Mercotowns (Mercocidades) and the much more intense society-society contacts. In addition, it seems to be much clearer that Mercosur/l has an implicit goal namely: the maintenance of an industrial basis inside its territory, creating conditions to sustain the ongoing presence of transnational corporations here.

Beyond these solid advances, Mercosur/l's agreements with other areas, such as Europe and Eastern Asia, bother the United States significantly. So, since the end of 1996, but especially after the commencement of Clinton's second mandate, Washington took to attacking the trade practices of Brazil and Mercosur/l, and their proximity to other processes of integration. During this acrimonious debate, Brazil has been arguing that

---

7. *Southern Africa and Mercosur/l: Reviewing the Relationship and Seeking Opportunities*, Seminar Report, October 2000.

Mercosur/l, which intends to create a common market, represents a much deeper process of integration than NAFTA that is only a free trade area. This fact alone is regarded as reason enough to justify Mercosur/l's survival, being preferable to a country to country agreement with NAFTA. The White House response has been to revamp NAFTA's power of attraction, embellishing it with the promise of obtaining fast track development, especially in relation to Chile. In its turn, cooperation with EU and Asia is being harshly attacked by the United States. This scenario can be deduced from Clinton's speech to the Senate in 1997, asking for the approval of fast track:

> *We need to act, to expand our exports to Latin America and Asia since these two regions are growing fast or we will be left behind as these economies strengthen their ties with other countries.*

In other words, the integration with the United States means to become importers of North American products.[8]

Therefore, priority has to be given to the fight for the liberalization of non-tariff barriers, gaining more access to the North American market, avoiding unilateral restrictions and dealing with the delicate issues present in the World Trade Organization, restraining the use of both issues of the environment and labor relations in trade matters. Inside Mercosur/l, it is essential to implement common rules to discipline foreign investments, controlling their volatility and to create coordinating mechanisms to avoid competition among Latin American countries to attract the same invest-ments. Although these are essential policies, it is also important to recog-nize that they are mainly reactions to the negative treatment of which our countries are the recipients and that a much more selective attitude from Washington can still lead to the break up of the Mercosur/l countries. In this sense, it is imperative to implement social reforms to redistribute income, to create a stronger economic framework, and to reject certain neoliberal paradigms that regulate globalization and the Scientific and Technological Third Industrial Revolution.

The *Real* Crisis and The Future of Mercosur/l

The association of Chile and Bolivia with Mercosur/l, the ongoing negotiations with other South American countries and the complete

8. Dossier "Alca," *Política Externa*, vol. 5 n° 4/vol. 6, n°1, Mar.–Aug. 1997.

absorption of the first country which seems to be very much on the cards, have bolstered the intensification of trade exchange and the other aspects of the integration which have clearly characterized Mercosur/l as a success. However, in 1997, the Asian financial crisis affected the region negatively, a situation that was worsened by the stock market collapses in Asia and Russia in 1998. This produced a flight of capital from the 'emerging markets', especially in Brazil (loss of 50 percent of exchange reserves). At the beginning of 1999, Brazil had to devalue the *real* heavily (two *reais* would account for one dollar). The high costs of Brazilian imports hit Argentina, which previously enjoyed a surplus with us, badly. It was the beginning of the so-called Mercosur/l crisis that some identified as the end of the regional integration process.

More than a crisis of the integration itself, this represented the erosion of an economic model and, especially, of the international context on which it was based. The world economic reality at the end of the 1990s was significantly different from the one at the beginning of the decade. The global financial instability, the slow down in the economic growth and also the recession in the region, the debacle of social indicators and the increase in unemployment altered the internal political situation, leading to the erosion of legitimacy of the governments of the Mercosur/l countries. Furthermore, the situation in Argentina worsened in the wake of its presidential elections. As soon as Fernando de La Rua, the opposition candidate, was elected, the rhetoric was one of conciliation and of reviving the integration process. The same thing happened in Uruguay, after Battle's victory. Moreover, because of the steady recession in Argentina, although exports to Brazil had diminished, imports from Brazil had not grown significantly.

Therefore, restoring the economic growth in the region is an essential condition by which to keep the integration process going, and governments are already well aware of this fact. On the other hand, the very real danger that Mercosur/l has had to endure forced various actors who are usually inactive and even critical of the integration process realize the damage that would be produced by its possible disappearance. With the dawning of this knowledge, they suddenly 'discovered' the virtues of the process. In fact, as many entrepreneurs have found out, the dismissal of Mercosur/l would generate a loss of confidence among its external investors and a demoralization that would adversely affect each country of the region individually. Not only entrepreneurs have discovered the advantages of Mercosur/l, also, somewhat later, its advantages have dawned on trade unions.

In a reality of worsening problems linked to globalization, there is a growing perception that Mercosur/l is a good instrument to articulate a new form of international projection for South American countries. Despite some lingering uncertainties, few actors question the essential character of the process. So, at the same time that the decision-making mechanisms and the institutions essential for an adequate functioning of Mercosur/l are re-evaluated, issues such as the strengthening and the enlargement of the process emerge as important strategic questions. Lastly, it is essential to answer the challenges of the hemispheric integration represented by the FTAA and of Mercosur/l's place inside it.

Examining the first aspect, it would be wrong to blame the institutions and the decision-making mechanisms of Mercosur/l for being responsible for the lack of a rapid solution to the present crisis. Their apparent limitations allowed a fast advance of the integration process in the past. However, this does not mean that they should not be reconsidered and that permanent and supranational institutions need to be created. But, in order to reach this stage, Brazil's commitment must grow and Argentina's suspicions must diminish. Come what may, the results of all these challenges depend mainly on some changes in the economic policies of the countries of the region, since there would be no individual survivors. The new governments that are coming into power in Argentina, Uruguay and Chile plus the relative changes in the power struggle inside the Brazilian government (produced by the premature succession fight) should generate a new positive environment for such actions. Social problems and the recovery of sustained economic growth should be the main issues to be addressed or we will face a deep crisis of government.

In any consideration of the enlargement of Mercosur/l, it is essential to take into account that the Southern Cone is already a developed area with moderate prospects of economic and demographic growth. In contrast, the Andean region, especially in its northern part (Colombia and Venezuela), represents a dynamic area with greater chances of growth, in spite of the crisis that affects it at the moment. The proximity to them, either through an association or by membership of Mercosur/l, makes SAFTA a real entity, although via different paths, creating a concentric circle radiating from the original hard core. Cogently, Southern African cooperation, as set out in ZPCSA and strengthened by President Mandela's Mercosur/l meeting in Ushuaia, in 1998 would represent the second concentric circle. Therefore, an area with considerable productive and technological capacity would be forged, rich in natural resources and with an attractive market conducive to regional activities and appealing to other zones.

The fulfillment of these objectives would help to create a power pole capable of taking part in the new multipolar international system that seems to be emerging in the beginning of the twenty-first century. But, in order to reach this point, it will be essential to maintain diversified relations with other poles of world power, such as the United States/NAFTA, the EU and East Asia. Here, there is an issue that must be dealt with realistically: the FTAA proposal. It would be suicidal to merge Mercosur/l into a hemispheric integration led by the first world power, but it would be unrealistic to turn its back upon it. With a strengthened Mercosur/l capable of negotiating as a bloc, it would be a viable alternative to search for some kind of hemispheric integration that might even help its international projection. To achieve this, it is of utmost importance to abandon a mere reactive and bargaining position, investing in the strategic importance of Mercosur/l's set of simultaneous multilateral relations. Therefore, at the turn of the century, Mercosur/l is facing a series of challenges that, if dealt with carefully, would help to strengthen it, leading to the exploration of the new potentialities in the international scenario.

The so-called Mercosur/l crisis was provoked by the flight of capital phenomenon that hit Brazil, plus the devaluation of the *Real*, the profound imbalance in our economy, combined with difficulties in expanding our exports outside the bloc, the tensions produced by the displacement of enterprises and workers in a moment of recession, and the loss (or the giving up) of the coordinating capacity of states and governments. According to Samuel Pinheiro Guimarães, Director of the Institute of International Relations Research of the Ministry of Foreign Affairs, an emergency program to overcome the crisis could be achieved by taking certain steps:

> a) common policies for the expansion of exports and the control of imports from third countries trying to obtain a surplus; b) a common program of identification and the elimination of barriers to Mercosur/l's exports; c) the creation of a special regime for sensitive products, such as sugar; d) the creation of an industrial restructuring fund and of a fund for technological development financed by the Common External Tariff resources; and e) the enlargement of timetables in common credit operations, eliminating the need for the use of a strong currency in the bilateral transactions and the freeing of transactions with other areas.[9]

---

9. Guimarães, *Quinhentos anos de periferia*, p. 25.

With the implementation of this minimum program, integration would be given a new boost, restoring certain strategic objectives of Brazil-Argentina's cooperation of the 1980s.

The Brasilia Summit and South American Integration

Facing this growing set of challenges, the reaction of Brazilian diplomacy has been to foster South American integration, promoting the Brasilia Summit. This initiative occurred at the same time that the United States was feeling the first signs of a recession and during its presidential elections. Therefore, since July 2000, Washington has been systematically launching a package of projects in order to block Brazilian advances and to accelerate the negotiations and the implementation of the FTAA.

The official sanctioning of Plan Colombia by the White House on August 31, 2000 to help in the war against narcotics, and the simultaneous realization of the Brasilia Summit, a joint meeting of South American governmental officials, made clear that two opposing (but related) trends were developing in South America. These trends represent two different kinds of answers to the issue of achieving the politico-economic stability that was reached at the beginning of the decade. This sort of stability was characterized by the primacy of market economy, the total openness of domestic markets as a way of taking part in the globalization process, and the adoption of neoliberal policies of privatization and deregulation in the domestic field. At the same time, the liberal democratic regime was strengthened after the end of the authoritarian rule and the resurgence of the left.

However, this new situation created serious social problems (in spite of the official rhetoric) that sooner rather than later began to influence the political and economic realms. This latest reality, long concealed by the financial stability, emerged in full force when the stock markets started to drop progressively in 1997, reaching their nadir at the beginning of 1999 with the flight of speculative capital and the devaluation of the *real*. During this period, several political crises erupted in Paraguay, Ecuador, Venezuela and, more recently, Peru. It goes without saying that in almost every country of the region social clashes have also been part of the scene.

As mentioned before, the USA launched Plan Colombia in this context, although Colombian problems (such as the left-wing guerrillas, drug trafficking, right-wing death squads) were already well known and there were no significant changes that could justify such a policy. Moreover, a prolonged, direct military intervention in the region, or even closer and more unequivocal support of Colombian security forces, would have saddled the White House with very high costs. Additionally, a discrete, selected and specialized American military presence is already present in the Andean region, without relation to Plan Colombia. So, what was the real meaning of this initiative?

Beyond the show of force in drug wars (and towards the left-wing guerrillas who control one-third of the country), and the support for President Pastrana's allied government, Washington intended to point out to other countries that it was aware of all the developments in the region, supporting allies and punishing 'strays'. Reminiscent of the Colombian situation, in Venezuela President Chávez not only peacefully dismantled the traditional political model shared by almost all of Latin America, he has also sketched a new internal regime and set out an autonomous diplomatic conduct, restoring the principles of nationalism and Third Worldism.

Panama is also being swept by a nationalist wave, whereas Ecuador is suffering a crisis of government (deposing of the president) while caught up in the throes of a powerful social mobilization This is a phenomenon also present in Bolivia. In its turn, in Peru, Fujimori did manage to get re-elected for the third time, in spite of U.S. wishes to the contrary, and started to implement a new foreign policy in order to break its imposed isolation, trying to consolidate the government. However, his resistance was undermined in the short run by the cutting of American and Japanese investments as well as by international accusations of corruption in the election that led his third mandate, which ended very quickly.

Paraguay has been afflicted by a well-entrenched political crisis for the last two years. On the other hand, Chile and Argentina, and their newly elected governments, show clear signs of how weak their previous political and economic stability was. Not so long ago, these countries were being pointed out as 'models'. Finally, Brazil is a double-edged problem for the USA: on one hand, the government is debilitated and the opposition is growing; on the other, arising from this situation and the *Real* crisis, this same government is outlining changes of track in the international context.

Brazil's decision to call the South American Summit, that proposed the creation of a South American Free Trade Area, in Brasilia at the very time that Mercosur/l's own survival was being questioned seemed to surprise some analysts. However, this process is easily understood and was rationally motivated by the crisis in which the country found itself, and because of the growing international and regional difficulties. Thus, Brazil needed to restore an autonomous (yet, non-confrontational) diplomatic dialogue, criticizing the "asymmetric globalization".

In part, the search for international alternatives was also motivated by the growing preoccupation of Brazil's business sectors, faced with a long-term recession and the risks that membership of the FTAA would bring. Taking a contradictory stance, the answer to the Mercosur/l crisis focused on the widening of the integration to all South America. Therefore, Brazil's previous 1993 initiative for the creation of the SAFTA seems to be taking shape via circuitous routes. In this sense, further talks were scheduled for October, in order to establish a free trade area that comprises Mercosur/l and the Andean Pact.

Beyond the present economic and political difficulties and the U.S. offensive for the creation of the FTAA (made easier by the Mercosur/l crisis), American pressures opposing Fujimori's re-election (and the way that this regime collapsed) and Plan Colombia are all seen as interference in the domestic affairs of South American countries. A growing militarization of Colombian domestic conflicts generating refugee flows and other problems is also worrying the countries of the region. So, this new proposal, besides covering economic needs, has a political dimension. In this context Brazil has found some room to exercise its regional leadership, in concert with its neighbors, even strengthening its virtual candidacy to a seat in a reformed UN Security Council.

The question is to find a way to avoid taking actions that achieve (of deliver) no results. As is widely known, the possibilities open to the Brazilian government and its ability to resist pressures are limited. This is even more true for other countries, such as Argentina, because of their tightly-knit integration into the current model. Yet, there are factors that are beyond their control. The economic history of Brazil shows that when faced with a deep crisis in the external sector that has prevented the country from obtaining convertible currencies, the country was obliged to reshape its economic model, its international stance and sometimes even its own political system. Whether or not the current predicaments will reach this point is something that we will find out in the future.

The FTAA and the Future of Mercosur/l

In the second half of 2000, in the midst of the Mercosur/l crisis, the American economy started to show signs of a slowdown. At the same time,

Brazil was furthering its South American initiative. Because of their loss in U.S. presidential elections, the Democrats tried to create new facts that would lock Bush's presidency into an acceleration of the FTAA negotiations. According to the economist Marcelo de Paiva Abreu,

> *hemispheric integration is, in fact, an extension of NAFTA. Regionalism's role for the USA is a clear sign of the so-called 'crowbar' policy. The expression was mentioned by Carla Hills (American negotiator): to break into closed markets.*[10]

Among the American actions that were taken to implement this strategy were the co-optation of Chile, renewing the old promise to integrate this country into NAFTA. Chile, a weak country, which does not present a strong economic presence, and which seems to be incapable of articulating a national project, pins all its hopes on this arrangement. Argentina, in its turn plunged in a deep economic and financial crisis, is also tempted to make huge concessions in the FTAA negotiations, in exchange for bilateral favors in its economic relations with the USA. Therefore, the external context has been disadvantageous to Brazil.

The possible creation of the FTAA would mean the end of Mercosur/l, once it reached the point of nullifying the advantages that the Common External Tariff (CET) offered the firms of member countries. Since Southern Cone integration is comprised only of developing countries, with limited competitiveness, its absorption into a bloc that included Canada and the United States would mean the collapse of productive chains, for it would grant the more competitive firms of the North the same conditions as the local ones. Besides, the end of CET would annihilate one of the factors that attract investments, the possibility to "jump" regional barriers, allowing the installation of industries inside somewhat protected countries. Moreover, for economies such as that of the Rio Grande do Sul, American cattle and agricultural exports would represent a real threat (especially soybean, rice, manufactured agricultural products, cattle and poultry farming).

The outcome of this dispute will depend very much on Brazilian diplomacy. Several analysts argue that, if Brazil did not take part in the FTAAs negotiation, it would be isolated. This is not true, since Latin American countries do not compete with Brazil on either the Latin American or on the North American market. Most of these countries have

---

10. Marcelo de Paiva Abreu, "Alca," p. 47.

already gained commercial privileges in the USA. As recalls Ambassador Samuel Pinheiro Guimarães:

> Considering South American countries, their limited industrial diversity and the size of their economies also restrain their ability to compete with Brazil in the American (and hemispheric) market. Moreover, their exports to the USA are different from Brazil's, focusing on primary products that we do not export, such as the Chilean copper, oil from Venezuela and Ecuador, Peruvian and Bolivian ores, etc. Argentina's case is more interesting, since it produces and exports the same products that the USA also exports in great quantities, grains and meat, and its priority market is the European Union. It is hard to see what Argentina might gain in the trade or in the field of investments with its participation in NAFTA or even in a future FTAA.[11]

Therefore, from our discussion, it should be noted that, despite all its limitations, Mercosur/l represents not only a trade initiative, but also a strategic one, which clashes with North American interests. Inside the FTAA (that is not a mere trading project), we would lose our legal capacity to make use of the mechanisms of industrial, technological and commercial policies to accelerate development. In Mercosur/l this would be possible as long as the national rulers could free themselves of their present ideological chains. Brazil, in its turn, needs to avoid the traps created by the despair of Argentina (which depends on the Brazilian market) and begin to mobilize its social and business sectors against the risks presented by the FTAA, rousing them from their lethargic condition and confronting the crux of this critical issue: regional integration. After ten years, there can be no doubt that Mercosur/l has been an appropriate strategic initiative and that, through it, paraphrasing the World Social Forum, which was held in Porto Alegre in 2001, "another integration is possible."

---

11. Interview on www.global21.com.br. 29 December 2000.

MERCOSUR/L AND LATIN AMERICAN INTEGRATION

Paul Cammack

Introduction

The argument advanced in this chapter is twofold. First, regional associations can in principle play a wide variety of roles, from the promotion of common regional interests to the reinforcement of domestic political projects; they may even contribute to processes of state formation and identity construction and transformation. Second, Mercosur/l has in fact played a number of such roles over the last decade, and should not be seen as a simple economic association; but at the same time the constraints imposed by its rigid structure (essentially a bilateral association between two mismatched economies whose governments are pursuing incompatible agendas) have limited the extent to which it can perform them effectively. It was able for conjunctural circumstances to contribute briefly to political stability and economic reform and integration in its early stages, but has little capacity to offer more, and may already be an obstacle to further progress on these fronts. Mercosur/l, in sum, is an ineffective regional association with little capacity to contribute to regional or global integration, and little capacity to promote other goals.

Regionalism and Subregionalism

In principle, regional associations may play a number of roles. Even if one assumes that they slot neatly into an institutional hierarchy in which already constituted states deal with *domestic* issues through their own national institutions, the regional associations address *regional* concerns, and international organizations take care of *global* issues, a wide range of political, economic and security objectives might still be pursued at regional level. In this context, regional associations might be understood as vehicles for the common pursuit of regional goals, and inter-regional linkages provide a forum within which the conflicting interests of already constituted regions can be addressed and perhaps reconciled. Even at this simple level of analysis, though, it is clear that 'common regional goals' emerge against a backdrop of rivalries and conflicting interests between states, contrasting priorities, and differing perceptions of how common interests once identified might be pursued. It might be better, then, to see regional associations as vehicles for the negotiation of conflicting interests, as much as for the pursuit of common interests.

However, the image of a neat compartmentalization of responsibilities, in which global issues correspond to global institutions, regional issues to regional institutions, and domestic issues to domestic institutions, is potentially misleading. After all, one of the leading assertions of the 'globalization' literature is that states are less able than once they were to secure their domestic objectives through national institutions, and are therefore obliged to pursue them through supra-national institution-building despite the danger of further loss of sovereignty as a consequence. Another is that in the shaping of the agendas of international organizations, the designs of some states weigh far more heavily than those of others. It follows that there is no reason to suppose either that regional associations will concern themselves principally with or be best understood in terms of purely regional issues, or that inter-regional initiatives will reflect and further the interests of the partners involved, in opposition to those of actors external to the inter-regional dialogue. Global, regional and national institutions are all equally sites of struggle between conflicting interests, and there is no knowing in advance who will control them, or to what purposes they will be turned. Payne and Gamble rightly assert, then, in their discussion of regionalism from the perspective of the 'new IPE', that the relationship between regionalism as a statist project and globalization as a social process is still in the balance, and that 'the reverse concepts, namely globalism defined as a state-led project and regionalization defined as a social process manifest at the regional level, cannot be excluded from the framework of analysis'.[1] Nor can we exclude the tendency for states to use regional and subregional association as a

---

1. A. Payne, and A. Gamble, "Introduction: ..." in Gamble and Payne, eds., *Regionalism ...,* pp. 1–20.

means to promote or reinforce strategies of class hegemony or capitalist development pursued at the domestic level. We should therefore expect regional and inter-regional initiatives to be criss-crossed by both domestic and global projects and concerns.

Finally, if one abandons the fiction that states are stable entities with fixed identities, and assumes instead that they are continually in a state of self-construction and identity formation, the possibility arises that regional associations might even play a fundamental role in the creation or redefinition of the identity of states. In other words, they may be vehicles for the construction or reconstruction of states and state identities, part of the institutional framework within which states are defined and redefined. In a sense, then, regional associations may construct states, as much as states construct regional associations.

A New Materialist Perspective

I approach the issue of regional and subregional association from a starting point of global political economy, within a 'new materialist' approach which seeks to restore the classical Marxist perspective as a comprehensive conceptual and theoretical framework within which the contemporary global political economy can be understood.[2] Within this framework 'globalization' is not new. It is a mystificatory euphemism for the global spread of capitalism and the rapidly advancing internalization of its imperatives (ranging from proletarianization and the creation of a global reserve army of labor to inter-capitalist competition) in virtually every society around the globe.[3] At its heart has been an increasingly conscious and systematic offensive over the last two decades, led by successive U.S. governments and the transformed Bretton Woods institutions, to reassert the sway of capital over labor, primarily by increasing the scope of action for financial capital on a global scale. Within this broad context, the new materialist approach follows Panitch in arguing that states *never* controlled global capitalism, but recognizing at the same time that globalization is *authored* by states in circumstances in which the *determining power of capital* is more powerful than ever before. In this context, states seek to construct international regimes which define and

---

2. P. Cammack, "Interpreting ASEM: ...," pp. 13–32.
3. P. Cammack, "Making Poverty Work."

guarantee the global and domestic rights of capital.[4] Regional and subregional associations, sitting as they do between the national and the global levels of regime construction, need to be evaluated with an eye to both.

Adopting this perspective, the new materialist approach accepts that capitalist-oriented states seek collectively to preserve and constantly extend the general conditions for capital accumulation through multilateral institutions and other mechanisms of international and inter-regional co-ordination. But it locates such efforts in a context in which states simultaneously seek individually to secure particular advantage over other states, within and beyond particular 'regions' of the global economy. In other words, it interprets the balance of conflict and cooperation between states in supranational institutions in terms of the need to cooperate to preserve a global capitalist economy while simultaneously competing with each other within it. Secondly, it starts from the assumption that as a consequence of the process of combined and uneven development, domestic configurations and spatial locations will vary from state to state, and give rise to distinct arrays of interests and distinct projects from state to state in the system. Thirdly, it sets this doubly complex picture of relations between states (shaped by combined and uneven development, and marked by a dynamic of competition and cooperation) in the context of the fundamental capitalist framework in which firms are obliged to compete with each other to lower the cost of labor and increase the individual rate of profit.

It argues that in the current context of the completion of the world market and the universalization of the imperatives of capitalist competition, firms compete and financial circuits operate on a global scale. As a result, autonomous projects for capitalist accumulation secured at the level of the state—briefly possible in a small number of cases in the past—are generally problematic. At the level of global economic management, this situation is reflected in the emergence of global regulatory agencies (international organizations) and regional and inter-regional initiatives sponsored and carried forward by state leaders in an effort to mitigate the difficulties they face in advancing what they take to be their 'national interest.' States naturally carry into this context their need to compete with each other, as well as their need to cooperate to establish the general conditions for the global hegemony of capitalism. It is in this specific

---

4. L. Panitch, "Rethinking the Role of the State," pp. 84–85.

sense that subregional, regional, inter-regional and global regulatory institutions are *sites of struggle* between competing projects sponsored to different degrees by states, capitalist firms and international agencies. As capitalist competition becomes global in scale and the imperatives it generates become universally binding, such initiatives may variously resist, modify or promote the logic of global capitalist competition. However, the tendency is for the logic of capitalist competition to assert itself on a global scale, and states, firms and international organizations are as much shaped by the process as shaping it.

In this environment of global competition for profit, states are increasingly driven towards making their territories hospitable to capitalist investment, whether domestic or foreign. This is the logic of the familiar neoliberal agenda which removes obstacles to the free range of capital by privatization and the removal of protection, and cuts the costs of its operation by reducing taxes and promoting 'efficient' systems of targeted welfare. At the heart of this process is a drive to bring workers directly under the control of capital—the promotion of what Marx called the real subsumption of labor to capital, or the creation of circumstances in which the majority are proletarianized, and have no option but to offer themselves for employment in a labor market thoroughly permeated by the logic of capitalist competition. This overall agenda is currently pressed at global level by such regulatory agencies as the IMF, the World Bank, and the World Trade Organization. Within this context, states have generally engaged in regional and inter-regional initiatives as much in order to restore, secure, maintain or reinforce the domestic hegemony of capital over labor, as to address the narrow agenda with which episodes of regional integration are sometimes associated. And the new materialist perspective suggests that in seeking to understand how regional associations can play a part in the construction of states and the transformation of state identities, priority should be given to their construction as competitive neoliberal states in a global capitalist economy. In other words, we should understand subregional and regional association, and engagement with global institutions, in terms of the construction and reinforcement at domestic level of the hegemony of capital over labor.

Regional and Local Contexts

The regional background to the creation of *Mercosur/l* is the project launched in the United States at the beginning of the 1970s with the closing of the gold window, given a brutal start in regional terms by what now seems intensely strategic support for Pinochet's neoliberal experiment from 1975, propelled onto a larger stage by Volcker's policy turn to a high-dollar, high interest-rate regime, and Brady's pioneering of bond-based lending, and perfected by Clinton and his economic advisers after 1993. This new 'Dollar-Wall Street Regime' established the domestic hegemony of financial capital, and transformed the Bretton Woods framework into an engine to impose its global domination.[5] The push towards a Free Trade Area for the Americas is part of it, but the increasingly systematic character of its global agenda is far more dramatically expressed by the sequence of U.S. initiatives which led from the APEC Summit in Seattle in 1993 through to the Bogor Declaration in 1994, and the Action Agenda at the 1995 summit in Osaka, to be reinforced by the creation of the WTO itself, and the energy expended in the same period to prevent an alternative project espoused by Japan from taking off. As the power of this disciplinary framework has spread, it has brought about a fundamental shift in social forces and relationships within states around the world, facilitating the rise to power of new elite's themselves committed to the same disciplinary regime.

Mercosur/l should be interpreted against this background in terms of the logic of advancement of domestic projects in Brazil and Argentina aimed at reorienting social relations in those countries and imposing the discipline of capital over labor—or, in broad terms, at exposing those societies to the global logic of capital. In specific terms, the objective was to bring the economies and societies of the region into line with an emerging regional pattern, a goal given a sense of urgency and common purpose as a consequence of a shared perception that considerable ground had already been lost to regional competitors such as Chile and Mexico. In this context, the inclusion of Paraguay and Uruguay barely affected what was essentially a bilateral arrangement.

It was a particular feature of the regional context that domestic projects of economic and social restructuring were being taken forward in the precarious context of a simultaneous efforts to restore liberal democratic political systems. In this case, all four members of Mercosur/l faced similar legacies—a history of military rule that had not only closed down liberal democratic institutions and instituted regimes of varying degrees of torture and terror, but had also failed in the end as vehicles for social and economic

---

5. P. Gowan, *The Global Gamble,* pp. 39–59.

restructuring. This was a specific conjuncture in which subregional association could strengthen nascent democratic regimes by expressing and supporting a common subregional aspiration to democracy. All in all, then, Mercosur/l was as much about creating and securing a particular kind of domestic social and political order as about establishing state positions in an emerging world order. Engagement in the subregional project, in short, has been intended to advance and reinforce emergent national political projects whose principal goal is to achieve bourgeois hegemony and relative state autonomy at the domestic level, and specifically to transform social relations in order to embed a neoliberal domestic order which it is possible to reproduce through liberal democratic political institutions: in this sense, the creation of the subregional association can be seen as an extension of domestic political economy.[6]

The key aspect of the regional context here was the final disappearance of the conditions for statist developmental projects (based on import-substitution) as a result of the debt crisis of the 1980s. This was made critical by the relative backwardness of both domestic adjustment and political institutionalization in Argentina and Brazil. These two countries had made little progress in restructuring their economies by 1990, and their processes of transition to democracy remained precarious and only weakly institutionalized. The genesis and consolidation of Mercosur/l coincided in time with the adoption of programs of neoliberal restructuring in Brazil in 1990 (under President Fernando Collor de Mello) and in Argentina in 1991 (under President Carlos Saúl Menem), against the background of repeated failures in the recent past. It was given urgency by concurrent moves to establish a USA-Canada free trade area in 1989, the first approaches from Mexico to the USA in March 1990, the launching by President Bush of the Enterprise for the Americas Initiative in June of the same year, and the signing of the NAFTA agreement in August 1992. Framework agreements with other Latin American states (including the Mercosur/l Four) were designed 'to set out and enforce new economic and political "rules of the game" in the hemisphere', reflecting '*the triumph of economic liberalism, of faith in export-led growth and of belief in the centrality of the private sector to the development process*'.[7] At this point, Argentina and Brazil were lagging seriously behind the processes of

---

6. P. Cammack "MERCOSUR/L: from Domestic Concerns to Regional Influence," pp. 96–97.
7. A. Payne, "The United States ...," in Gamble and Payne, eds., *Regionalism ...*, p. 106.

neoliberal reform in Mexico and Chile, as commentators on the region widely noted. Despite their repressive character (particularly acute in the case of Argentina) neither military regime abandoned the populist legacy of the post-1930 period nor established a more liberal economy; nor did they forge ahead with reducing the role of the state. In the case of Argentina, intense social conflict combined with division among elite's and among the military themselves meant that no clear new state project was consistently pursued: on two occasions, 1966–1970 and 1976–1980, a single military leader remained in office for four years, but in each case a nascent national project broke down. A protracted transition followed by temporizing and economic crisis under Alfonsin deepened the sense of urgency. In the case of Brazil, a rather different trajectory led to a similar position at the end of the 1980s. The Brazilian military, in power for twenty-one years, showed more continuity and achieved more success in economic policy than was the case in Argentina. However, their period of greatest success, featuring high rates of growth between the late 1960s and the 1970s, was based upon an intensification of the state-interventionist policies of the populist period, rather than upon a turn towards a more neoliberal approach. A strategy based upon heavy state investment, particularly in such key areas as energy, heavy industry, and capital goods and arms production, was then intensified rather than abandoned after the first oil crisis: the Second Development Plan of 1974, implemented by General Ernesto Geisel, was a deliberate attempt to use a counter-cyclical policy of large-scale state investment to keep growth moving forward in adverse global conditions, and its failure left the military with an economic crisis which intensified in the period of drift after 1979. Sarney, like Alfonsin, prolonged the crisis to the end of the 1980s.

In both Argentina and Brazil, then, the new regimes which took over at the end of the 1980s faced conditions of severe economic instability. Each launched programs of economic liberalization, which combined renewed currency reform with tariff reductions and privatization. In Argentina, a privatization programme was launched in 1990, a series of measures were taken to undermine job stability, and, after an unsuccessful initial experiment, the appointment of Domingo Cavallo as Minister of the Economy in January 1991 was followed by the linking of the austral to the U.S. dollar, and then by the abandonment of the ill-fated austral, and a return to a new (and newly stable) peso. In Brazil, a programme of tariff reduction (from 1990) and privatization (from 1991) began to construct Collor de Mello's proposed 'New Brazil', but inflation hovered at 450-550 per cent per annum through 1991 and 1992, and the prospects for stabilization were severely jolted by the impeachment and removal from office of President Collor on charges of corruption in 1992. Most significantly, a report published in 1991 by the Argentine Foreign Ministry identified the lack of 'labor flexibility' as the pressing problem in both Argentina and Brazil. On all counts, the two were badly placed to compete with their neighbors.

In the context described above, the establishment of Mercosur/l in the early 1990s was clearly aligned with a long delayed comprehensive programme of domestic economic reform which sought to promote and consolidate economic liberalization. Priority was attached to the creation of Mercosur/l in Argentina and Brazil as a consequence of the launching of neoliberal economic projects at the end of the 1980s. As seen above, the economic context was made critical by a combination of long-term and short-term factors: over the long-term each country had pursued a pattern of predominantly state-led development since the Second War, and an alternative liberal model of development had proved unsustainable when it had been attempted. In the short term, each government had found itself in the grip of a deepening economic crisis, and felt itself to be losing ground, in an increasingly competitive global environment, against rivals who had apparently adjusted to new circumstances with greater success. The depth of the political and institutional crisis in each country was if anything greater. In the long-term perspective, civilian and military liberals alike had proved politically weak throughout the period. In particular, no political party with an agenda of economic liberalism enjoyed success in either country after 1930. When liberal projects were devised in the late 1980s, therefore, there was not only no immediate party political support for them, but virtually no plausible political vehicle for them in living memory. Crucially, in each case, the hold of the regime of organized labor was precarious. In Argentina, the combative legacy of Peronism had not been extinguished, while in Brazil the emergence of the PT (Workers' Party) after 1979 had created the first independent mass party of labor.

In these circumstances, each of the political regimes under which reform was advanced was fragile. In Argentina, Carlos Menem was elected by the Peronists—the political tradition defined by labor militancy and opposition to a liberal orientation in economic affairs. In Brazil, Fernando Collor de Mello was elected by a coalition united only by opposition to 'Lula'—Luis Inacio da Silva, the leader of the Workers' Party—and was backed initially only by a minuscule party of his own creation. In summary, a long-term crisis of political liberalism was resolved by carrying liberal projects forward on the basis of personal projects which lacked committed institutional or ideological support. This greatly reinforced commitment to Mercosur/l. Menem and Collor had strong motivation to offer each other mutual support, and to seek to strengthen commitment to the liberal project by furthering subregional cooperation. It is essential, therefore, that the depth of the historical crisis of political liberalism in each country is appreciated. Developmentalist, corporatist and interventionist ideas had enjoyed ideological hegemony in each country since 1930, and in both countries liberalism had proved equally weak in civilian party politics and within the military. In Argentina, liberal civilian traditions have been virtually excluded from power since the 1940s by the electoral weight of Peronism, while the military was split between liberal and corporatist factions, with the latter tending to predominate. In Brazil, liberalism surfaced briefly with the election of Quadros by the UDN (União Democratica Nacional) in 1961, and in an authoritarian guise under Castello Branco, but the military soon accentuated the statist and developmentalist aspect of their project. Liberalism as an ideological project, therefore, enjoyed little institutional support in either Argentina or Brazil at the end of the 1980s. At this point involvement in Mercosur/ l was invoked to provide support for specific political projects committed to the introduction and consolidation of systematic programs of neoliberal economic reform. In particular, subregional engagement in Mercosur/l provided support for local projects of political democratization.[8]

Mercosur/l Today: Diverging Goals and Diminishing Returns

Mercosur/l should still be regarded today primarily as a symbol of political commitment to neoliberalism, and as an auxiliary means of sustaining democracy and imposing discipline within the domestic economy. However, it could never have been expected to do more than create some breathing space within which more enduring domestic economic, political, social and institutional reform could be achieved. It remains essentially a bilateral union (given the minimal economic impact of Uruguay and Paraguay) which unites two economies with different economic strategies and diverging regional projects.

---

8. J. Grugel, "Latin America ..." in A. Gamble and A. Payne eds., *Regionalism ...*, pp. 131–167.

With this in mind, we may now return to the analytical framework set out at the beginning of this chapter. It was suggested there that regional (or subregional) associations might serve for the pursuit of common regional interests or the negotiation of conflicting regional interests. In addition, a number of other projects were identified to which participation in a regional or subregional institution might contribute in varying circumstances, ranging from domestic economic and social restructuring to the construction or transformation of state identity.

In this context, two principal conclusions have emerged from examination of Mercosur/l as a subregional association. First, it suffers from severe structural limitations. It is essentially a bilateral arrangement between unequal partners, Brazil and Argentina, onto which two much smaller countries, Uruguay and Paraguay, have been grafted. For all practical purposes, the latter are unable to influence the character or direction of the association, although at times they may be able to derive minor benefits from membership of it. Second, the early 1990s, in which the association came into being, presented a conjuncture in which a number of overlapping and mutually supporting short-term considerations made the association briefly useful for a whole range of reasons, but this was a short-lived combination of circumstances which is now over and which is not likely to reappear. This is partly because the moment of shared interests across a range of issues was a brief one that has given way to divergent projects and interests, and partly because such common goals as remain would always have had to be achieved in the longer run either by more soundly established domestic processes, or as a consequence of more robust international regimes. If this is so, Mercosur/l has lost a large part of its purpose, and may be expected in the future to play a minor role as a forum for the pursuit of minor trade concerns.

The basic issue here remains the structural rigidity of an arrangement which brings together four economies, two of which contribute 96 per cent of total GDP shared unequally between them in a proportion of roughly three parts for Brazil to one for Argentina. Given the predominance of Brazil, and the overwhelming weight of bilateral concerns, broader goals are always likely to be pushed aside by the unavoidable salience of immediate and often conflicting bilateral concerns. This aspect of the association has been highlighted in recent years by the devastating institutional effects of wildly divergent economic strategies, best exemplified by Argentina's pursuit of virtual dollarization through the medium of the currency board, while Brazil has sought to boost global competitiveness through devaluation. When the imperatives of each strategy collide, Brazil simply acts unilaterally and in breach of its obligations, and its partners, Argentina included, have little option but to accept its unilateral action. Such specific policy clashes bring into the open a deeper divergence which was temporarily obscured in the conjuncture of the early 1990s, when both Brazil and Argentina were seeking cover for delayed and precarious processes of economic liberalisation and privatization. It was the case then, and remains so now, that Brazil seeks regional leadership as a potential basis for resistance to the creation of a Free Trade Area of the Americas devised in Washington, whereas Argentina seeks to avoid subordination to Brazil's regional pretensions, and seeks a future within as large a regional free trade area as is available.

The conflicts of interest that are already apparent in Mercosur/l are likely, then, to become more apparent as the projected Free Trade Area of the Americas comes closer to being a reality. In the meantime, the need for support for integration from a subregional association has diminished. This is in part because headway of a modest kind has been made and continues to be made on a common tariff and other aspects of integration. Mostly, however, it arises from the creation and consolidation of the World Trade Organization and the substantially increased powers of surveillance and intervention developed over the last decade by the IMF and the World Bank, which have eclipsed any limited contribution Mercosur/l might have made to global regulation and integration. In particular, the disciplinary framework put together jointly by the IMF and the World Bank, through the 'international financial architecture' and the extended regime of global intervention developed out of poverty reduction strategies and 'letters of development strategy' makes Mercosur/l and other such associations redundant as auxiliary means to the assurance of neoliberal discipline.[9] To the extent that the Mercosur/l partners look for external alliances in order to consolidate neoliberal projects at home, they will now look beyond Mercosur/l. And finally, whatever assessment one makes of the extent of consolidation of democracy among the Mercosur/l partners, it is hard to argue that the association plays any continuing role in sustaining democracy. In short, the broader goals to which Mercosur/l

9. P. Cammack, " 'The Mother of All Governments' ..." in S. Hughes and R. Wilkinson, eds., *Engaging Global Governance* ...

might initially have contributed have moved beyond its reach, and the more the association is reduced to its core identity as an extended bilateral trade regime, the more the incompatibility of its principal partners will make it a forum which draws attention to conflicts over projects of economic integration. In these circumstances, its ability to contribute to larger goals will be further curtailed. All in all, it appears to be an institution with its best days are behind it.

WHO IS INTEGRATING WHOM?
TRADE IN THE PERENNIAL NORTH-SOUTH CONFLICT

Marianne L. Wiesebron

"Barbarism is not only the cowardice of terrorism, but also intolerance or the imposition of unilateral policies on a planetary scale," stated the Brazilian President, Fernando Henrique Cardoso, while addressing the French National Assembly, on October 30th, 2001.[1]

The Fourth Ministerial Meeting of the WTO at Doha, Qatar, November 2001 and its Consequences

While Afghanistan is being bombed and the media resounding to the war against terrorism, other wars are also going on very quietly, but with consequences that are perhaps even more far-reaching. These other wars are happening on the trade fronts, but can be as deadly or deadlier than battles being fought in the air and on the ground. The most recent crucial moment was the Fourth Ministerial Meeting of the WTO, held at Doha, Qatar, from November 9 until 14, where it was decided that a new round of trade negotiations will take place, and what its agenda will be. Among the most prominent issues are agriculture and patents. Food supply, or its lack, is a most powerful weapon. Every day, over 35,000 children starve to death in poor countries, according to the statistics of the UN Food and Agriculture Organization. Policies imposed by the IMF and World Bank are partly to blame, and so are WTO regulations. Whereas quite some people in Third World countries previously produced enough food to sustain their livelihood, they now have to compete in the world market, to

---

1. *Estado de São Paulo*, " O discurso de FHC na França," 30 October 2001.

comply with structural adjustment policies. As a consequence, they now produce crops for export to pay their debts and for their food imports from the First World. As a result starvation now occurs in places where it was rare in the past. While many Third World Countries had to reduce or abolish their subsidies for agriculture altogether, the EU and the USA, on the contrary, continue or even increase their subsidies for agriculture.

Agriculture

In fact, the USA has just voted to give substantial help to its own agricultural sector, as this country exports more agricultural produce than industrial products. As Mattie Sharpless, Acting Administrator, Foreign Agriculture Service of the U.S. Department of Agriculture, recently told the Senate Agriculture Committee: "*Dollar for dollar, America exports more meat than steel, more corn than cosmetics, more wheat than coal, more bakery products than motor boats, and more fruits and vegetables than household appliances.*" Sharpless added that agriculture is one of the few sectors of the U.S. economy that consistently contributes a surplus to its trade balance. That may explain why there is a new Farm Bill pending before the U.S. Congress, which would provide U.S. $170 billion in subsidies to American agriculture in the next ten years. This amount is quite shocking, all the more so when Third World Countries are required, time and time again, not to give subsidies or cheap credits.[2]

The United States is not the only party assisting its agricultural sector. The European Union had a similar bad reputation for quite some years, and has also been attacked by the USA for its CAP. The EU provides subsidies to its farmers as does the USA, but in a somewhat different way. Although not as important in this area as the USA and the EU, Japan also protects its farmers with heavy subsidies and difficult access to its markets. The First World disburses about $1billion dollars per day to its farmers, in one way or another, supplementing incomes in some sectors, providing cheap credits, or subsidizing exports, all of which distort the world market. For the EU, agriculture involves more than just the purely commercial side, namely landscape, environment, as well as cultural aspects, but for other countries, these arguments were added to up the ante.

---

2. Devinder Sharma, "World Food Supremacy, America's other war," *Deccan Herald*, 18 October 2001.

Besides the two foremost players, the United States and the European Union, the Cairns Group also plays an important role in these discussions. This Group consists of eighteen agricultural exporting countries, which account for one-third of the world's agricultural exports. As it happens, they are mostly opposed to the protective policies of the EU, while, strangely enough, the USA often sides with the Group. The Mercosur/l countries and its associated partners are members of this Group. Colombia, Costa Rica and Guatemala are the other Latin American members, although far less important economically. Among the other member states are Third World countries, such as South Africa, and Southeast Asian countries, like Indonesia, Malaysia, the Philippines, Thailand, but also Australia and New Zealand. Since its establishment in 1986, the Cairns Group has succeeded in putting agriculture on the multilateral trade agenda and keeping it there. It was largely as a result of the Group's efforts that a framework for reform in agricultural trade was established in the Uruguay Round and agriculture was for the first time subject to some trade liberalizing rules, set out in the WTO Agreement on agriculture.

In Qatar, agriculture was one of the toughest issues, nearly becoming a breaking point; especially as the EU was unwilling to even start discussions on subsidies. The French government was even more reluctant than usual to touch this topic, as there are elections next year. The Irish, Finnish and Germans backed the French position. In the end, the EU agreed to start discussions on agriculture, after it was agreed that the outcome could not be determined beforehand. Furthermore, the EU also put non-trade issues on the agenda for the coming round.

However, even if some progress was made, the big battle on agriculture has still to be fought. The final agreement reached at Doha provides possibilities for better access to American and European agricultural markets. Still, quite some ground will have to be covered before the Cairns Group and others interested in better market access for their agricultural produce will see some of their demands accepted. This might take many years, even if this new round is concluded by 2005 as scheduled, which seems improbable.

Patents

Another matter which set the First and the Third World against each other, and which was considered one of the toughest issues of the Doha meeting, was surprisingly settled in a manner acceptable to most parties: the issue of patents in the area of health.

The governments of South Africa and other African countries are fighting a desperate battle against AIDS. The government of Brazil has succeeded in controlling this disease, thanks to the use of generic medicines. For all these governments health and human lives have a greater priority than the huge profits the pharmaceutical companies enjoy. In this, they are supported by NGOs concerned with health. African countries do not produce generic medicine themselves, but both Brazil and India are able to produce good quality, cheap generic medicines. African countries are in need of cheap medicine, but access is restricted because of the TRIPs, the WTO agreement on patents and intellectual property. Kenya, for instance, might wish to buy a cheap generic drug in India to fight against infant pneumonia, but is not allowed to according to the TRIPs rule, and has to buy the five times more expensive American medicine at prices it cannot afford. As a consequence, this disease alone kills two million children each year—when their lives could have been saved easily. NGOs were recently joined by the Pope who stressed that human life was a fundamental human right and ought to be more important than profits and should therefore be placed first. However, U.S. companies make a net yearly profit of about $23 billion in the area of patents and intellectual property worldwide, so the stakes are very high. Pharmaceutical companies from the USA, Switzerland and some other European Union member states used their powerful lobbies to prevent an agreement that might have a negative influence on their profits. In the end an agreement was reached that gives governments the possibility to choose a cheaper alternative in case of a public health emergency. Part of the reason for the willingness of governments of some rich countries to make concessions must be sought in the recent anthrax outbreaks in the USA. The U.S. government appeared willing to weaken the stranglehold of the patent system in order to be assured of sufficient supplies at affordable prices. In the end the pharmaceutical company concerned was prepared to lower the prices of such products substantially, to avoid weakening the patent system. Only after being confronted with an emergency itself was the USA more conciliatory in negotiations in which Brazil was the major representative of the position adopted by about fifty Third World countries. Some NGOs estimated that the final Doha declaration did not go far enough in the area of health and human rights, but the official view of the Brazilian government argued that this declaration would achieve the desired result.

From a larger perspective it must be kept in mind that the number of patents is increasing at an alarming rate. Companies from Western countries have started patenting, amongst others, plants from tropical forests or remedies that have been used indigenously for centuries. This makes these remedies unaffordable, or even unobtainable in the Third World countries from where they originated. These patents are not based on original research, which patents were originally designed to protect. The Doha Meeting agreed to examine the relationship between the TRIPs Agreement and the Convention on Biological Diversity, the protection of traditional knowledge and folklore, but it remains to be seen what the result will be. Furthermore, companies sometimes change the composition of the original (natural) ingredients slightly, thereby obtaining patent protection for their product for many more years. Therefore we are confronted with a problem with wide ramifications that needs to be tackled as currently, cheaper medicines can only be used in case of a medical emergency. The division between rich and poor countries is most apparent in the area of the technological gap, in addition to the continuing brain drain. The First World makes abundant use of the brainpower of the South, with India having become especially famous as an able producer in the area of information technology. While in recent years there has been more talk about correcting the existing imbalances between North and South, and rich and poor, in reality the gaps are becoming wider, both between countries, but also within the population of countries themselves.

The Next "Round"

Many other topics were discussed and placed on the agenda for the coming years, such as the relationship between trade and investment and transparency in government procurement. However, care was taken to exclude other important topics such as the functioning of transnational companies. A number of well-known NGOs such as OXFAM were present in Doha during the meeting, but others, known to be vocal critics of the WTO, who are fighting for globalization with a human face, and criticizing the WTO for its lack of transparency and democratic procedures, were not allowed to enter Qatar. What was also surprising was the lack of coverage of the Doha meeting in the global media, despite its impact on the future global development. The (economic) prophets gathering in the desert of Doha did not make their voice heard, and this is not a good omen. Transparency, or rather lack of it, was not only an issue at Doha—

the Chinese government took great care to play down the implications of China's WTO accession on the Chinese economy as a whole, and its consequences for individual Chinese in particular.

At this Fourth WTO Ministerial Meeting, China became a full member of the WTO, as did Taiwan, which has the status of a customs union, increasing the number of WTO members to 144. Chinese membership has generally been welcome, but the impact on other Asian countries, in particular other giant developing countries such as India and also Brazil can only be judged years from now.

Although it is hazardous to venture predictions, one may notice that rich countries should gain greater access to Third World markets, while demands by India, supported by Pakistan, for a reduction of restrictions on their textile exports were refused. The WTO still needs to demonstrate that it is not just the rich men's club it is often made out to be. One of the jewels in the crown of the WTO, the Dispute Settlement Understanding, has lost its luster for quite a while now. Settlement procedures take place under heavy political pressure behind closed doors, and even if granted sanctions as a remedy for breaches of agreement by rich countries, sanctions by a poor country are likely to be shrugged off by its stronger adversary. A balanced development of the global economy cannot be achieved without democracy and greater transparency in global institutions being established to supervise the fair functioning of global markets.

Furthering Integration

It would be wrong to construe lines of division in the global economy in a simple manner as 'rich' against 'poor'. Competition among developing countries remains fierce, and the impact of WTO driven globalization may differ vastly in various parts of the world. As repeatedly stated by various contributors to this volume, competition encourages integration, but patterns of integration in (South) East Asia, Latin America, and Europe are highly dissimilar. In addition to the negotiations under WTO auspices, numerous other negotiations are taking place at bilateral and multilateral levels which will have repercussions for the WTO process. The Brazilian government has just started consultations with Japan on the creation of a Free Trade Area between that country and Mercosur/l. That would be the first free trade link between Mercosur/l and East Asia. Meanwhile, negotiations between Mercosur/l and the European Union are continuing, likely resulting in a Free Trade Area between these two blocs by 2005.

Incidentally, this is the same year for which the establishment of the FTAA has been scheduled. These are major developments, which receive little attention in the media.

Concerning the FTAA, Brazil prefers to negotiate within the WTO rather than within the FTAA framework. This is quite revealing of the nature of negotiations within the FTAA. There are expectations that the WTO process will make it easier for Brazil to deal with U.S. 'anti-dumping' measures and other, mostly non-tariff barriers restricting Brazilian exports to the USA. The USA did agree under much pressure to put anti-dumping on the WTO agenda, although getting results might be quite a different matter. Mexican membership in NAFTA has given some indication about the future workings of the FTAA, which the USA considers to be an extension of NAFTA.

Economic and political crises in Argentina weaken the hands of Mercosur/l, but even Chile, its associated member, seems to have decided now to support the consolidation of the Mercosur/l process. Regional integration, after all, seems an indispensable means to survive global competition. In Asia, the ASEAN Plus Three process does not rank as a road towards regional 'integration', rather it is set of procedures towards intra-regional cooperation, especially in the field of capital markets and the stabilization of regional currencies. Here, too, global competition is the driving factor behind strengthening regional cooperation. Unlike South America and Europe, strategic divisions, mainly between China and the USA, plus tensions on the Korean Peninsula, but also strategic competition between China and India, and the fluid security situation in Central and Southwest Asia, prevent the creation of a genuine regional identity, without which regional integration will remain a mere dream. The APEC meeting in Shanghai in October 2001 did give a new lease of life to that gathering, but its membership remains too diverse to contribute to the creation of an 'Asia-Pacific Community'. Perhaps its main function is to allow the USA to remain deeply involved in processes affecting moves towards regional integration in Asia.

Yet regional integration may also create new fault lines in international politics and economics. The EU looks as if it has awakened to the danger of the FTAA, therefore it plans to sign free trade agreements with all the different economic blocs of Latin America. Meanwhile, President Bush hopes to get the TPA (Trade Promotion Authority), the successor of the fast track procedure, he needs to add momentum to U.S. leadership in the drive towards the FTAA. The fact that Bush has focused almost exclusively on the fight against terrorism might not be helpful in times of rising unemployment. First indications are that if Bush does get the TPA, it will be conditional on the implementation of a considerable number of protectionist measures. These might reduce rather than enhance his negotiations powers and might also affect negatively the results of the WTO Round.

However, if successful, the FTAA has the potential to result in a mega-power, probably dominated by the USA, and would form, together with an enlarged EU, two blocs with an economic clout unrivalled on the globe. (South) East Asia would probably not be able to produce a similar bloc, in spite of its huge potential, in the short term.

Conclusion

Globalization is a multilayered affair, in which numerous institutional-ized negotiation processes coexist, sometimes rivaling, sometimes supple-menting each other. In addition to the WTO process, roughly two hun-dred new bilateral or multilateral agreements have been concluded re-cently, but the USA has participated in only about ten such agreements. This was one of the reasons why the USA put its full weight behind achiev-ing a minimal consensus at Doha to assure the WTO's increased leading role in the process of globalized competition and integration. There seem to be contradictory developments: improving general trade rules while fostering preferential trade agreements, which imply exceptions to the general rules. Trade agreements, monetary unions, the creation of new common markets and free trade areas, monetary cooperation such as ini-tiated in Asia, and other forms of preferential treatment, vie with each other. What does this imply for the future structure of the (economic) global order? Will this lead to the establishment of a series of 'islands' of very different sizes and power, in which the dividing lines between 'north' and 'south' may become quite different? A new form of integration has started: between countries from the First World and the Third World. The impact of these processes should be studied carefully. But, it must not be forgotten that a significant part of the global population, especially in the forty-eight poorest countries, the LDCs (Least Developed Countries), have no part in these new developments. The agreement by the EU to wave their debts by 2009 seems too little, too late. It remains to be seen if the notice the WTO takes of LDCs goes beyond official speeches. Quite apart from the human dimension of poverty, history has frequently shown the disastrous consequences of ignoring the suffering of the poor. The future will show whether mankind has internalized that lesson.

BIBLIOGRAPHY

"Dossier Alca," *Política Externa*, Vol. 5, n° 4 and Vol. 6, n° 1, Mar.–Aug. 1997, pp. 27–123.

Abbott, Frederick M., *China's Accession to the WTO*, available from: http://www.asil.org/insigh13.htm.

Abreu, Marcelo de Paiva, "Dossier Alca", *Política Externa*, Vol. 5, n° 4 and Vol. 6, n° 1, Mar.–Aug. 1997.

Agence Europe, "UE/Argentine/euro", 22 June 2001, p. 23.

Agence Europe, "UE/MERCOSUR: l'EU a presenté au Mercosur une offre pour la libéralisation du 90% de l'agriculture et 100% de l'industrie en dix ans", 5 July 2001.

Aguirre, Mariano, "Narcotrafic, l'alibi de Washington," *Manière de Voir* 36, Nov.–Dec. 1997, pp. 71–72.

Albuquerque, José Guilhon, ed., *ALCA: Relações Internacionais e sua construção jurídica*, São Paulo: FTD, 1998, 3 vols.

Almeida, Paulo Roberto de, *O Mercosul no contexto regional e internacional*, São Paulo: Aduaneiras, 1993.

Ambrose, Stephen E., *Rise to Globalism, American Foreign Policy since 1938*, New York: Penguin Books, 1985 (4th rev. ed.).

APEC, *Achieving the APEC Vision—Free and Open Trade in the Asia Pacific*, Singapore, Second Report of the Eminent Persons Group, Aug. 1994.

Baldwin, R., "The Political Economy of Postwar U.S. Trade Policy," in: *The Bulletin*, 4, New York: New York University, Center for the Study of Financial Institutions, 1976.

Bandeira, Moniz, *O eixo Argentina-Brasil: o processo de integração da América Latina*, Brasília: Editora da UnB, 1987.

Banega, Cyro, et al., "The New Regionalism in South America," in M. Schulz et al., ed., *Regionalization in a Globalized World: A Comparative Perspective on Forms, Actors and Processes*, London: Zed Books, 2001, pp. 234–249.

Bank of International Settlements, *Bank of International Settlements 71st Annual Report, 1 Apr. 2000–31 Mar. 2001*, Basle, 2001.

Beinstein, George, "Entre dettes et pillages, une économie a genoux", *Le Monde Diplomatique,* July 2001, pp. 12–13.

Belen, Balanya, *Europe Inc.: Regional and Global Restructuring and the Rise of Corporate Power*, London: Pluto Press, 2000.

Berthelot, Jacques, paper presented to the Symposium on issues confronting the world trading system, World Trade Organization–Geneva, July 6–7, 2001 (obtained from J. Berthelot, berthelot@ensat.fr.)

Bhagwati, J. and Hudec, R.E., eds., *Fair Trade and Harmonization*, Vol. I, Economic Analysis, Cambridge Mass., MIT Press 1996.

Bhagwati, J., "The Demands to Reduce Domestic Diversity among Trading Nations", in: J. Bhagwati and R.E. Hudec, eds., *Fair Trade and Harmonization,* pp. 9–41.

Bhagwati, J., "The Agenda of the WTO", in: Van Dijck and Faber, eds., *Challenges to ...*, pp. 27–61.

Bhagwati, J., Krishna, P.,and Pangariya, A., eds., *Trading Blocs,* Cambridge, Mass.: MIT Press, 1999.

Blowers, A. and Glasbergen, P., eds., *Environmental Policy in an International Context*, London: Arnold, 1996.

Bowring, Philip, "Foreign-Invested Enterprises Account for Half of China's Exports," *International Herald Tribune*, 29 June 2001.

Brown, Lester R., *Who Will Feed China?* Washington D.C.: World Watch Institute, 1996.

Browne, Harry, et al., *For Richer, For Poorer. Shaping US-Mexican Integration*, Albuquerque/London: Resource Center Press/Latin American Bureau, 1994.

Bulmer-Thomas, Victor, ed., *The New Economic Model in Latin America and its Impact on Income Distribution and Poverty*, London: Macmillan/ ILAS, 1996.

Business Roundtable, *The Case for U.S. Trade Leadership: The United States is Falling Behind,* Washington D.C., 9 February 2001.

Buve, Raymond y Wiesebron, Marianne L. eds., *Procesos de integración en América Latina: Perspectivas y experiencias latinoamericanas y europeas*, Amsterdam/Mexico: CEDLA/UIA, 1999.

Buzan, Barry, *People, States, and Fear: An Agenda for International Security Studies in the Post-Cold War Era*, 2d. ed., Boulder: Lynne Rienner, 1991.

Camargo, Sônia de, and Vasquez Ocampo, Jose, *Autoritarismo e Democracia na Argentina e Brasil: uma década de política exterior (1973–1984)*, São Paulo: Convívio, 1988.

Cammack, Paul, " 'The Mother of All Governments': The World Bank's Matrix for Global Governance", in S. Hughes and R. Wilkinson, eds., *Engaging Global Governance: Towards a New Agenda*, London: Routledge: forthcoming.

Cammack, Paul, "Interpreting ASEM: Interregionalism and the New Materialism", *Journal of the Asia Pacific Economy*, 4, 1, 1999, pp. 13–32.

Cammack, Paul, "Making Poverty Work", in *Socialist Register 2001*, Rendleshem: Merlin Press, forthcoming.

Cammack, Paul, "MERCOSUR: From Domestic Concerns to Regional Influence", in G. Hook and I. Kearns, eds., *Subregionalism and World Order*, Rendlesham: Merlin Press, 1999, pp. 95–115.

Cammack, Paul, and Richards, G.A., "Introduction: ASEM and Interregionalism," *Journal of the Asia Pacific Economy*, 4, 1, 1999, pp. 1–12.

Cardoso, Fernando Henrique, *Política Externa em tempos de mudança*, Brasilia: FUNAG/Ministério de Relações Exteriores, 1994.

Caroit, Jean-Marie, "L'initiative pour les Amériques fait des inquiets," *Manière de Voir* 36, Nov.–Dec. 1997, pp. 38–40.

Carrillo, Jorge, ed., *Mercados de trabajo en la industria maquiladora*, 2d. ed., Mexico: Plaza y Valdés, 2001.

Carrion, Raul & Vizentini Paulo, *Globalização, neoliberalismo, privatizações: quem decide este jogo?*, Porto Alegre: Ed. Universidade/UFRGS, 1997.

Carta capital, "MERCOSUL, um parceiro conveniente. A adesão do Peru traz novas oportunidades ao Brasil, apesar da turbulencia politica", Vol. II, No 50, 11 June, 1997.

Casadio, Gian Paolo, *Transatlantic Trade; USA-EEC Confrontation in the GATT Negotiations*, Farnborough: Hants Saxon House, 1973.

Cervo, Amado Luis, ed., *O desafio internacional: a política exterior do Brasil de 1930 a nossos dias*, Brasilia: Ed. UnB, 1994.

Chernick, Marc, "The Crisis of Human Rights in Colombia. It's Time to Internationalize the Peace Process", *LASA Forum*, XXVIII, 3, 1997, pp. 20–23.

Chia Siow Yue and Tan, J., eds., *ASEAN and EU—Forging New Linkages and Strategic Alliances*, Singapore: ISEAS, 1997.

China On Line, Available from: *http://www.chinaonline.com/issues/wto/currentnews/open/b200010520-SS.asp.*

China Statistic Bureau, "Analysis Report Foreign Trade," available from: http://www.stats.gov.cn/news/year50/year5013.htm.

Chomsky, Noam, *Year 501: The Conquest Continues,* Boston: South End Press, 1993.

Chossudovsky, Michel, "Au Coeur de la crise, le pillage. Recolonisation programmée au Brésil," *Le Monde Diplomatique,* Mar. 1999, p. 20.

Commission of the European Communities, *Perspectives and Priorities for the ASEM Process (Asia Europe Meeting) into the New Decade,* Brussels: Commission Working Document, COM (2000) 241 final, 18 Apr. 2000.

Commission of the European Communities, *The New WTO Round,* Brussels: Informal Discussion Paper for EU Trade Ministers, Berlin, 9–10 May, 1999.

Corden, W. Max, *Trade Policy and Economic Welfare,* Oxford: Clarendon Press, 1974.

Couffignal, Georges, "Mexíque. L'heure du pluralisme," in *L'état du Monde, 1998,* pp. 220–225.

Couffignal, Georges, ed., *Amérique Latine, tournant de siècle,* Paris: La Découverte, 1997.

Coyle, William, *The Impact of China and Taiwan Joining the WTO,* available from: http://www.econ.ag.gov/briefing/wto/Wang/wang.htm.

Declaración de Santiago, 20 de abril 1998, Santiago: Segunda Cumbre de las Américas, 18–19 Apr., 1998.

Deng, Zhihai, et al., eds., *Shimao zuzhi wenti jieda* [Questions and answers concerning the WTO], Beijing: Zhongguo duiwai jingji maoyi Publishers, 2000.

Dijck, Pitou van, and Faber, Gerrit, eds., *The External Economic Dimension of the European Union,* The Hague: Kluwer Law International, 2000.

Dijck, Pitou van, and Faber, Gerrit, "The EU in the World Economy: New Policies and Partnerships," in: P. van Dijck, and G. Faber, eds., *The External Economic Dimension ...,* pp. 1–51.

Dijck, Pitou van, "Meeting Asia and Latin America in a New Setting," in: P. van Dijck and G. Faber, eds., *The External Economic Dimension...,* pp. 293–319.

Dijck, Pitou van, and Faber, Gerrit, eds., *Challenges to the New World Trade Organization,* The Hague: Kluwer Law International, 1996.

Dijck, Pitou van, and Faber, Gerrit, "Introduction," in: P. van Dijck and G.Faber, eds., *Challenges to ...*, pp. 1–25.

Dijck, Pitou van, "NAFTA: A model for the WTO", in: P. van Dijck and G. Faber, eds., *Challenges to ...*, pp. 127–153.

Dijck, Pitou van, and Gerrit Faber, "After the Failure of Seattle: New Challenges to the EU", in: *European Foreign Affairs Review*, Vol. 5, 2000, pp. 217–355.

Dijk van, M.P. and S. Sideri, eds., *Multilateralism versus Regionalism: Trade Issues After the Uruguay Round*, London: Frank Cass, 1996.

Dombrowski, Peter and Rice, Tom, "Changing Identities and International Relations Theory: a Cautionary Note," in *Nationalism and Ethnic Politics*, Vol.6, No.4 (Winter 2000), pp. 83–105.

Drysdale, Peter, Elek, A. and House, B., "Europe and East Asia: A Shared Global Agenda?" in: P. Drysdale and D. Vines, eds., *Europe, East Asia and APEC—A Shared Global Agenda?*, Cambridge: Cambridge University Press, 1998.

Drysdale, Peter and Ligang, Song, eds., *China's Entry to the WTO: Strategic Issues and Quantitative Assessments*, London, New York: Routledge 2000.

Economic Commission for Latin America and the Caribbean (ECLAC), *Preliminary Overview of the Economies of Latin America and the Caribbean 1999*, Santiago: ECLAC, 1999.

Economic Commission for Latin America and the Caribbean (ECLAC), *Foreign Investment in Latin America and the Caribbean 1998*, and *1999*, Santiago: ECLAC, 1998 and 1999.

Economic Daily, 20 February 2000.

Economist, The, "All Goods Must Slow Down," 7 March 1998, pp. 71–72.

Economist, The, "Argentina's Economic Crises. Austerity or Bust," 21 July 2001, p. 43.

Economist, The, "Brazil's Foreign Policy: Southern Crossroads," 26 August 2000, p. 44.

Economist, The, "Breaking Foreign Policy Taboos," 26 August 2000, pp. 43–44.

Economist, The, "Chile. Battening Down," 4 July 1998, p. 54.

Economist, The, "Dirt Poor. A Survey of Development and the Environment," 21 March 1998.

Economist, The, "Ecuador, Now the Hard Part," 18 July 1998, pp. 54–55.

Economist, The, "Ecuador, Still Fragile," 2 September 2000 p. 52.

Economist, The, "It's all Chávez," 4 July 1998, pp. 54–55.

Economist, The, "Mexico's Once-Ruling Party Faces the Shock of Opposition," 15 July 2000, pp. 55–56.

Economist, The, "Paraguay, Deadlock" and "A Message from the People," 12 December 1998, pp. 63–64.

Economist, The, "The Gringos Land in Colombia," 2 September 2000, p. 51–52.

Economist, The, "The War of 1898," 3 January 1998, pp. 48–50.

Economist, The, "To Decertify or not," 21 February 1998, p. 14.

Economist, The, "Zedillo's Legacy to Fox," 9 September 2000, pp. 71–72.

Economist, The, 26 April 1997.

Economist, The, 9 November 1996.

Eichengreen, B., *Globalizing Capital: A History of the International Monetary System,* Princeton: Princeton University Press, 1996.

Eicher, L., "Technical regulations and standards," in: J.M. Finger and A. Olechowski, eds., *The Uruguay Round; A Handbook on the Multilateral Trade Negotiations,* Washington, D.C.: The World Bank, 1987, pp. 137–143.

España, Iñigo de Palácio, and Vizentini, Paulo, eds., *Seminário União Européia-Mercosul: Acordo Marco Inter-Regional de Cooperação,* Porto Alegre: Presidência Espanhola da União Européia, 1996.

Estado de São Paulo, "O discurso de FHC na França," 30 October 2001.

Esty, Daniel C., *Greening the GATT,* Washington, D.C.: Institute for International Economics, 1994.

État du Monde 1993, L'Annuaire économique et géopolitique mondial, Paris, La Découverte, 1992.

État du Monde 1998, L'Annuaire économique et géopolitique mondial, Paris: La Découverte, 1997.

État du Monde 1999, L'Annuaire économique et géopolitique mondial, Paris: La Découverte, 1998.

État du Monde 2000, L'Annuaire économique et géopolitique mondial, Paris: La Découverte, 1999.

Europa-América Latina: 20 años de documentos oficiales (1976–1996), Madrid: IRELA 1996.

Evans, J.W., *The Kennedy Round in American Trade Policy: The Twilight of the GATT?,* Cambridge, Mass: MIT Press, 1971.

Faber, Gerrit, "International Trade and Environmental Policies", in: A. Blowers and P. Glasbergen, eds., *Environmental ...,* pp. 79–105.

Faber, Gerrit, "Towards a Pan-European-Mediterranean Free Trade Area?" in: P. van Dijck and G. Faber, eds., *The External Economic...*, pp. 245–271.

Fawcett, Louise and Hurrell, Andrew, eds., *Regionalism in World Politics*, Oxford University Press, 1995.

Fawcett, Louise, "Regionalism in Historical Perspective," in L. Fawcett and A. Hurrell, eds., *Regionalism in World Politics*.

Feghali, Jandira, "Neoliberalismo no Brasil: as reformas da Previdência, Administrativa e da Saúde", in R. Carrion and P. Vizentini, *Globalização, neoliberalismo ...*, pp. 254–296.

Fewsmith, Joseph, *China and the WTO: The Politics behind the Agreement*, the National Bureau of Asian Research, available from: http://www.nbr.org/publications/report.htm.

Finger, J. Michael and Olechowski, A., eds., *The Uruguay Round; A Handbook on the Multilateral Trade Negotiations*, Washington, D.C.: World Bank, 1987.

Finger, J. Michael and Winters, L. Allan, "What Can the WTO Do for Developing Countries', in: A. Krueger, ed., *The WTO as an International Organization*, Chicago: University of Chicago Press, 1998, pp. 365–397.

Fischer, T.C., *The United States, the European Union, and the "Globalization" of World Trade*, Westport, CT and London: Quorum Books, 2000.

Florêncio, Sérgio Abreu, e Lima and Araújo, Ernesto Henrique Fraga *Mercosul hoje*, São Paulo: Alfa-Omega, 1996.

Fonseca Junior, Gelson, and Castro, Sérgio Nabuco de, eds., *Temas de Política Externa Brasileira II*, São Paulo: Paz e Terra, 1994. 2 vols.

Foroutan, Faezeh, "Does Membership in A Regional Preferential Trade Arrangement Make a Country More or Less Protectionist?" working paper, World Bank, April 1998, at *www.worldbank.org/html/dec/Publications/Workpapers/WPS1800series/wps1898/wps1898.pdf*.

Frankel, Jeffrey A., and Wei, Shang-Jin, "The New Regionalism and Asia: Impact and Options," in: A. Panagariya, M.G. Quibria and N.Rao, eds., *The Global Trading System ...*, pp. 94–104.

Fujime, Kazuya, "Long-term Outlook of Energy Supply and Demand in East Asia", paper presented to the International Symposium on APEC Cooperation for Sustainable Development held on June 18–19 1997, organized by Institute of Developing Economies, Tokyo, 1997.

Gaceta mercantil, "Sul-americanos formam bloque para enfrentar Alca," 10 July 2001.

Gaceta mercantil, 10 July 2001.

Gamble, Andrew and Payne, Anthony, eds., *Regionalism and World Order*, London: Macmillan, 1996.

Gansler, J.S., *Affording Defense*, MIT Press, Cambridge, MA. 1989.

Garcia Munhoz, Dércio, "As reformas e as mudanças na Previdência Social," in R. Carrion & P. Vizentini, *Globalização, neoliberalismo ...*, pp. 241–253.

GATT, *The Results of the Uruguay Round of Multilateral Trade Negotiations, The Legal Texts*, Geneva: GATT, 1994.

Gilpin, Robert, in D. Unger and P. Blackburn eds., *Japan's Global Role*, Boulder: Lynne Rienner, 1993.

Gowan, P., *The Global Gamble: Washington's Faustian Bid for World Dominance*, London: Verso, 1999.

Green, Duncan, *Silent Revolution. The Rise of Market Economics in Latin America*, London: Latin American Bureau, 1995.

Gresh, Alain, "L'ombres des inégalités," *Le Monde Diplomatique*, Sept., 1997, p. 1.

Grieco, Joseph M., "Systemic Sources of Variation in Regional Institutionalization in Western Europe, East Asia and the Americas," in E.D. Mansfield,. and H.V. Milner, eds., *The Political Economy ...*, pp. 164–185.

Grimwade, Nigel, *International Trade Policy*, London: Routledge, 1996.

Groombridge, Mark A., *Tiger by the Tail: China and the World Trade Organization*, Washington, D.C.: AEI Press, 1999.

Grossman, G.M. and Helpman E., *Protection for Sale*, CEPR Discussion Paper No. 827; 1993.

Gruber, Lloyd, *Ruling the World. Power Politics and the Rise of Supranational Institutions*. Princeton: Princeton University Press, 2000.

Grugel, Jean, "Latin America and the Remaking of the Americas," in A. Gamble and A. Payne eds., *Regionalism ...*, pp. 131–167.

Guimarães, Samuel Pinheiro, ed., *ALCA e Mercosul: riscos e oportunidades para o Brasil*. Brasilia: IPRI/FUNAG/MRE, 1999.

Guimarães, Samuel Pinheiro, ed., *Estratégias Índia e Brasil*, Brasília: Instituto de pesquisa de Relações Internacionais/Fundação Alexandre Gusmão, 1997.

Guimarães, Samuel Pinheiro, *Quinhentos anos de periferia*, Porto Alegre/ Rio de Janeiro: Ed. da Universidade/UFRGS/ Contraponto, 1999.

Haggard, Stephan, *Developing Nations and the Politics of Global Integration*, Washington: The Brookings Institutions, 1995.

Haggard, Stephan, *The Political Economy of the Asian Financial Crisis*, Washington: Institute of International Economics, 2001.

Het Financiële Dagblad, 25 April 2000.

Hooghe, Ingrid d', "Het ASEM-forum en de samenwerking tussen Azië en Europa: is er toekomst voor de politieke dialoog?" *Internationale Spectator*, jaargang 55, nr 6, June 2001, pp. 324–328.

Hook, G. and Kearns, I., *Subregionalism and World Order*, London: Macmillan, 1999.

Hosono, Akio, "Ratenamerika Chiiki to Kokusai Shihon-ido (International Capital Movements and Latin America), in *Kaigaitoshi Kenkyujo Ho*, Tokyo: Research Institute for International Investment and Development, Nov. 1996.

Hou, Shusen, *WTO gei zhongguo baixing dailai sheme?* [How will the WTO affect ordinary Chinese people?], Beijing: Jingji Ribao Publishers, 2000.

      http://www.chinamarket.com.cn.

      http://www.chinaonline.com/issues/wto/currentnews/open/ b200010520-SS.asp.

      http://www.stats.gov.cn/news/year50/year5013.htm.

      http://www.stats.gov.cn/news/year50/year5013.htm.

Hudec, R.E., *Enforcing International Trade Law: The Evolution of the Modern GATT Legal System*, Salem, NH: Butterworth Legal Publishers, 1993.

Hufbauer, G.C. and J. Schott, *Western Hemisphere Economic Integration*, Washington, D.C.: Institute for International Economics, 1994.

Hughes, S. and Wilkinson, R., eds., *Engaging Global Governance: Towards a New Agenda*, London: Routledge, forthcoming.

Hurrell, Andrew, "Regionalism in Theoretical Perspective," in Louise Fawcett and Andrew Hurrell, eds., *Regionalism in World Politics*.

IMF, *Direction of Trade Statistics Yearbook*, Washington D.C.: IMF., 1992 to 1998.

Institute of Developing Economies (JETRO*)*, *The Study on Industrial Networks in Asia*, Mexico/Tokyo: IDE/JETRO, 2000.

Inter-American Development Bank (IDB), *Integration and Trade in the Americas*, Periodic Note, Washington D.C.: IDB, Dec. 1997.

International Business Daily, 15 February 2001.

International Herald Tribune, The, "Brazil Braces for Phone Firm Sale", 27 July 1998.

IRELA (Institute for European-Latin American Relations), *Prospects for an EU-MERCOSUR Free Trade Agreement and US Policy Options*, Madrid: Irela Special Report, Nov. 1999.

IRELA, "Constructing the Free Trade Area of the Americas: A European Perspective," Brussels: Irela Briefing BRF 97/3–FTAA, 19 June 1997, pp. 1–8.

IRELA, *Economic Relations between Mercosur and the EU: Prospects for the Lomé Decade*, Madrid: Irela Special Report, 22 November 1999.

IRELA, *Mercosur: Prospects for an Emerging Bloc*, Brussels: Irela Dossier 61, Aug. 1997.

ISTOÉ, "Mississipi brasileiro," 5 August 1998, pp. 55–57.

ISTOÉ, "Um gosto amargo de saquê Recessão no Japão reduzira expansão econômica do mundo para 2.4%. Brasil terá de buscar novos mercados," 24 June 1998, pp. 108–110.

James, H., *International Monetary Cooperation since Bretton Woods*, New York: Oxford University Press, 1996.

Japan External Trade Organization, *JETRO White Paper on Foreign Direct Investment 1999*, Tokyo: JETRO, 1999.

Japan International Cooperation Agency (JICA), *The Country Study for Japan's Official Development Assistance to the Republic of Peru*, Tokyo: The Committee on the Country Study for Japan's Official Development Assistance to the Republic of Peru, Nov. 1998.

Kagami, Mitsuhiro and Masatsugu Tsuji, eds., *Privatization, Deregulation and Economic Efficiency. A Comparative Analysis of Asia, Europe and the Americas,* Tokyo, Japan: Institute of Developing Economies, Japan External Trade Organization, 1999.

Kagami, Mitsuhiro and Masatsugu Tsuji, eds., *Privatization, Deregulation and Economic Efficiency: A Comparative Analysis of Asia, Europe and the Americas*, Aldershot: Edward Elgar Publishing Ltd., 2000.

Kagami, Mitsuhiro, "Europe and Asia: Too Faraway?" in: P. van Dijck and G. Faber, eds., *The External Economic Dimension ...*, pp. 341–353.

Kagami, Mitsuhiro, *The Voice of East Asia: Development Implications for Latin America*, Tokyo: JETRO, 1995.

Kahle, Günter, "Grundprobleme der Integration in Lateinamerika seit der Unabhängigkeit (1810–1948), in M. Mols, *Integration und Kooperation ...*, pp. 27–51.

Karlsson, Weine and Malaki, Akhil, *Growth, Trade and Integration in Latin America*, Stockholm: Institute of Latin American Studies, 1997.

Kerremans Bart and Switky Bob, eds., *The Political Importance of Regional Trading Blocs*, Aldershot: Ashgate, 2000.

Kikuchi, Tsutomu, "ASEAN Plus Three Backgrounds and Tasks," *Kokusai Mondai* (Japan Institute of International Affairs), May 2001. (in Japanese).

Kopinak, Kathryn, *Desert Capitalism: what are the maquiladoras?*, Montreal/New York/ London: Black Rose Books, 1997.

Krueger, A., ed., *The WTO as an International Organization*, Chicago: University of Chicago Press, 1998.

La Sociedad Civil del Mercosur y Chile en la Asociación con la Unión Europea, Santiago: CELARE, 2000.

Lake, David A. and Morgan, Patrick M., *Regional Orders: Building Security in a New World*, Pennsylvania: The Pennsylvania University Press, 1997.

Laredo, Iris M., ed., *Estado, Mercado y Sociedad en el Mercosur*, Rosario: Universidad Nacional de Rosario, 1996/2000, 6 vols.

Leebron, D.W., "Lying Down with Procrustes: An Analysis of Harmonization Claims," in: J. Bhagwati and R.E. Hudec, eds., *Fair Trade and ...*, pp. 41–118.

Lemoine, Maurice, "Au Coeur de la plus vielle guerilla d'Amérique latine. En Colombie, une nation, deux états," *Le Monde Diplomatique*, May 2000, pp. 18–19.

Lemoine, Maurice, *Les 100 Portes de l'Amérique Latine*, Paris: Les Editions de l'Atelier, 1997.

Lousada, Manuel, "Normas e barreira técnicas: um campo de cooperação," in S.P. Guimarães, ed., *Estratégias Índia e Brasil ...*, pp. 555–561.

Lovett, William Anthony, et al., *U.S. Trade Policy: History, Theory, and the WTO*, N.Y.: Armonk, M.E. Sharpe, 1999.

Lozano, Claudio, "Los efectos del ajuste neoliberal: bloque dominante, desempleo y pobreza en la Argentina actual," in R. Carrion and P. Vizentini, *Globalização, neoliberalismo, privatizações ...*, pp. 148–169.

Mansfield, Edward D and. Milner, Helen V., ed., *The Political Economy of Regionalism*, New York: Columbia University Press, 1997.

Markusen, A.R. and Costigan, S.S., eds., *Arming the Future: A Defense Industry for the 21st Century*, New York: Council on Foreign Relations Press, 1999.

Martins, Luciano, et al., "ALCA: uma pauta para discussão," in "Dossier ALCA," *Política Externa,* Vol. 5, n° 4 and Vol. 6, no 1, Mar.–Aug. 1997.

Mathis, James H., "The Community's External Regional Policy in the WTO," in: P. van Dijck and G. Faber, eds., *The External Economic Dimension ...,* pp. 127–151.

Mayer, Frederick W., *Interpreting NAFTA: The Science and Art of Political Analysis,* New York: Columbia Press University, 1998.

McNaugher, T.L., *New Weapons, Old Politics: America's Military Procurement Muddle,* Washington D.C.: Brookings Institution, 1989.

Medeiros, Marcelo de Almeida, "Relações Exteriores do Mercosul: uma abordagem brasileira," in *Revista Brasileira de Política Internacional,* Vol. 38, n° 2, 1995.

MERCOSUL: acordos e protocolos na área jurídica, Porto Alegre: Livraria do Advogado, 1996.

Mercosul: Legislação e Textos Básicos, Brasília: Senado Federal, 1996 (2d ed,).

Mestries, Francis, "Mexique," in *L'Etat du Monde,* 2000, pp. 377–383.

Middlemas, Keith, *Orchestrating Europe. The Informal Politics of European Union 1973–1995,* London: Fontana Press, 1995.

Ministry of Foreign Affairs, *Official Development Assistence: Annual Report 1996,* Tokyo: MFA, 1997.

Ministry of Foreign Trade and Economic Cooperation (MOFTEC-Beijing), *Statistic Data,* available from: http://www.moftec.gov.cn/htm/government/data_trade.

Ministry of Foreign Trade and Economic Cooperation, "Economic and Trade News," 2 February 2000, available from: http://www.chinamarket.com.cn.

Ministry of Trade and Industry (Tokyo), *Japan Trade White Book,* Years 1955–1975, Tokyo: MITI.

Mitra, D., "Endogenous Lobby Formation and Endogenous Protection: A Long-Run Model of Trade Policy Determination," in: *American Economic Review,* Vol. 89, no. 5, 1999, pp. 1116–1135.

Mols, Manfred, *Integration und Kooperation in Lateinamerika,* Paderborn: Ferdinand Schöningh, 1981.

Moussis, Nicholas, *Access to European Union, Laws, Economics, Policies,* Genval: EDIT-EUR, 1999 (9th rev. ed.).

Nagarajan, N., *The Millennium Round: An Economic Appraisal,* Economic Papers, Number 139, ECFIN/659/99–Rev. EN, European Commission, Brussels, Nov. 1999.

Nishijima, Shoji and Smith, Peter H., ed., *Cooperation or Rivalry? Regional Integration in the Americas and the Pacific Rim*, Boulder: Westview Press, 1996.

Noland, M., *Pacific Basin Developing Countries, Prospects for the Future*, Washington, D.C .: Institute for International Economics, 1990.

NRC-Handelsblad, "Tanend enthousiasme voor Amerikaanse vrijhandel," 18 April 1998.

NRC-Handelsblad, "Zuid-Amerika boert nu achteruit," 4 September 2000.

Ogus, A, *Regulation. Legal Form and Economic Theory*, Oxford: Oxford University Press, 1994.

Oldsman, Eric, *Making Business Development Work: Lessons from the Enterprise Development Center in Rafaela, Argentina*, Best Practices Series, Washington D.C.: Inter-American Development Bank, 2000.

Orme, Jr., William A., *Understanding NAFTA: Mexico, Free Trade and the New North America*, Austin: University of Texas Press, 1996.

Ostry, S., *Reinforcing the WTO*, Group of Thirty. Occasional Paper No. 56. Washington D.C. 1998.

Palam, R. and Abbot, J., *State Strategies in the Global Political Economy*, London: Printer, 1999.

Panagariya, A., Quibria, M. G., and Rao, N., eds., *The Global Trading System and Developing Asia*, Oxford: Oxford University Press, 1997.

Panitch, Leo and Leys, Colin, eds., *Global Capitalism versus Democracy: Socialist Register 1999*, Rendlesham: Merlin Press, 1999.

Panitch, Leo, "Rethinking the Role of the State," in J. Mittelman, ed., *Globalization: Critical Perspectives*, Boulder, Co: Lynne Rienner, 1996, pp. 83–113.

Pánuco-Laguette, Humberto and Székely, Miguel, "Income Distribution and Poverty in Mexico," in V. Bulmer-Thomas, ed., *The New Economic Model in Latin America ...*, pp. 185–222.

Papas, Leslie, and Macleod, Lijia, "The Numbers Game," *Newsweek*, 24 January 2000.

Pape, Wolfgang, *Models of Integration in Asia and Europe: Generating Public Space for our Common Futures*. Report from the seminar jointly organized by the Forward Studies Unit of the European Commission and the Institute for the Integrated Studies of Future Generations, Kyoto, held from 19 to 21 October 1999 in Brussels, Copyright: European Communities, 2001.

Paradiso, José, et al., *Política externa na América do Sul*, São Paulo: Fundação Konrad Adenauer, 2000.

Pastore, Mario, "Democracy, Defense, Integration and Development. A Long Run View of Latin America," *LASA Forum*, XXVII, 3, 1996.

Payne, Anthony and Gamble, Andrew, "Introduction: The Political Economy of Regionalism and World Order," in A. Gamble and A. Payne, eds., *Regionalism* ..., pp. 1–20.

Payne, Anthony, "The United States and its Enterprise for the Americas,, in A. Gamble and A. Payne, eds., *Regionalism* ..., pp. 93–129.

Peck, Merton J. and Scherer, F.M., *The Weapons Acquisition Process: An Economic Analysis*, Cambridge, MA: Harvard University Press, 1962.

Pelkmans, Jacques, "A Bond in Search of More Substance: Reflections on the EU's ASEAN Policy," in: Chia Siow Yue and J. Tan, eds., *ASEAN and EU—Forging New Linkages* ..., Singapore: ISEAS, 1997.

Pelkmans, Jacques, *European Integration. Methods and Economic Analysis*, Harlow: Addison Wesley Longman, 1997.

People's Daily (Beijing), 2 February 2000.

People's Daily (Beijing), 17 January 2001.

Peschard-Sverdrup, A.B., "The U.S.-Mexico Fresh Winter Tomato Trade Dispute: the Broader Implications," *Entrecaminos*, Vol. 2., Spring 1997, pp. 51–66.

Pietschmann, Horst, "Integration und Bürokratie," in M. Mols, ed., *Integration und* ..., pp. 60–74.

Pischel, Gerhard, "Trade, Treaties and Treason: Some Underlying Aspects of the Difficult Relationship Between the EU and the WTO," in *European Foreign Affairs Review*, vol. 6, No. 1, Spring 2001, pp. 103–133.

Plá, Juan Algorta, ed., *O Mercosul e a Comunidade Européia: uma abordagem comparativa,* Porto Alegre: Ed. da Universidade/UFRGS, Instituto Goethe/ICBA, 1994.

Prolongeau, Hubert et Rampal, Jean-Christophe, "En Amérique Latine, l'industrie des enlèvements," *Le Monde Diplomatique*, Nov. 1997, p. 3.

Prolongeau, Hubert, "Violences dans les rues et dans les têtes," *Manière de Voir* 36, Nov.–Dec. 1997, pp. 68–70.

Przeworski, A. and Vreeland, J.R., "The Effect of IMF Programs on Economic Growth," *Journal of Development Economics,* Vol. 62, Issue 2, Aug. 2000, pp. 385–421.

Rapoport, Mario y Musacchio, Andrés, eds., *La Comunidad europea y el Mercosur: una evaluación comparada*, Buenos Aires: Fundación Konrad Adenauer/ FIHES, 1993.

Reiterer, Michael, "ASEM–The Third Summit in Seoul 2000: A Roadmap to Consolidate the Partnership between Asia and Europe," in *European Foreign Affairs Review*, Vol.6, No.1, Spring 2001, pp.1–30.

Relaciones America Latina-Union Europea: nuevas perspectivas. Documentación de base, Santiago: CELARE, 1995.

Revelli, Philippe, "La résistance des 'sans terres' du Brésil," *Le Monde Diplomatique*, Sept. 1997, pp. 14–15.

Rizzo Romano, Alfredo, y Melo, Artemio Luis, eds., *Las relaciones Argentina-Estados Unidos (1983–1993)*, Rosário: Homo Sapiens, 1993.

Rood, Jan, "Transatlantic Economic Relations in a New Era," in: P. van Dijck and G. Faber, eds., *The External Economic Dimension ...*, pp. 177–195.

Rosen, Daniel H., *China and WTO: An Economic Balance Sheet*, available from: http://www.iie.com/NEWSLETTER/news99-6.htm.

Ruigrok, Winfried and Tulder, Rob van, *The Logic of International Restructuring*, 1995, London: Routledge,

Ruttley, P.L., Mac Vey, I. and George, C., eds., *The WTO and International Trade Regulation*, London: Cameron May, 1998.

Saavedra-Rivano, Neandro, "Chile and Regional Integration," in Shoji Nishijima and Peter H. Smith, ed., *Cooperation or Rivalry ...*, pp. 97–111.

Sampson, Gary P., *Trade, Environment, and the WTO: the post-Seattle Agenda*, Washington, D.C.: Overseas Development Council; Baltimore: Johns Hopkins University Press, 2000.

Sanger, David, "A Great Bargain," *Foreign Affairs*, Vol. 80, No. 1, Jan./ Febr. 2001, pp. 65–75.

Scammel, W.M., *International Monetary Policy*, Second Edition, London: MacMillan, 1961.

Schulz, Michael, Söderbaum, Fredrik and Öjendal, Joakim, eds., *Regionalization in a Globalized World: a Comparative Perspective on Forms, Actors and Processes*, London: Zed Books, 2001.

Segal, Gerald, "Does China matter?" *Foreign Affairs*, Vol. 78, No. 9/10, 1999.

Sharma, Devinder, "World Food Supremacy, America's other war," *Deccan Herald*, 18 October 2001.

Shrybman, Steven, *The World Trade Organization: a Citizen's Guide*, Ottawa/Toronto: The Canadian Centre for Policy Alternatives/James Lorimer and Co. Ltd., 1999.

Skidmore, Thomas E. and Smith, Peter H., *Modern Latin America*, New York/Oxford: Oxford University Press, 1997 (4th ed.).

Slaughter, M.J., *Global Investment, American Returns. Mainstay III: A Report on the Domestic Contributions of American Companies with Global Operations.* Washington D.C.: Emergency Committee for the American Trade, 1998.

Smith, M. and S. Woolcock, "European Commercial Policy: A Leadership Role in the New Millennium?" in: *European Foreign Affairs Review*, Vol. 4, No. 3, 1999, pp. 439–462.

Solingen, Etol, "Economic Liberalization, Political Coalitions, and Emerging Regional Orders," in D.A. Lake and P.M. Morgan, *Regional Orders ...*, pp. 68–100.

Solinger, Dorothy J., "Globalization and the Paradox of Participation: The Chinese case," in *Global Governance*, Vol.2, 2, Apr.-June 2001, pp. 173–196.

Solís, Mireya, *Mexico and Japan: The Opportunities of Free Trade*, Study prepared for Subsecretaría de Negociaciones Comerciales e Internacionales, Mexico: SECOFI, Apr. 2000.

Southern Africa and Mercosur/l: Reviewing the Relationship and Seeking Opportunities, Seminar Report, Oct. 2000, Johannesburg: Konrad Adenauer Stiftung, 2000.

Srinivasan, T.N., "International Trade and Labour Standards from an Economic Perspective," in: P. van Dijck and G. Faber, eds., *Challenges ...*, pp. 219–245.

Steger, D.P., "WTO Dispute Settlement," in: P.L. Ruttley, I. Mac Vey and C, George, eds., *The WTO and International Trade Regulation*, London: Cameron May, 1998.

Stern, R. and B. Hoekman, "The Codes Approach," in: J.Michael and A. Olechowski, eds., *The Uruguay Round...*, pp. 59–69.

Stiglitz, Joseph, "What I Learned at the World Economic Crisis," *The New Republic* (www.thenewrepublic.com/041700/stiglitz041700.html), 17 April 2000.

Takahashi, Yasuo, *Shin sekai chitujo*, Tokyo: Soogoo hoorei Publishers, 1999.

The Financial Times, 20 March 2001, 23 July 2001.

Thurow, Lester, *Yomiuri Shinbun*, 25 April 2000.

Tims, W., "New Standards in World Trade Agreements: Two Bridges too Far. A Comment," in: P. van Dijck and G. Faber, eds., *Challenges ...*, pp. 307–317.

Transatlantic Business Dialogue, *CEO Conference Briefing Book*, Cincinnati, 1999.

Tratado de Libre Comercio de América del Norte, Texto oficial, Mexico: SECOFI, 1994.

Tsuji, Masatsugu, Sanford Berg and Michael Pollitt, *Private Initiatives in Infrastructure: Priorities, Incentives and Performance*, Tokyo: JETRO, 2000.

Unger, D. and Blackburn, P., eds., *Japan's Global Role*, Boulder: Lynne Rienner, 1993.

Valadaõ, Alfredo, "Ordem Mundial: a estrátegia da lagosta," in *L'Etat du Monde 1993, Annuaire économique et géopolitique mondial*, Paris: La Découverte, 1992, p. 22.

Ventura Dias, V., "Managing Access to Markets: the EU and Latin America," in: P. van Dijck and G. Faber, eds., *The External Economic Dimension ...*, pp. 319–341.

Verdier, D., *Democracy and International Trade: Britain, France and the United States*, Princeton: Princeton University Press, 1994.

Viner, Jacob, "Conflicts of Principle in Drafting a Trade Charter," in: *Foreign Affairs*, July 1947, Vol. 25, no. 4, pp. 612–628.

Vizentini, Paulo and Rodrigues, Gabriela, *O dragão chinês e os tigres asiáticos*, Porto Alegre: Novo Século, 2000.

Vizentini, Paulo, "A Ascenção da Ásia Oriental e sua Projeção Internacional: novas dimensões do desenvolvimento e segurança," *Ciências & Letras*, FAPA 19, Aug. 1997.

Vizentini, Paulo, "Brazil-Asia Relations and their Perspectives," *IIAS Newsletter*, 16, Summer 1998, p. 4.

Vizentini, Paulo, "Mercosul: A Brazilian Strategy towards the World Reorganization," in M.L. Wiesebron, ed., *Mercosul: facing a New Millenium*.

Vizentini, Paulo, *A política externa do regime militar brasileiro. Multilateralização, desenvolvimento e construção de uma potência média (1964–1985)*, Porto Alegre: Ed. da Universidade/UFRGS, 1998.

Vogel, D., *Trading Up; Consumer and Environmental Regulation in a Global Economy*, Cambridge, Mass.: Harvard University Press, 1995.

Ward, John, *Latin America, Development and Conflict*, London/New York: Routledge, 1997.

Wiemann, J., "Green Protectionism: A Threat to Third World Exports?" in: P. van Dijk and S. Sideri, eds., *Multilateralism versus Regionalism ...*, pp. 91–120.

Wiesebron, Marianne L., ed., *Mercosul: facing a New Millenium*, Leiden/ The Hague: Leiden University/Clingendael Institute, 1999.

Wiesebron, Marianne L., ed., *Brasil 500 anos. Recent developments and perspectives*, Leiden/The Hague: Leiden University/Clingendael Institute, 2000.

Wiesebron, Marianne L., "Brazilian Democracy at a Municipal Level," in M.L. Wiesebron, ed., *Brasil 500 anos*, pp. 27–40.

Wilkinson, Rorden, *Multilateralism and the World Trade Organization: The Architecture and Extension of International Trade Regulation*, London and New York: Routledge, 2001.

Winters, L. Allan, "Trade and Poverty: Is There a Connection?" in: *WTO, Trade, Income Disparity and Poverty*, Special Studies 5, Geneva: WTO 2000 (taken from the internet).

Witker, Jorge, "Evaluación de los aspectos jurídicos del Tratado de Libre Comercio en América del Norte," in R. Buve and M.L. Wiesebron, eds., *Procesos de integración ...*, pp. 80–89.

World Bank, The, "Development and the Environment," in: *World Development Report 1992*, Oxford: Oxford University Press, 1992.

World Bank, The, *2000 World Bank Atlas*, Oxford: Oxford University Press.

World Bank, The, *The East Asian Miracle—Economic Growth and Public Policy*, Oxford: Oxford University Press, 2000.

World Bank, The, *World Development Report 1998–1999*, Oxford: Oxford University Press, 1999.

World Bank, The, *World Development Report 1999–2000*, Oxford: Oxford University Press, 2000.

World Trade Organization, *Annual Report* 1997 and 2000, Geneva: WTO Secretariat.

Wouters, Mieke, "De vermoorde Democratie. Colombia zoekt internationale bemiddeling bij conflict," *ALERTA*, No. 238, Oct. 1997, pp. 12–23.

Yamazawa Ippei (chief researcher) Research Report, *21seiki no nikkan keizai kankei wa ika ni arubeki ka* [Proposals for Japanese-Korean Relations in the Twenty-first Century], Nihon booeki shinkookai- Ajia keizai kenkyuujo, 2000.

Yoonosuke, Hara, *Ajiagata keizai shisutemu*, Chuuoo kooron Shinsha, 2000 [Chuukoo shinsho, 1555].

Zhi, Wang, "The Impact of China's WTO Entry on the World Labor-Intensive Export Market: A Recursive Dynamic CGE Analysis," *World Economy*, 22, 3, May 1999, pp. 379–405.

ABOUT THE AUTHORS

Paul Cammack is Professor of Government at the University of Manchester, UK. He specializes in Latin American and comparative politics, and international political economy, and has recently been working on the political economy of comparative regionalism in East and Southeast Asia and Latin America. He is the author of *Capitalism and Democracy in the Third World*, London: Cassell, 1997; "Mercosur: From Domestic Concerns to Regional Influence," in G. Hook and I. Kearns, eds., *Subregionalism and World Order*, London: Macmillan, 1999, pp. 95–115; "Interpreting ASEM: inter-regionalism and the new materialism," *Journal of Asia Pacific Economy*, 4, 1, January, 1999, pp. 13–32. He is currently working on a Marxist interpretation of contemporary political economy, with reference to regional integration in Asia and Latin America, and global regulation through the World Bank.

Pitou van Dijck is Associate Professor of Economics at the Center for Latin American Research and Documentation (CEDLA) at the University of Amsterdam. His main fields of interest are industrialization and trade policies in Latin America and Asia, and multilateral and regional rule systems for international trade. Among his book publications are *Latin America's New Insertion in the World Economy* (co-edited with R. Buitelaar), *Challenges to the New World Trade Organization* and *The External Economic Dimension of the European Union* (both co-edited with G. Faber).

Gerrit Faber is Associate Professor of International Economics at Utrecht University, the Netherlands. His main research interests are trade-policy issues related to European integration and development co-operation. Among his most recent book publications are *Challenges to the New World Trade Organization* and *The External Economic Dimension of the European Union* (both co-edited with P. van Dijck) and co-author (with A. Sarma and P.K. Mehta) of *Meeting the Challenges of the European Union—Prospects of Indian Exports*.

Raymond Feddema is Senior Lecturer in International Relations at the University of Amsterdam. He received his Ph.D. (A Society in Crisis. Continuity and Change in the Tonkin Delta, 1802-1927) at the same university. At present his main fields of research are the political economies of Southeast and East Asian countries in relation to their particular cultures and their links to the global economy. Recently he edited with Kurt Radtke *Comprehensive Security in Asia. Views from Asia and the West on a Changing Security Environment,* Leiden: Brill, 2000.

Mitsuhiro Kagami was born in 1943, educated at International Christian University, obtained an M.A. in economics at Stanford University, and a Ph.D. at Hiroshima University. He is now executive vice president of the Institute of Developing Economies, Japan External Trade Organization. He worked for the UN Economic Commission for Latin America and the Caribbean(1982-86), and served as a visiting researcher at the Inter-American Development Bank (1991–93). He is the co-editor of *Privatization, Deregulation and Economic Efficiency: A Comparative Analysis of Asia, Europe and the Americas,* Aldershot: Edward Elgar Publishing Ltd., 2000.

Tsutomu Kikuchi is Professor of International Relations at the Department of International Politics, Aoyama-Gakuin University, Tokyo. He has been an adjunct research fellow of the Japan Institute of International Affairs (JIIA), Tokyo. He obtained his doctoral degree at Hitotsubashi University, Tokyo. He has been actively involved in the Track 2 dialogues such as CSCAP and PECC among others.

Kurt W. Radtke is Professor of Japanese and Chinese Studies at Waseda University, Institute of Asia-Pacific Studies, Tokyo. His major fields are politics and society in East Asia, as well as comparative studies of Chinese and Japanese culture. His published books include *China's Relations with Japan, 1945-83: the role of Liao Chengzhi* Manchester: Manchester University Press, 1990 and *Comprehensive Security,* co-edited with R. Feddema, Leiden: Brill, 2000.

Paulo G. F. Vizentini is Professor of History at the Universidade Federal do Rio Grande do Sul, Porto Alegre Brazil. He is also Director of the Institute of Latin American Advanced Studies. He is specialized in International Relations, in particular Brazilian Foreign Policy, and international relations in Latin America. He followed a post-doctoral program on international relations at the London School of Economics. He wrote: *Relações Internacionais e Desenvolvimento no Brasil O Nacionalismo e a Política Externa Independente (1951–1964)*, Vozes, 1995; *A Política Externa do Regime Militar Brasileiro: multilateralização, desenvolvimento e a construção de uma potência média (1964-1985)*, Porto Alegre, 1998; *Dez anos que abalaram o Século XX. Política internacional 1989–1999*, Porto Alegre, 1999.

Marianne L. Wiesebron is Assistant Professor of History at the Department of Latin American Studies at Leiden University. She specializes in Brazilian history, politics and society. Recently, she has been working on current economic and political developments in Latin America, on problems of regional integration, with a focus on social aspects, and in particular on Mercosul, including comparisons with NAFTA and the European Union. Some recent publications are: *Procesos de integración en América Latina: Perspectivas y experiencias latinoamericanas y europeas*, co-edited with Raymond Buve, Amsterdam, México D.F., 1999; *Brasil 500 anos. Developments and Perspectives*, Wiesebron, ed., Leiden, Den Haag, 2000.

Yang Zerui has Master degree from Beijing University and Waseda University (Tokyo) where he is a Ph.D. candidate. He is co-author of *Economic Cooperation in Northeast Asia*, China Foreign Trade Press, 1995, and *Focus on Shanghai—APEC's Progress and Perspective*, Economic Management Press, 2001 (both published in Chinese).

Index